# THE CANADIAN COMMERCIAL REVOLUTION

## 1845-1851

BY

GILBERT NORMAN TUCKER 1898-1955.

ARCHON BOOKS
1971

ISBN: 0-208-010262



Library of Congress Catalog Card Number: 71-147378
*Printed In The United States Of America*

TO

THE MEMORY OF

THE VERY REVEREND L. NORMAN TUCKER

# PREFACE

THIS is a study in the field of British colonial history. The period from 1845 to 1851 is an interesting and critical one, both in the history of the British Empire, and in that of Canada as a colony within it. It was during those years that the distinctive political and economic design of the self-governing part of that empire was stamped upon it. In many ways the Province of Canada during those years was the most notable of the colonies of settlement, and much careful study has been devoted to the political events which occurred there. No less important, however, though perhaps less visible and certainly not equally well-known, are the economic conditions and problems of the time. The present work, which in an earlier form was accepted as a doctoral dissertation by the University of Cambridge, is an attempt to examine this economic background. The chapter on the famine migration, in an earlier form, has appeared in the *American Historical Review.*

Sincerely and very gratefully I thank each one of the host of kind friends who have helped me in season and out of season, enduring boredom unspeakable for friendship's sake. I regret that space forbids me to mention them all by name; but a very few I must so mention. I owe especially abundant thanks to Professor H. W. V. Temperley, for his interest and invaluable advice. To Professors A. P. Newton and Lillian Penson I am also exceedingly grateful for their generous assistance. I must acknowledge the great kindness of the late Doctors Adam Shortt and A. G. Doughty. Last but not least I thank my colleague Professor Leonard W. Labaree, the editor of this series, for expert help unstintingly given.

G. N. T.

*Branford College, Yale University,*
*January, 1936.*

## CONTENTS

## LIST OF ILLUSTRATIONS

# THE CANADIAN COMMERCIAL REVOLUTION

## I

## INTRODUCTION

The colony of a civilized nation which takes possession, either of a waste country or of one so thinly inhabited, that the natives easily give place to the new settlers, advances more rapidly in wealth and greatness than any other human society. ADAM SMITH.

THE Industrial Revolution introduced a technique of production so extraordinarily efficient that it enabled commodities of every sort to be made in any quantity, and caused marketing to become the principal problem of industry. The greater the scale of production, the lower the cost tends to be, and the wider the market; while an expanding market makes possible still greater production, and so it goes on. With increased productive power a society multiplies its wants and its means to satisfy them; but never fast enough to keep pace with the relentless machines. Thus a highly industrialized society always has an actual or potential surplus of goods for consumption, which it must, if possible, dispose of to less economically mature neighbors—compassing heaven and earth to find customers. Commerce and finance are the handmaidens of industry and wait upon her. The world is large and its wants are many, and undreamed of wealth awaits him who is in a position to satisfy them. In our own day the industrialized society is becoming the normal type, and we do not know what the end of the story will be; but it has not always been so.

The Britain of ninety years ago was the only great industrial community, and the markets of the whole world were the prize for which she strove. Her great natural advantages and magnificent technical equipment gave self-confidence to her resourceful and energetic business men. Free competition is the creed of the strong, and the business world set out to convert the politicians to it—the gospel was successfully preached, and the era of free trade began.

Yet in national even as in individual life, a line of action has not one result, but many, and wisdom can never foresee all the effects of what is about to be done. Great Britain was the world's workshop, yet she was also the metropolis of a widespread empire. The latter had been organized on mercantilist lines, and imperial preference had hitherto been regarded as its life-blood. The old empire was a *Zollverein*, encircled by a golden band of economic interest, wherefore it was not possible for the *laissez faire* policy to triumph in Britain without introducing into the imperial organization changes of a most drastic and far-reaching character. With the inauguration of her new commercial policy in and after 1846, the mother country made in effect an economic declaration of independence. This, to the disappointed imperialist of that day, was at best unnecessary and dangerous, and might in the worse event prove to have been a kind of imperial suicide. The free trader however, cheerfully faced the alleged risks, partly because Manchester thought more in terms of economics than of politics, and its aspirations were far removed from those of the imperialists. Moreover it was often assumed by free traders and others that colonies of settlement were inevitably destined to political independence.[1] In addition to this, *laissez faire* was both a creed and a panacea, and a creed is of paramount importance to its devotees, while from the application of a panacea no ill results are to be feared. So to free trade England turned with a completeness and an obedience to theory uncommon in her history, nor can there be much doubt that in so doing she served her immediate material interests.

1. See C. A. Bodelsen, *Studies in Mid-Victorian Imperialism* (Copenhagen, 1924), pp. 32 ff.

The economic features of the old colonial system had been exceedingly unpopular in the thirteen colonies which became independent in 1783. With the commercial organization of the empire during the last phase of the old system, on the contrary, the colonists were well content. Their external trade was under restraint, for imperial tariff and navigation laws confined its current to a limited number of channels; yet these were not unnatural channels, and a monopoly of the British market was sugar-coating enough for almost any pill. Industrialized Britain indeed provided such a market for food and raw materials as had never before been known, while she and her northern colonies were now complementary to each other in the economic sense to a much greater extent than ever before. The commercial code was not unreasonably framed, and was administered in a statesmanlike way. The nineteenth century colonists too, whatever may have been the reasons, seem to have been a more docile, contented, and diffident breed than the inhabitants of the thirteen earlier colonies, while such grievances as they had were political rather than economic. Their feelings were not far removed from panic when they learned that the whole imperial economic system—the very base and foundation on which they conceived their economic life to rest—was to be swept away.

The Province of Canada was much the largest and most important of the colonies, and possessed great natural advantages; but was also beset by certain difficulties mainly due to the mixed character of its population and the severity of its climate. Remote from the sea, and, as it were, in the very arms of the United States, the province was not, like most colonies, within the orbit of a single great nation, but of two. During the previous decade the colony had experienced that most dire of all social calamities, civil war. As there were in reality two Canadas, a division into two for purposes of government had been tried without success; yet political union was proving to be unsatisfactory also. A conflict over fundamental constitutional issues was being fought to a finish, and the province was not only the largest responsibility which the Colonial Office had, but its greatest cause of anxiety also. These were the concluding and decisive years of the "struggle for responsible government"—that is to say for the unconditional application of the British parliamentary system to dominions in embryo. The Province of Canada was a laboratory in which this important experiment was carried out. About the experiment and its results very much has been said and written.

The Canada of the eighteen-forties was a reasonably prosperous community of the normal colonial type, with a number of features largely peculiar to itself. The geographical position of the province in relation to the rest of the continent and to the St. Lawrence and Mohawk valleys with their respective potentialities as trade routes is one of the two major clues to the economic significance of those years. The word "waterway" was continually upon the lips of the Canadian politician and business man of that day, and this was because they knew very well that an adequate means of communication with the ocean was absolutely essential to their prosperity. Yet this was by no means all. It also seemed obvious to Canadians and others of that day, and the weight of the available evidence was on their side, that the unmeasured generosity of Providence had designed the Province of Canada to be, by means of its great river, the channel for the whole of the trade of the Great Lakes region on both sides of the international boundary. The fulfilment of this apparently reasonable hope promised to clothe the province in such a garment of prosperity as it had never known. That these hopes might be turned into realities, in the period after 1845 the provincial government was completing a very ambitious program of waterway development, designed to make the St. Lawrence River navigable throughout its entire length.

The whole waterway question is not only of the greatest importance as a key to the economic life of the colony in the period, but it also differentiated it from all its sister colonies, and furnished problems and interests peculiar to itself. This fact was fully recognized in Britain, with the result that imperial policy had accorded to that particular colony an especially favored status both in law and in practice. A few years before the British government had guaranteed the interest on a large Canadian loan, the proceeds of which were to be spent on the St. Lawrence waterway. This, while it was not a unique concession, was a very unusual one. The Canada Corn Act of 1843 admitted Canadian wheat, and Canadian-milled flour regardless of its origin, to the British market on unusually favorable terms. Thus from 1843 to 1846 the province stood on a privileged footing not only as compared with foreign countries but with the other colonies also. The needs of the Canadian waterway too, exercised a definite influence in bringing about the repeal of the Navigation Laws.

The second of the two major clues to the problem of the economic life of Canada in the period, is the fact that that country, like most colonies, had to find an external market for its staples. In certain other ways too the province was an exceptional case. It was the principal colonial producer of wheat and timber. Both these commodities enjoyed under the old colonial system a substantial preference in the British market. Only on condition that the province were able to sell these products, and to transport them to their market, would its economic mechanism be complete in all its parts and able to function satisfactorily. The near presence of the United States too had an important influence upon Canada, as upon the other British North American colonies. Comparisons were inevitably drawn between the respective political constitutions and degrees of material well-being, and since the United States was relatively prosperous in the period this influence was strong and is frequently visible. The famine migration of 1847 came almost entirely to Canada, and its effects were in consequence peculiar to that country. In some respects the province had gone further in the direction of maturity than any other colony, and had been the first to come face to face with problems which in the long run proved to be generic.

The improvement of the St. Lawrence waterway had been undertaken on the assumption that imperial preference was an immutable thing. Everyone in the colony had been optimistically talking and thinking canals, and hopes had been raised to the highest pitch by the action of the imperial parliament in passing the Canada Corn Act. These customary certainties were thrown on to the scales of doubt by the new trade policy of Britain, and colonial fears painted a dark prophetic picture of what would follow. Nor did prophecy ever receive a more immediate fulfilment, for the inauguration of the new commercial policy was succeeded by one of the worst depressions in Canadian history. The year 1846 saw a serious decline in business activity in the colony. The following year was rendered memorable by the most disastrous tidal wave of immigration that the country has ever experienced. In 1848 lowered economic vitality produced serious results on the public finances. Continued depression characterized the year 1849, accompanied by the only important and organized movement on behalf of separation and annexation that Canada has seen. Meanwhile in Britain *laissez faire* went on from strength to strength, and it seemed likely that free trade, which many Canadians regarded as the cause of their troubles, had come to stay. Consequently numerous other remedies began to be advocated in Canada, each of them strictly guaranteed to transform a very sick colony into a healthy one again. The depression ran its course, and in due time prosperity returned once more.

At this time therefore, the province was restless and troubled politically, while in the economic sphere it looked anxiously from a difficult and unprosperous present toward an uncertain future. Three important and particular factors were at work however, making for stability and safety during a trying time. One was the economic self-sufficiency, and the steadiness and discipline of the French Canadians. Another was the character and prestige of the provincial government. The third was the governor-general,[2] whose courage and tact made many rough places smooth.

James Bruce, eighth Earl of Elgin, who succeeded Lord Cathcart as representative of the crown in the colony, arrived there early in 1847, and held office until 1854, during which time he played a part in provincial affairs that was always important and sometimes decisive.[3] The third Earl Grey was secretary of state for war and the colonies in Lord John Russell's government from 1846 to 1852, succeeding W. E. Gladstone in that position. There was an election in the province in the winter of 1847–48 which returned to the legislative assembly a Reform majority of more than two to one, the Upper Canada representatives being about evenly divided, while Lower Canada returned thirty-five Reformers and only seven Tories. The Draper government resigned, thus bringing to a close a long period of Tory rule, and was succeeded by the Reform or Liberal administration of Baldwin and Lafontaine, which remained in power until 1851.

The real leader of the Tory party was Sir Allan MacNab, who was speaker of the assembly from 1844 to 1848, and subsequently leader of the opposition. Their inspector-general,[4] when they held office, was William Cayley, who had received a legal education in England. The Reform government after 1847 contained a number of unusually able men, and is sometimes referred to as the

2. Officially he was Governor of Canada and Governor-General of the North American Provinces.

3. "For the eight years which ensued [after he became governor-general] the life of Lord Elgin and the history of Canada are one; in all the events of first-rate importance during these years he was the chief actor, and, taken together, they constitute the most influential chapter, since 1763, in British North American history." J. L. Morison, *The Eighth Earl of Elgin* (London, 1928), p. 79.

4. The Inspector-General of Accounts was the provincial Chancellor of the Exchequer. His official interests however were wider than those of the corresponding British minister.

"great administration." Its leaders, who represented the English and French parts of the province respectively, were Robert Baldwin and Louis Hippolyte Lafontaine. The Reform inspector-general was Francis Hincks, a brilliant Irishman of forceful personality, who probably understood the economic condition and needs of the colony better than any other man of his day. William Hamilton Merritt, the unwearying champion of the waterways, was also a member of the Reform government, first as president of the executive council, and later as commissioner of public works.[5]

When, after the Union of 1840 we speak of the Province of Canada, we mean the older and more settled parts of what are now the provinces of Quebec and Ontario, that is to say the valley of the St. Lawrence River, together with the triangle of land lying between the Great Lakes on the south and west, and the Laurentian Barrier to the northward. Some of the inhabited area had recently been a wilderness, and a slow but steady process of further settlement was going on, so that there existed a more or less well-defined and ever-moving fringe where the forest of yesterday was being transformed into the farms of tomorrow. The countryside was probably more beautiful than it is now, for the trees were more numerous and finer, and the streams and rivers larger and cleaner; while the railway, the telegraph-pole, the transmission-line, and the roadside sign, were rare or non-existent. Factories had only begun to set their disfiguring imprint upon the land, and the farm buildings may have more than made amends for their rough-hewn appearance by the picturesqueness which travellers often attributed to them.

Despite the Act of Union the colony was still divided, both racially and in the parlance of the time into Lower and Upper Canada.[6] The former was several times larger than the latter in area; but much of it was uninhabitable.

5. The political life of Canada at this time is well described in Morison, *Eighth Earl of Elgin*, Ch. III.

6. Or Canada East and Canada West.

The population of the two together in 1846 amounted to nearly 1,400,000, and was increasing steadily and rapidly; for though the death-rate was higher than it is now, the birth-rate was also higher, and immigration helped to swell the total.[7] Upper Canada, hitherto the less populous part of the province, was about to equal and then surpass Lower Canada in this respect, for although the latter had the greater natural increase it had also the higher death-rate, while Upper Canada received most of the immigrants.[8] There was also a considerable emigration from Lower Canada to the United States. About 15,000 Indians lived in the province.

Of the people of Lower Canada some three-quarters were French Canadians. These descendants of the colonists of the old régime had a conception of life that was half mediaeval. The *habitant* practised the economy of self-sufficiency, for he contrived to live almost entirely on what his farm produced. He and his proverbially large family ate the food grown in their own fields, and spun from the wool of their sheep yarn wherewith to weave cloth for their own use. The woodlot supplied building materials, fuel, and sugar. The French Canadian was a man of few and simple wants, apparently more interested in persons than in things, and the materialism which emphasizes expenditure, multiplies wants, and maintains a restlessly objective attitude toward the physical environment, was wholly alien to him. The inhabitants of French Canada had indeed preserved more or less intact the social and intellectual order of an earlier day, and they were devout and disciplined, ignorant, static, and happy. The whole nineteenth-century mode of thought, sceptical, scientific, and materialistic, with its shibboleths of freedom, democracy, progress, and the rest of it, had passed them by, save only where city life or emigration had changed them.

7. See the table of population. Appendix C.

8. Births in 1851, in Lower Canada 36,739, in Upper Canada 32,681. Deaths in 1851, in Lower Canada, 11,674, in Upper Canada 7,775. *Census of the Canadas, 1851–2*, II, 5.

They were more ready to build churches than canals, and in a sane and wholesome kind of squalor lived the life which the sages have recommended. Theirs were the qualities which make for stability and self-sufficiency, and in consequence for cultural and economic isolation. In the story about to be told it will be noticed that the French Canadians play a very minor part; yet this will cause no surprise if it is considered, not only what manner of people they were, but the following facts as well. Lower Canada was not a wheat-exporting country, partly as a result of its multi-cellular economic organization. Its staple trade in timber was less affected than might have been expected by the untoward events of these years, and the population as a whole was largely independent of its staple. The French Canadians too, since they lived on the lower and naturally more navigable parts of the great river, possessed easy means of communication with their neighbors in the valley, and ready access to the sea beyond, though of this they had but little need. They seem to have been more apt to think in political than in economic terms, were passionately conscious of their nationality, and resolved at any cost to prevent its being submerged beneath the surrounding ocean of English-speaking civilization. French Canadians often complained that their neighbors were being anglicized,[9] and this indeed was a reasonable fear, since the survival of their culture, and doubtless the salvation of their souls also, depended upon a rigid exclusion of everything that was not French and Roman Catholic. The conditions and events about to be dealt with, mainly concerned the inhabitants of Upper Canada, the Eastern Townships, and the cities of Montreal and Quebec.

The population of Canada West was more diverse in character than that of Lower Canada,[10] and the English-

9. *E.g.* "Comment à présent, je vous le demande, soupirer en français auprès d'une Canadienne qui vous répondra en anglais! . . . C'est décourageant, ma foi!" "Nisus" in *l'Avenir,* Dec. 2, 1848.

10. The principal population groups were represented in approximately the following percentages:—Native Canadians not of French origin, 55;

speaking Canadians were unlike their French fellow-citizens in nearly every respect in which differences of mental and moral attitude are possible. They were a United Empire Loyalist population heavily diluted by direct migration from the British Isles, and greatly influenced in their ideas and ways by their American neighbors.[11] They were energetic, progressive and materialistic, and thoroughly of their day and generation. In many ways they were less fortunate than are those who compose a mature society. It was not theirs to inherit from bygone generations a land made smooth for gracious living and equipped with all the appliances of civilization. Their harder lot it was to subdue an unfriendly wilderness and tame it to their use. As became their environment they were strong and shrewd men disdainful of theories, and interested chiefly in the material realities of life. The speech of the field, the wharf, and the market-place was on their lips. A universal preoccupation with business had established the mercantile code of honor among them, and the money motive was unduly prominent.[12] The range of their interests was narrow, and in urbanity of manner they did not excel. They were both more and less provincial than their French fellow-subjects who formed a small and largely self-contained cultural unit, for they were integrated with one of the great world cultures, in a very subordinate yet participating capacity. Together with a local *esprit-de-corps* they entertained a strong sentimental regard for their relation to Great Britain. They were British colonists of the usual type, modified by their particular environment.

A newly settled colony must normally obtain its wealth

Irish, 18½; English and Welsh, 8⅔; Scottish, 8; American, 4½; French Canadians, 2¾. (Percentages based on returns of *Census of 1851–2*, I, 36–37.) The proportion of Irish had been greatly increased by the famine immigration of the year 1847. The percentage of Americans was probably diminishing.

11. It must be remembered that the typical U.E. Loyalist was different from his revolutionary fellow-colonist only with respect to political opinions.

12. "A lax commercial morality is, in effect, the barbarism of a young commercial nation." Goldwin Smith.

almost entirely from agriculture, and Canada was not a community of town-dwellers. The greater part of the population—almost ninety per cent—lived on the farms and in the villages, and was directly interested in agriculture. It is necessary to realize what this implies. Such a society, unless, as in the case of the French Canadians, it does not possess a modern standard of wants, is necessarily far from being self-sufficient. For since practically no industry exists, production is one-sided, and the quantity of goods exported and imported will therefore have to be relatively very large. Upon a community of this kind the economic winds and tides which move across the world tend to exercise a decisive and uncontrollable influence. A monopoly in the production of a staple, such as their vast fields of snow-white cotton used to confer upon the southern states of the American Union, may be a passport to prosperity. For then in the event of poor crops the producer can take refuge behind the level of prices, and there will be no marketing problem; but millennial conditions such as these are rare. More commonly the staple is not a natural monopoly, and the level of prosperity is then subject to the capricious influence of world prices, unless the producing country can diversify its agriculture, industrialize itself, or obtain a political monopoly in place of the natural one which it does not possess. Yet, although vulnerable in the way described, a not over-dense population of farmers, particularly of land-owning farmers, has a basic economic stability, and is unlikely to encounter social and economic problems of the worst type. It will not experience acute distress in times of depression, for it can draw its belt very tight, and the elementary necessaries of life are not likely to be lacking. A farmer has a stoicism all his own, and it may in part be due to the ultimate economic security of his occupation.

In a recently settled agricultural community—a colony in the economic sense—the per capita production of wealth is very large. In such lands nature is generous, and the law of diminishing returns does not operate. Methods and plant are new, and tend to conform closely to existing requirements. Manual labor is well rewarded; but hours are likely to be long, for there is much to be done.[13] The proportion of productive workers is very high,[14] and no stigma attaches to work as such, which in taking on a new dignity acquires perhaps an added efficiency therewith. Taxation is low, and the standard of living high.

Canada was a poor man's country. Cheap and available land tapped the reservoir of labor. A hard-working and reliable man was sure to find employment, and likely in that uncrystallized society to improve his lot greatly. A clergyman with several years' experience in an Upper Canada parish stated that he "never knew a really industrious, honest, sober, mechanic to be in want."[15] A skilled worker could earn from four to six shillings a day, or about four pounds a month and his board: unskilled work was worth from two to three shillings a day. A farm laborer's wage was usually about two shillings or half-a-crown a day, and by the year some twenty to twenty-three pounds and board. Maid-servants, who were scarce, earned from seven to sixteen pounds a year with board and lodging provided, and there were many complaints as to their quality.[16] The general level of wages was rather higher in Upper than in Lower Canada. Everywhere in the colony foodstuffs were fairly cheap; but rents in the towns were often higher than in Britain. The following are samples of entries made in his day-book by a business man living in Canada West, and they give a fair idea of

13. "With regard to the hours of labour, it may be stated generally that they are somewhat longer, and the application is closer, than in Britain." J. B. Brown, *Views of Canada and the Colonists* (2nd ed., Edinburgh and London, 1851), p. 357.

14. "The non-producing population of the Province is very small, not amounting at the outside to 8000 souls in all." Appendix to the "First Report of the Board of Registration and Statistics," *Sessional Papers, 1849,* Appendix B. (C.O. 45: 236).

15. G. W. Warr, *Canada as It is* (London, 1847), p. 103.

16. These wages are quoted in pounds sterling. Unless otherwise stated however, values are given in "currency." £1 4*s.* 4*d.* currency was equal in value to £1 sterling.

retail prices paid for articles of good quality. "Paid for one pair of socks, 1/3; for breakfast at Dophin's Inn, 11¼d.; postage of a Letter, 1/2; 2½ yds. grey cloth, 7/½; 1 pair of shoes, 6/3; 1 lbs. of Tea, 2/6; 1 lbs of sugar, 6 d.; a broom, 9¼d.; a toothbrush, 7½d.; 1 barrel of Flour, £1-8-9; 1 lbs. butter, 7½d.; a penknife, 2/6."[17]

Excellent however as were the prospects offered by the province to the working-class settler, the gentleman who came thither for the purpose of eking out a diminished fortune was likely to be disillusioned, unless he could obtain a salaried position in one of the towns. The colony was essentially a community of land-owning farmers who did most of their own work. The complicated old land-tenures, of feudal origin, were about to disappear from Lower Canada, and into Canada West they had never been introduced, so that fee simple reigned supreme. The normal farm in Upper Canada comprised from one to two hundred acres, in Lower Canada something less. A would-be settler might buy land directly from the government, or from one of the land companies. The most rapid settlement in the period was taking place on the Huron Tract, controlled by the Canada Land Company, which concern seems to have enjoyed a large measure of public good-will. Some settlers bought farms from private individuals, and, as might be expected, a certain amount of land was held for speculative purposes. If the prospective purchaser wished to settle on unimproved land, he could obtain it at from two-and-sixpence to eight shillings an acre. As Canada West had the better and more plentiful land, most of the settlement was taking place in that part of the colony. Land was consequently a little more expensive there than in Lower Canada.

Most of the country in its natural state was thickly wooded, and the first task of the settler on an unimproved tract was to remove the trees and underbrush from a small

17. Askin Papers, Vol. 51. These entries are taken out of a long list, and are in some cases abbreviated.

portion of his holding, and to build a modest house. On the area selected for clearing, the smaller trees and undergrowth were first cut down and piled in heaps. Then the larger trees to be used for building the house were felled, cut into suitable lengths, and either drawn by oxen or moved on rollers to the site of the projected building. When the material was ready the neighbors usually came together to help to put up the house, and by this means the work might be nearly finished in the course of a single day.

The distinguishing feature of the architecture of the colony, for obvious reasons, was the general use of wood. The settler's first home was the "shanty," a very small and roughly built structure made of whole logs with the bark left on them; or sometimes, if the trunks were very large, of logs split in two. The roof was often made of basswood[18] stems split down the centre and hollowed out into a sort of trough. A layer of these was laid side by side, sloping, with the troughlike hollows facing upward. A second layer was then laid over the first, with the convex sides on top, in such a way as to shed the rain from their upper surfaces into the sloping hollows of the lower layer. The shanty was intended to shelter the settler until his resources should enable him to build a larger and more comfortable dwelling. After the rough shanty came the "log-house," made of logs laid horizontally and notched at the ends in such a way as to hold the walls together at the corners. The spaces between the logs were pointed with mortar or clay, and the chimney was built of stone, or of clay reinforced with wood. The walls were often lined with boards. A fairly large log-house built by a settler in the Peterborough district was thus described by its owner. "The dimensions were thirty-six feet in length, and thirty-two in breadth, which gave us a nice parlour, a kitchen, and two small bedrooms, which were divided by plank partitions. Pantry or storeroom there was none; some rough shelves in the kitchen, and a deal cupboard in the

18. *Tilia americana,* a variety of linden.

corner of the parlour, being the extent of our accommodations in that way."[19]

After the log-house came the painted or rough-cast frame house, which is still the normal Canadian farm dwelling. In the older-settled parts of the colony these were already very common.[20] A typical one was built on a stone foundation, and was thirty-eight feet long and twenty-six feet wide. Later a forty-by-twenty-foot wing was added, together with a veranda nine feet wide along the front and one end. This house was lathed and plastered inside. In and near the towns, brick or stone as well as frame buildings were frequently to be seen, stone being more commonly used in Lower than in Upper Canada. The evolution of the barn was from logs to frame. The walls of the frame barns consisted of rough boards fastened to a skeleton of heavy hand-hewn beams, which were secured at the ends by mortise and tenon joints held in place by strong wooden pegs. In Lower Canada these barns were long and low; those of Upper Canada were broader in proportion to their length, and higher. With so extensive a use of wood, it is not to be wondered at that fires were common and much to be dreaded, and that insurance rates were very high.

The settler however did not live by house and barn alone, and his land, or a considerable part of it, had to be cleared for cultivation and fenced. The double process cost from two pounds ten to four pounds per acre, the trees of course providing abundant material for fences. Sometimes the initial fence consisted of logs, stumps, or stones piled up; but the standard type was the "snake" fence, a zig-zag structure made of wooden rails about

19. Susanna Moodie, *Roughing it in the Bush* (London and New York, 1852), II, 24–25.

20. "Sawmills are so numerous in Upper Canada that no difficulty will be experienced in getting all the timber which may be required cut, and that, too, without laying out money; for the Canadian system of milling is to deduct a toll—one half of timber and every twelfth bushel of grain." G. W. Warr, *Canada as It is*, p. 95.

twelve feet long and some four inches thick, resting upon each other. In Lower Canada a type of post-and-rail fence was often used, sometimes in combination with a low stone wall. The stumps, and large stones if there were any, were removed as soon as possible from the field in prospect, to permit of cultivation. Except when the land lay close to some larger watercourse, the trees which remained after the buildings and fences had been constructed could not be sold as lumber on account of the difficulty and cost of transportation. They were piled up and burned, and the ashes could be converted into potash which was easy to dispose of, being valuable in proportion to its bulk and weight. For his first crop, maize and potatoes were the standby of the settler since they would grow in freshly broken ground. Maize might even be sown before the stumps had been removed, for this crop did not absolutely require either previous ploughing or cultivation during growth. In a cleared field maize was planted in "hills" about three feet apart each way, a hill consisting of four or five grains planted in a hole made with a hoe. Sometimes pumpkins were grown along with maize. Both maize and potatoes were cultivated with the hoe. In new settlements, during the warmer half of the year, cattle and horses were turned loose to pick up a living on the uncleared part of the farm or on the adjoining wild land. There they could get plenty to eat; but were difficult to find when wanted. In the winter, of course, shelter and fodder had to be provided for them.

The Lower Canadian staple was timber. Behind the settled areas, and particularly up the Ottawa River, tall, straight trees, chiefly pines, were to be found in abundance, growing by the side of large rivers down which they could be floated. Here an extensive and normally profitable lumber industry was carried on. Work in the lumber camps could be combined with farming, for the cutting and drawing of the logs was done in the winter when farm work was practically at a standstill. This older part of the colony however, produced only a relatively small amount of wheat. The way of life of the French Canadians induced them to practise mixed and therefore self-sufficient farming. The fact too that the greater part of their soil had undergone long cultivation probably helped to force mixed farming upon them, as it has so often upon similar communities elsewhere.

In Canada West on the other hand, wherever the land had been properly broken in, wheat, usually autumn-sown, was the favorite crop, and formed the all-important staple of that part of the colony. Rust and the Hessian fly were already there, and in some years did considerable damage; nevertheless on those rich flat acres good crops were the rule. Great quantities of oats and potatoes were also grown, as well as maize, barley, peas, rye, buckwheat, and turnips. Over limited areas, chiefly in the western peninsula, hemp, flax, and tobacco were cultivated; the latter being said to have been first introduced by runaway slaves. Numerous nurseries existed in the colony, selling seeds and seedlings of good quality. Good seedling fruit-trees, already grafted, might be had for a shilling each. Many sorts of fruit might be grown, though all did not succeed equally well in every part of the country. There were apples and pears in great variety, as well as cherries, plums, currants, gooseberries, and strawberries. Near the Niagara River peaches and grapes were grown, and already the Niagara Peninsula was beginning to be noted for its fruit. The dairy and the farm garden provided additional resources. So too did hives of bees, and honey was put to more varied uses than it is now, being to some extent a substitute for sugar. A settler thus described the capture of a swarm of wild bees out in the woods. "Cutting down the tree, cross-cutting it above and below the swarm with a saw, getting it home after being all of us well stung, setting it up as a hive, with a board at each end, and fomenting our swollen hands and faces, occupied the greatest part of the day, and, as it turned out, it was far from unprofitably employed, as I have now a valuable stock from it."[21] Another very important substitute for sugar was obtained from the sap of the sugar-maple. Cattle, hogs, horses, and sheep were kept, of course, and their numbers were increasing, those of the sheep and horses with great rapidity. In many places, especially in the newly-settled areas, hunting was a useful supplement to farming, and could be carried on in the comparatively idle winter-time, the result being meat, and sometimes with luck a profitable fur also. In many parts of the province not too near the towns, there were deer in the woods; but in such places the cry of the wolves could still be heard in the night, and these, as well as bears, sometimes took toll of the livestock. There were many other sorts of game to be shot, bird as well as beast,[22] and the beautiful little passenger pigeon, which once in its myriads had seemed to fill the sky, and which is now extinct, was still numerous, though noticeably less so than formerly.[23] Fishing was another resource, particularly along the lower reaches of the St. Lawrence. Laws for the protection of game, wildfowl, and fish, had already made their appearance.

Farm machinery was not yet in general use, both the reaper and the mower first appearing in the period. The sound of the threshing flail was still heard in the land, for though threshing-machines were known, they were very uncommon. Yet if hand-work was laborious, it left the farmer more independent economically than he is now. The device of combined labor was often employed, all the neighbors coming together for a day to do a particular piece of work on an individual farm. These free contributions of labor were expected to be returned in kind. The

21. Anonymous, *The Emigrant to North America* (Edinburgh and London, 1844), p. 35.

22. Partridges, woodcock, snipe, plover, wild ducks, and geese, also in some places wild turkeys and quail. Rabbits were common.

23. "The passenger-pigeon is not so large as the wild pigeon of Europe. It is slender in form, having a very long forked tail. Its plumage is a bluish-grey, and it has a lovely pink breast. It is, indeed, a very elegant bird." Samuel Strickland, *Twenty-seven Years in Canada West* (London, 1853), I, 297.

"bee" as it was called enabled the most formidable tasks to be undertaken lightheartedly, gave scope for experienced judgment and special aptitudes, and was an eagerly anticipated social event. There were building, logging, and chopping, as well as mowing and cradling bees, to say nothing of bees in the kitchens when the problem of jam and preserves for the winter was attacked in mass formation. Agricultural societies existed in both parts of the province for the purpose of encouraging and facilitating the use of improved methods.

The farmer in the colony enjoyed certain great advantages. In much of Canada West at least, the soil was very fertile, and, except in the long-settled areas, it contained the accumulated assets of the ages. Land was cheap to buy, and there was a fair chance that more of it could be obtained if needed. The rapid development of the community practically ensured a rise in the capital value of any given piece of settled land; while most of the very laborious and not immediately remunerative work which the purchaser of uncleared land was obliged to do, added considerably to the value of his property. The farmer in the colony too, since he had no rent to pay, could afford when the price of what he produced was low, to hold back his crop in hope of a better bargain later on. Taxation was very light. His social position too was enviable, for he was his own master, and a little capitalist in his own right. For him and for his children, in that liquid and equalitarian society, very few ambitions that stayed within the bounds of reason, could be pronounced incapable of fulfilment. Yet the farmers of the province were not without their own more or less peculiar difficulties. Insufficient capital, particularly in the case of recent settlers, was one of these. Another was the lack of good roads, and in some cases, of any roads at all. Hired labor was scarce, and often poor in quality. Too large a proportion of the year's work had to be crowded into that short hot Canadian summer; while the long and severe winter imposed a very serious handicap on stock-raising. Forest and ground fires were at times, and particularly in certain localities, a serious menace. Insect pests required much less control than they do now; but weeds were an important problem, particularly in the pastures.

Of goods in domestic use, a comparatively large proportion were made in the home. Even in Upper Canada this applied to such commodities as soap, candles, and sugar. Wool produced on the farm was sent to a mill to be carded, and was then spun at home, and sometimes the women of the house wove as well as spun. Professional weavers were sometimes hired to come in and do the work at the rate of five or six pence per yard of cloth woven. These country weavers, of whom there were quite a number, made a very good living working for the farmers and cultivating a piece of land for themselves. Home-made cloth, usually grey in color, was strong and warm, and home-made vegetable dyes were often used. The colonists however bought a certain amount of factory-made textiles, and cloth woven at home was often sent to a fuller to be finished off. Baking was of course a domestic industry, and the bread might be raised with yeast from the hop-vine which climbed up the wall of the house. Cheese and butter were home-made. An immense amount of preserved fruit was eaten, and shelves well-stocked with this commodity were the rule.[24] The farm usually afforded wood for the farmhouse stoves; but the towns of Upper Canada were beginning to use coal imported from the United States. Trade by barter was very common, and borrowing from the neighbors a habitual abuse. All this however was nearly a century ago, and one of the newspapers in the Colony was running *Dombey & Son* as a serial story.

The province possessed a number of small towns and cities, and for the most part travellers spoke well of them. The most important were Montreal, Quebec, Toronto, Kingston, and Hamilton. Foremost among them all stood

24. "They generally make four meals *per diem;* and at every meal they introduce preserves in some one shape or other." G. W. Warr, *Canada as It is*, p. 50.

the rather impressive little city of Montreal, about which a good deal will have to be said in due time. Quebec, unlike all the other cities and towns, was in appearance very much what it is now, and was the most important harbor in the colony, with a practical monopoly of the export trade in timber. Toronto, which had supplanted Kingston as the principal town in Upper Canada, is thus described by a contemporary: "Entering the spacious harbour, the appearance of Toronto, lying closely along the shore, and extending backwards, produces a very favourable impression in the mind of the traveller as to the prosperity and importance of this part of Canada. A close mass of houses, with several spires, warehouses, market-houses, and public works, meet the eye; and towards the upper part of the city, fronting the lake, are the fort, houses of legislature, and several excellent private residences and public hotels." The streets were arranged at right-angles, and were flanked with sidewalks made of thick planks laid transversely and sloping toward the roadway which also was of plank. That all was not yet entirely metropolitan may be gathered from the fact that cows and pigs were occasionally to be seen running loose about the streets. Kingston was a solid-looking place with a tradition, and it possessed even then its two characteristic institutions, Queen's College and a penitentiary. Together with Hamilton at the other end of Lake Ontario it received the status of a city in 1846. Bytown, up the Ottawa, the future federal capital, received the following description from a visitor who saw it in 1842. "Fifteen years ago there was not a tree cut in the forest where Bytown stands, and it now, I am told, numbers upwards of 3000 inhabitants. The effect of this rapid growth is very curious (as regards the appearance of the place)—it is, in fact, half a town and half a wood: the stumps are scattered through the gardens of the houses, and pine-trees through the streets, so that points of view might actually be selected in the middle of the town where you would almost lose sight of buildings altogether, and might fancy yourself in the primeval

LONDON, CANADA WEST, 1844.

forest." There were, of course, many lesser places, as "the village of Varennes, pleasingly situated on the banks of the St. Lawrence," and "the quaint French village of Longueuil," the "enterprising and flourishing village of Sarnia," the "thriving small town of Barrie," and the "large and prosperous village of Paris." Ancaster was "a very pretty little village, with two churches, and composed principally of wooden houses." Woodstock was "a long village, neatly and chiefly built of wood." London was "a very large, well laid-out town." Along the north shore of Lake Erie lay a series of little harbor villages, Ports Colborne, Maitland, Dover, Burwell, and Stanley.

As has already been stated, industries had been but little developed; yet they existed. Since early in the eighteenth century there had been an iron-works at St. Maurice a few miles north of the St. Lawrence behind Three Rivers. In the period the Forges St. Maurice were operated on a considerable scale—they produced iron of very good quality, and stoves made there were extensively used throughout Lower Canada. The sand of which the moulds were made was brought from England. Elsewhere in the colony, iron-works were increasing in number, and the foundation of an agricultural implement industry had also been laid. Articles of household furniture of every sort were manufactured locally. There were many distilleries in the province. In addition to the saw-mills which have already been mentioned as having been very numerous, the colony possessed a large number of flour and woolen mills, run by water-power. A Scottish mill-worker described "flour mills in Canada that surpass anything of the kind I have ever seen in Scotland—some of them very large."[25] It will be noted that the majority of these industries were engaged in the production of goods for use in the home.

In Lower Canada education of the masses was not desired; while in Canada West it was hampered by sparse-

25. William Thomson, *A Tradesman's Travels, in the United States and Canada* (Edinburgh, 1842), p. 102.

ness of population and lack of money. Anything approaching a really good formal education, or a first-rate professional training, was far beyond the educational resources of the province. More important still, perhaps, there was a lack, partial in Lower Canada, and very nearly complete in Canada West, of a socially privileged and leisured minority. There was, in Upper Canada at least, no indigenous class whose position was unassailable, in which training was as much dependent upon the home as upon the school, and amongst nearly all of whose members a high degree of education in the broad and non-curricular sense might be taken for granted. This does not imply a complete sameness—in the towns and cities, at least, differentiation existed. Nevertheless the generalisation holds true that there was a marked degree of cultural uniformity at a rather low level. Indeed how could it have been otherwise? Great vocational versatility was common. William Hamilton Merritt of St. Catharines at different times was farmer and shop-keeper, ran mills, a salt-works, a potashery, a mineral spring, and a distillery, and was a promoter and politician. One Samuel Shaw, who had a shop at 75 Yonge Street, Toronto, sold both surgical instruments and axes. A contemporary advertisement reads: "Beddome's Desideratum for the Gout and Rheumatism. . . . A large supply of this celebrated Indian Remedy just received by THOMAS MACLEAR, Bookseller." In the French part of the colony a characteristic dialect had developed, and this was true of English Canada also. The inhabitants of the latter region had evolved a way of speaking which was probably very similar to that of their American neighbors. A visiting stranger described their speech as rapid, vehement, and nasal, and delivered in a majestic manner as though with each and every statement a matter of the greatest importance were being communicated. According to the same witness the women's voices were musical and pleasant.[26]

26. James Taylor, *Narrative of a Voyage to, and Travels in Upper Canada* (Hull, 1846), pp. 49–50.

The women of the colony were hard-working, and exposed to a comparatively rough life. The province was probably unusually healthy for those of its inhabitants who were fairly robust to begin with; but a bad place for such of the delicate as survived, and probably also for the old. Medicinal water enjoyed a vogue, and there were mineral springs at Varennes, and near Kingston, and elsewhere. The newspapers were full of advertisements for patent medicines. Medical schools of a sort[27] existed at Montreal, Quebec, and Toronto.

It was on the whole a very religious community—among the French the influence of the Roman Catholic Church was almost unbounded—while nearly all of the English-speaking inhabitants belonged to one or other of the religious communions, Protestant or Roman, the more evangelical sects seeming to possess the stronger appeal. Everywhere, in addition to their spiritual functions, the churches were essential channels of social intercourse, to a far greater extent than in more urban communities. Religious differences were a constant source of strife, since in Lower Canada there was acute friction between the Roman Catholic majority and the Protestant minority, while in Canada West the jealously guarded privileges of the Church of England aroused the bitter and active resentment of the numerically preponderant nonconformists. The domestic virtues were strongly in evidence. Crimes against property were rare—those against the person were comparatively frequent, and were almost invariably simple assaults rather than crimes of a more sophisticated type. Contemporary accounts are unanimous in selecting intemperance as the prevailing vice, and in declaring it to have been widespread and menacing. Spirits, particularly whisky, were the favorite drink. They were exceedingly cheap and easy to procure; though

27. This advertisement appeared in 1847: "Toronto Medical School. Will re-open on *the first Monday in November,* and be conducted as usual, by Dr. Workman, Dr. Morrison, Dr. Wright, of Markham, and the Subscriber, John Rolph."

whether this fact contributed to, or was a result of, the prevailing tendency to drink too much, or whether the two phenomena were unconnected, it is not easy to say. These were the palmy days of Père Chiniquy, the John B. Gough of Lower Canada. The standard of generosity and hospitality was high.

As with inland colonies generally, the greatest problem was that of transportation. Water is a natural highway, and with waterways of various kinds Canada was well supplied; consequently both travel and transportation by water were very much commoner than they are now. On the St. Lawrence and the Great Lakes, comfortable and swift passenger-ships plied their trade,[28] while the gradual completion of a system of canals on the St. Lawrence and the Ottawa, was facilitating trade as well as travel on those rivers. In 1846 it took twenty-four hours to go from Kingston to Montreal, and the fare from Montreal to Quebec was a dollar, which included a comfortable berth and a good supper.

Nature sometimes supplies rivers; but roads must be built, and this was a serious problem due to insufficiency of capital, scarcity of labor, and the scattered nature of the population. The normal road was a beaten track, fairly level but not surfaced, except perhaps that in swampy places it might be made firm by means of logs laid side by side. Such roads were not good; the degree of their badness however, varied greatly.[29] The extent to which inferior roads affect the marketing of bulky products is obvious. In the winter however, the frost provided the roads with a foundation and the snow surfaced them, so that in that season they were good, except immediately

28. "Nothing can exceed the comfort and style of some of these vessels." Sir Richard Bonnycastle, *The Canadas in 1841* (London, 1841–2), I, 138.

29. "The great hill to the south-west of the Delaware Bridge, becomes impassable in the rainy seasons, and on those occasions the Mails are carried through fields for the space of four or five miles. There are also many other ill-conditioned places, between London and Delaware." Report of the Commissioners of Public Works, 1848. *Sess. Papers, 1849,* App. B.B., (C.O. 45:237).

after a heavy fall of snow or during a thaw. Highways were often improved by the use of gravel or plank. The plank road was suggested by its low labor cost and the abundance of timber. In its construction longitudinal sleepers were laid upon a graded surface, thick boards being spiked crosswise upon them, and a thin layer of gravel spread upon the top. Such a road was exceedingly cheap to construct, and excellent to ride over when in good condition; its great drawback however was that it deteriorated very rapidly. It was only good for about ten years, and when old it became dangerous. Gravel or stones were sometimes used where the traffic was heavy. Considerable sums of money were being spent on roads, which were noticeably improving, and joint-stock companies or private individuals were often authorized to build roads or bridges and to charge tolls for their use. Ferries were common. This was still the day of the stage-coach, and the inns of the province as a rule were very poor.

In the picture of the two Canadas which has been presented, there is doubtless much to excite admiration and praise, and much also to criticize. The praise may in fairness be unreservedly bestowed; but not so the criticism. A nation is not built in a day. The colonists were engaged in a magnificent effort to perform one of the hardest tasks that have ever confronted mankind. They were husbandmen who had come in the first hour to the vineyard, and were laboring diligently in the heat of the day. They had done much; yet very much remained to be done by them and by their successors.

Such a sketch as this of the ways of a people necessarily rests upon a very varied documentary foundation. In this case, contemporary personal accounts constitute the most useful single type of material; and of these, dealing with the Province of Canada in the eighteen-forties, there is a surprisingly large supply. Such accounts, in printed form, are more than two dozen in number, and these books have one feature in common which is rather curious and interesting. Only one native colonist left such a record. Americans visited the colony, and settled there in considerable numbers; but they did not write. Frenchmen from France did not go to the Canadas. All the accounts, save one, are by old-country people. Travellers who saw and went their way; army officers stationed in the province; clergymen with charges there; settlers, particularly women—these and others wrote personal accounts. They confine their descriptions almost entirely to the English districts, consequently the French Canadian scene is relatively difficult to paint. A writer on this subject who intends to lean heavily upon this type of document, is consequently forced to overemphasize Upper Canada, and thus to distort the picture. In this particular case, however, such a lack of symmetry has a kind of logic in it, since the story about to be told concerns Upper Canada chiefly.

An attempt has here been made to afford a general idea of what it must have been like to live in the Province of Canada, especially the English part of it, nearly a century ago. The sources of information are local, and so is the picture which emerges from them. Yet, although a few of the features are peculiar, it is obvious that a strikingly similar picture could be and has often been painted elsewhere. The problems which faced the early settler almost everywhere in the northeastern part of English-speaking North America, were of the same general kind, and were solved in much the same way.

## II

# THE IMPROVEMENT OF THE WATERWAYS

Et maintenant en la présente navigation, faicte par vostre roial commandement, en la descouverture des terres occidantalles, estantes soubz les clymatz et paralelles de vos pays et roiaulme, non auparavant à vous ny à nous congneues, pourrez veoirs et savoir la bonté et fertillité d'icelle, la innumerable cantité des peuples y habitans, la bonté et paisibleté d'iceulx, et pareillement la fécondité du grant fleuve qui decourt et arouse le parmy d'icelles voz terres, qui est le plus grant sans conparaison, que on saiche jamais avoir veu. JACQUES CARTIER.

THE St. Lawrence River, which Cartier not unnaturally described to his sovereign with great enthusiasm, is indeed a "grant fleuve"—vast in volume, although exceeded in length by many of the world's very large rivers. It drains about 415,000 square miles above Quebec.[1] The banks are steep, and the bed often takes the form of parallel grooves, resulting in long, narrow sandbanks or islands of which Anticosti is the largest. These grooves provide excellent channels for navigation, and another French pioneer described it as: "le Fleuve le plus naviguable de l'Univers." The average discharge over a sixty-year period has been 247,000 cubic feet per second. The flow is unusually uniform, the ratio of maximum to minimum discharges being less than two to one. A report on the flow of the river states that: "The discharge of the St. Lawrence, even without any artificial regulation, is so steady, and the fluctuations in level day in and day out are so slight, that so far as the flow in the open-water months are [*sic*] concerned, the conditions for

1. *Statement and Engineers' Report by the Hydro-Electric Power Commission of Ontario* (Toronto, 1925).

constructing or operating a power plant or navigation canal are unequalled, and may be fairly characterized as almost ideal."[2]

It is the common lot of immature colonies to suffer more or less from lack of adequate transportation facilities. The settlements in the St. Lawrence Valley and north of the Great Lakes were remote from the sea; yet they lay in the depression worn down during the ages by the great river, and this afforded them a rare and valuable advantage—the means of communication with each other and with the sea. It is only a slight exaggeration to say that what the Nile has been to Egypt and the Sudan, that the St. Lawrence system was to the Canadas. It enabled the settler to reach his destination. It then afforded him facilities for exporting and importing goods, a way by which to reach his neighbors, and protection in time of war. The whole history of Canada from the time of Cartier until the building of the railways, was based on and conditioned by the St. Lawrence and its tributary waterways.[3]

Yet the St. Lawrence was not an entirely perfect means of communicating with the ocean. Before the conquest the French colonists were faced with the fact that they had rivals whose contact with the sea, being more direct, was superior to their own. In 1750 their Governor the Marquis de la Gallissonière wrote that: "Quoique ces colonies puissent fournir à l'Europe et aux Isles de l'Amérique, les mêmes marchandises que la nouvelle angleterre, il ne faut pas se flatter qu'ils puissent jamais le faire à aussi bon marché, surtout celles d'un grand encombrement, qui font d'ordinaire le principal et le plus sure objet du commerce, différence qui vient de la difficulté de la navigation des deux fleuves, de la longeur des traversées, et de ce qu'on ne peut aller en Canada, qu'en une certaine saison de l'année, ce qui en rendant la navigation plus longue, plus dispendieuse, plus difficile, et exposée à plus de danger, rehausse en même tems le prix des assurances."[4] This

2. *Ibid., Engineers' Report,* p. 56. 3. See map following index.

4. Marquis de la Gallissonière, "Mémoire sur les Colonies de la France

is no mere statement of a temporary condition: on the contrary a great part of the perennial Canadian waterway problem is here set forth. The shipping facilities of the St. Lawrence ports, relative to those of the harbors on the northeastern seaboard of the United States, were to remain a constant and important factor in the economic history of the settlements that lay beside the great river.

Nor was this all, for another serious difficulty remained to be faced. On Oct. 3, 1535, as Cartier and his companions stood on Mount Royal on the Island of Montreal, they saw "ung sault d'eaue, le plus impetueulx qu'il soit possible de veoir, lequel ne nous fut possible de passer." Indeed there were rapids impossible for any type of craft to ascend, at intervals all the way between Montreal and Lake Ontario, and as in course of time the canoe gave place to the batteau and the latter to the ship as the principal means of transportation, the problem created by these rapids became a very serious one.

The engineer's answer to a rapid is a canal. The process of circumventing the St. Lawrence rapids by means of canals was first begun in a small way about the year 1779, and by 1800 there were locks at Coteau du Lac, Split Rock, Mill Rapid, and the Cascades. The locks were small, and being only a partial success soon fell into disrepair.[5]

At the turn of the century the question attracted the attention of Sir Alexander Mackenzie. In a memorandum dated December, 1801, the great explorer unburdened himself on the subject. The memorandum is entitled: "Concerning a Canal projected by the American States from Albany to Lake Ontario, and a Canal between Lake Ontario and Montreal, by which the former would be rendered fruitless."[6] He wrote: "The People of the State of New York have long had, and still have in contempla-

dans l'Amérique Septentrionale." Décembre, 1750. Archives du Département des Affaires Etrangères—Mémoirs et Documents, Fonds Divers, Amérique II, 21–44.

5. Report by Col. Gother Mann, Dec. 24, 1800. Dominion Archives, Series C., Vol. 38.

6. Copy of Memorandum, *ibid.*, pp. 31–38.

tion, to open a Canal communication from the North River at Albany to Shinactady [*sic*] along the Mohawke river, and thence to Wood creek and Waters emptying into Lake Ontario; in order to make Albany what Montreal is intended by Nature to be, the Emporium of all the Trade and Commerce of the immense Territory and improving Country, round the great Lakes of Canada, so as to counteract by art the very great and many advantages which the latter has over the former by means of the Navigation of the St. Lawrence; . . ." He expressed a desire to deter English capitalists from helping to finance the American canal, and enlarged upon the natural advantages of the St. Lawrence. He considered that the New York route would have the single advantage of two months more of open season in the year. Mackenzie also suggested ways and means of improving the St. Lawrence by constructing canals, and added: "Thus would the Natural advantages which the Canadas are possessed of . . . be employed not only in their own Commerce but in that of all the citizens of the American States bordering on and Inhabiting the Vicinity of the Rivers communicating with or falling into the Lakes: . . ."

It has already been stated that the St. Lawrence river system was capable of affording to the inhabitants of the colony, not only valuable economic advantages, but a considerable degree of military security also. In the Indian wars of the seventeenth century the river had often enabled the colonists to escape from their relentless enemies, or to concentrate and move against them. In the middle of the eighteenth century, English control of the river had led to the conquest of New France. After 1762 Canada was to be the colony of the country which wielded the trident and could at all times bring decisive force to bear at any point to which warships could come unobstructed from the ocean. With a waterway navigable for small war and supply vessels up to the Great Lakes, Canada would be comparatively easy to protect. Otherwise the task was a very difficult one. During the War of 1812 the lesson was driven home. The lake fleets depended very largely on the resources of the lake ports, and the Americans won that part of the war. At that time also the importance of superiority on the lakes as a prerequisite to a successful land war was enunciated by no less an authority than the Duke of Wellington. "I believe," he wrote, "that the defence of Canada, and the co-operation of the Indians, depends upon the navigation of the lakes; . . . Any offensive operation founded upon Canada must be preceded by the establishment of a naval superiority on the lakes."[7] Nor, needless to say, were the military authorities responsible for the defense of the colony unaware of the problem. Toward the end of the war the commissary general addressed the following warning to the governor and commander-in-chief, Sir George Prevost. "The difficulties experienced in the transport of Stores and Provisions during the last Season for the construction, armament, and equipment of His Majesty's Ships on Lake Ontario, and for the Supply of the Troops in Upper Canada imperiously demand that means be promptly devised for a more certain conveyance of the innumerable Articles necessary for maintaining in that Province the great, and increasing, Naval and Military Force requisite for its defence." He added that "the practicability of making a Canal between Montreal and La Chine should be immediately ascertained."[8]

The construction of canals along the St. Lawrence itself between Montreal and Lake Ontario, was the most obvious solution of the problem; but the line of the St. Lawrence was practically incapable of defense in time of war. It seemed feasible however to construct a much less vulnerable waterway between the same two points by way of the Ottawa and Rideau Rivers, and the military authorities now began to consider this alternative scheme. The Ot-

7. Wellington to Lord Bathurst, Feb. 22, 1814. Gurwood, *Dispatches of the Duke of Wellington, 1799 to 1838* (London, 1838), XI, 525.

8. Commissary General to Sir George Prevost, Montreal, Nov. 14, 1814. Dom. Archives, Series C., 38, pp. 88–93.

tawa-Rideau route was being examined as early as 1815; but the difficulties connected with it were thought at first to be almost insuperable, and for a number of years nothing further was done. Meanwhile the Americans were not idle, and in the year 1825 the Erie Canal was completed, running from Buffalo to Albany on the Hudson, and designed to provide water communication between Lake Erie and the city of New York.

The government of Upper Canada in the year 1824 caused an estimate to be made of the cost of constructing a canal on the Rideau. Two years later the home government, seeing the necessity of such a canal in the event of war with the United States, sent Lieutenant Colonel John By, R.E., to the colony. In the same year, 1826, Colonel By made a survey and reported to his superior officer.[9] He stated that steamboat navigation from the St. Lawrence to the lakes would deprive the Americans of the means of attacking Canada, and would give Great Britain control of the trade of the whole Great Lakes area, even in spite of the expensive American canals. He feared that the existing plans for the improvement of the Canadian waterways visualized canals which would prove to be too small. Both for commercial and military purposes he thought that these ought to be capable of accommodating good-sized steamboats—vessels from a hundred and ten to a hundred and thirty feet long with a forty-or-fifty-foot beam, drawing eight feet of water when loaded, and capable of being armed should the need arise. More specifically and very strongly he urged that the Welland, Rideau, and Grenville canals be constructed on the necessary scale. This, with one or two minor improvements would be "the means of making the River St. Lawrence the great out-let for all the produce of that vast tract of land connected with the Lakes"; and this notwithstanding strong efforts on the part of the Americans to draw it their way by constructing various canals. The St. Law-

9. Copy of Col. By's Report on the Military Defence of Canada. Dom. Arch., Series C., 42, pp. 58–67.

rence was to be improved on the north side of the Island of Montreal, and Colonel By thought that Three Rivers, "being the finest roadstay in the St. Lawrence," would eventually become the general rendezvous for shipping. He was confident that canal tolls would not only defray interest charges, but would in a few years repay the capital investments also. His estimate of the cost was: Welland Canal, £400,000 sterling; Rideau, £400,000; Grenville, £100,000; improvement of navigation north of the Island of Montreal, £150,000. The imperial government decided to undertake the construction of the Ottawa and Rideau canals. Colonel By was put in charge of the latter, and the work was expected to occupy about four years.

The task proved to be a formidable one, and the actual cost of construction greatly exceeded the estimates. Colonel By decided to run his canal into the Ottawa just below the Chaudière Falls, and Bytown came into existence as a construction camp. Those who owned land along the proposed route thought that the millennium had come at last, and Colonel By had many problems other than engineering ones to deal with. Litigation in connection with land for the canal right-of-way was still going on long after the work had been completed. The difficulties were overcome however, and the canal was built both rapidly and well at a cost of something over £800,000. Its dimensions were rather less than those which By had recommended. It provided about a hundred and fifty miles of navigable water between Bytown and Kingston.

The Carillon, Chute à Blondeau, and Grenville canals on the Ottawa were also constructed; but less rapidly and well than in the case of the Rideau. Due to a change in policy after its completion, the Grenville Canal was shallower than the others, and the smallest lock in a system of canals is like the weakest link in a chain. The Royal Engineers built the Ottawa-Rideau canals, and the home government paid for them. They were a great asset to the two colonies from the military point of view, and were commercially advantageous also. They might possibly have been able to handle the grain export trade of the Great Lakes area had there been no Erie Canal; but with the latter they could not compete. A good contemporary description of these canals, written by an engineer officer of high rank resident in the colony, is to be found in Bonnycastle's *The Canadas in 1841.*[10]

In the meantime, further to the west, a work of great importance had been undertaken. From the head of the St. Lawrence where it flows from Lake Ontario, ships could sail along that lake and through to Lakes Erie, Huron and Michigan, unobstructed save by the famous obstacle in the Niagara River. The Welland, perhaps the most important of all the Canadian canals, joined Lake Ontario to Lake Erie by cutting through the Niagara Peninsula. It was an essential part of any comprehensive plan for a Canadian waterway to the sea, for it extended uninterrupted navigation on the St. Lawrence and Great Lakes system several hundred miles further toward the west. The position of the Welland was a commanding one, as this canal formed an integral part of each of the three canal systems dealt with in this chapter—the Ottawa-Rideau and the St. Lawrence systems, and the Erie.

Unlike the Rideau, the Welland Canal was originally a private venture. A few enterprising people in Upper Canada early foresaw how important the Erie Canal might prove to be. By and by, from the tip of the Niagara Peninsula, the sound of the workers on the Erie could almost be heard, and ideas are no respecters of international frontiers. As in the case of the Rideau, the Welland Canal is associated to a considerable extent with the name of one man. The Colonel By of the Welland was William Hamilton Merritt, and no adequate account of Canada political and economic in the middle of the last century could be written without mentioning his name in more than one connection. Merritt came of United Empire Loyalist stock, and was born in New York State in the

10. Sir Richard Bonnycastle, *The Canadas in 1841* (London, 1841–42), II, Ch. V.

year 1793.[11] When he was three years old his parents moved to Upper Canada, and settled in the Niagara district. At the age of fifteen he went down the river to Montreal and Quebec, proceeding thence to Halifax and the West Indies. He served with some distinction during the War of 1812, and before it was over again visited Montreal. After the war he went into business. According to his biographer, "Mr. Merritt . . . said that riding along the Niagara River from Chippewa to the ferry, first suggested the idea of a canal to his mind." In 1818 he began running surveys with a view to obtaining water for his mill from the Chippewa or Welland River, and he soon began to take the lead among the local inhabitants in urging upon the provincial government the need for a canal. In 1823 attempts were made to interest local men and capital in the project, and in January of the following year a company was incorporated to build the canal.

Two great difficulties presented themselves from the start. The first was the choice of a route. As in the case of the Rideau, the local inhabitants evinced more selfishness than public spirit or enlightened self-interest. Nearly everyone seems to have insisted upon a route which would enhance the value of his own particular property or business.[12] The other problem was that of securing capital—there was never quite enough—there seldom is. Money was scarce in the provinces; nevertheless a certain amount of stock was subscribed for locally. A number of private individuals in England took shares, among them the Duke of Wellington, and Huskisson. The former contributed £16,000 and also loaned money on a generous scale. A staunch supporter and liberal investor was also found in J. B. Yates of New York, and American capital from other sources proved to be available.[13] The greater part

11. These details from the Merritt Papers, and from J. P. Merritt, *Biography of the Hon. W. H. Merritt, M. P.* (St. Catharine's, 1875).

12. At a promotion meeting held in November, 1824, "Every person present was disposed to take shares, provided it should terminate at the Niagara river." J. P. Merritt, *Biography,* p. 68.

13. "Called on Jacob Astor, a German, who thinks well of it [the Wel-

of the weight however was borne by the governments, imperial and colonial. At the end of 1837 the investments were probably held as follows:

| | |
|---|---|
| Shares held by private parties | £117,800 |
| Loan and shares held by Upper Canada Government | £275,644 |
| Shares held by Lower Canada Government | £ 25,000 |
| Loan by Imperial Government | £ 55,555 |
| Total | £473,999[14] |

Thus almost exactly seventy-five per cent of what had started out as a purely private concern, was government-owned by 1837. Two years later the government of Upper Canada took over all the private shares.

In the final arrangement a canal was dug from Lake Ontario to the Welland River. From a point a little to the south of the Welland a feeder ran to Dunville on the Grand River, while a second canal ran from the junction of the feeder to Port Colborne on Lake Erie. The canal was about fifty-six feet wide at the top, twenty-six at the bottom, and supposed to contain eight feet of water. The locks, thirty-nine in number, were made of wood. The first ship passed through in the late autumn of 1829, and the canal was fully open by 1832. In 1841 enlargement of the entire work was begun, and the canal from start to finish cost about £1,400,000.[15]

Like a faint and feeble echo of the Welland was the Desjardins Canal, built by a company incorporated in 1826. This little canal ran from Burlington Bay at the western end of Lake Ontario, to Dundas, a distance of something over three miles, and accommodated vessels

land Canal]." From an entry in Merritt's diary for Mar. 13, 1828, quoted in the biography.

14. "Report of Commissioners of Public Works, 1848." App. N. *Sess. Papers, 1849*. App. B.B. (C.O. 45: 237). Also Sir George Arthur to Lord Normanby, No. 131, of June 8, 1839. MS. Room, Dominion Archives.

15. In 1826 Col. By had estimated the cost of the Welland Canal at £400,000 sterling.

drawing up to seven and a half feet of water. It was opened in 1837. It never paid its way, the provincial government became involved, and by the end of 1848 was a creditor of the company to the tune of £30,000.

The first ship-canal on the St. Lawrence was built in the Lower Province, at Lachine on the Island of Montreal, where Jacques Cartier had seen the rapids three hundred years before. A joint-stock company incorporated by a provincial act made preliminary surveys in 1819. The following year the provincial government purchased the rights of the company, and commissioners were appointed to superintend the work. The undertaking was authorised[16] and construction was begun in 1821. The canal, which ran from the village of Lachine at the lower end of Lake St. Louis to Montreal, was completed in 1825 at a cost of over £100,000. It was eight and a half miles long, and was originally built to handle vessels drawing four and a half feet of water. The province furnished all the capital, except £10,000 sterling which was contributed by the home government in exchange for the right to convey troops and military stores through the canal free of charge.

The completion of the Welland and Rideau canals, and of those on the Ottawa and at Lachine, made continuous water transit possible all the way between the ocean and Lake Superior. The Ottawa-Rideau canals however were designed primarily for military purposes. They were not owned or controlled by the province, but by the imperial government acting through the military authorities in the colony. Defense was an imperial responsibility, and the provincial authorities paid no attention to it at all. The military canals were circuitous, and contained a large number of locks. Also they were not very large, while, as time went on, bigger ships were built. The local authorities therefore decided to devote their attention to improving the St. Lawrence route, which, though vulnerable

16. By I Geo. IV, c. 6 (L.C.).

from the soldier's point of view, promised a great commercial advantage. A large program of construction was undertaken, based on the theory that the St. Lawrence waterway was naturally superior to any of its rivals.

In the year 1821 the legislature of Upper Canada had appointed a commission to report on the internal navigation of the province. The Welland Canal, from the time when it was first opened in 1832, provided a powerful argument in favor of the improvement of the St. Lawrence below it. In 1833 the legislatures of both provinces took steps to obtain information in the matter, and two American engineers were asked to examine the St. Lawrence and report on the practicability and probable expense of improving it by means of canals. Early in the following year one of them wrote: "It is certain to my mind that with such a canal as I have projected along the St. Lawrence; and Welland Canal in good order, that all the products of the soil from all the upper Lakes can be carried to tide water *a good deal cheaper by this route than can ever be done by the Erie Canal or any other work.*"[17]

That able diagnostician of sick colonies, Lord Durham, during his famous survey of the Canadas formed an exceedingly high estimate of the importance of a good system of canals on the St. Lawrence. On July 10, 1838, the great proconsul left Montreal for a journey through Upper Canada. He travelled, of necessity, very largely by water. Like La Salle before him, he was greatly impressed by the economic possibilities of Kingston, thinking it could be made the depôt of the western trade seeking an outlet to the Gulf.[18]

Sailing westward up Lake Ontario Durham noted with admiration the thriving town of Buffalo, with its fine buildings and the forest of masts in its harbor. "This prosperity," he wrote, "is owing to the Erie Canal which commences at Buffalo, and thus makes it the depot of all

17. Benjamin Wright to Joseph Bloomfield Esq., New York, April 1, 1834. Quoted in appendix to Col. Phillpotts' First Report.

18. Durham to Glenelg, No. 24, of July 12, 1838. Dom. Arch. MS. Room.

the trade of the West flowing to New York. All these advantages might be ours by the judicious application of not a large expenditure."[19] Durham went on to recommend to the Colonial Office the completion of the Welland Canal which he considered to be potentially superior to the Erie, and the construction of a canal in the St. Lawrence, "which has become necessary in consequence of our incredible abandonment of Barnhart's Island[20] to the United States. . . ."[21] Then would the western trade pass down the St. Lawrence to the sea, "and enrich all the Towns and districts through which it was carried." Lord Durham suggested a grant of money by the imperial government for the purpose, on the same principle by which grants-in-aid were voted for public works in England. He thought that the canal tolls would soon repay the principal, and added: "I believe, My Lord, I am not too sanguine when I assert that such a step taken would at once put an end to all discontents and disturbances in the Canadas." Lord Durham's suggestions and pleas were not without effect. Replying to the despatches referred to above, the colonial secretary requested Durham to communicate with the ordnance authorities with a view to the employment of a well-qualified engineer to examine the Welland Canal, "and such works as may open water communication between Lake Erie and the Sea," and to report in full for the information of His Majesty's Government.[22] Glenelg added that the latter was not thereby bound to propose financial assistance to parliament. Durham therefore gave instructions to Major (afterwards Lieutenant Colonel) George Phillpotts, R.E., to carry out the work mentioned in Lord Glenelg's despatch.

Phillpotts went ahead with his survey, and although the governor-general, Lord Sydenham, seemed to think him

19. Durham to Glenelg, No. 25, of July 16, 1838. Dom. Arch. MS. Room.

20. Opposite the Cornwall Canal.

21. W. H. Malloy, *Treaties, Conventions, . . . between the United States and other Powers* (Washington, 1910), I, 621.

22. Glenelg to Durham, No. 94, of Aug. 23, 1838. Dom. Arch. MS. Room.

slow and rather acquisitive, he wrote two very workmanlike reports,[23] which are documents of great value for the study of the Canadian canals. The first report was made late in 1839 and the second one the following year. Phillpotts was very enthusiastic about the St. Lawrence route, and recommended that an extensive program of canal construction be undertaken. Like many competent observers before and after him, he thought that by this means the St. Lawrence route could obtain the western trade.[24] Like Lord Durham he considered it to be a matter of imperial concern. He thought that revenue from tolls would suffice to pay the interest on the capital investment, and that improvement of the St. Lawrence navigation would make for good feeling and peace between the British Empire and the United States. He also thought that migration to the colony, and property values therein, would by this means be greatly increased. The recommendation was also made that any canals which might be constructed should be large enough for freight steamers of considerable size. The total estimated cost of the necessary canal works was £2,200,000 sterling. Phillpotts' reports frequently refer to the competitive possibilities of the Erie Canal.

Phillpotts considered the Ottawa-Rideau system to be excellent as a military line of communication; but that it could not compete with the Erie, nor do much to develop the Canadas commercially. Nevertheless, as a very poor second best to the development of the St. Lawrence, he suggested that the military canals be put in the best shape possible.

The Act of Union of 1840 effected an increase in the

23. Reports on the Inland Navigation of the Canadas. (C.O. 42:498).

24. He reinforced this opinion by quoting from a letter written by a business firm in Cleveland, Ohio, in which the following sentence occurs: "As to which of the two great routes from the West to the Atlantic (after the completion of yours) will obtain the preference, we give it as our opinion that 'in as much as that of the St Lawrence *must* be the cheapest so it must be preferred, and we look forward to its completion with great pleasure, believing as we do that it will be of incalculable benefit to the West.'" Messrs. Pease and Allen to Lt.-Col. Phillpotts, Aug. 22, 1839. First Report.

joint resources of the two Canadas, and made it easier for them to deal intelligently and comprehensively with their waterway problem. Soon after the union was brought about, and after Phillpotts' reports were written, and before the construction of canals on the St. Lawrence had been carried very far, a Board of Works was established by the provincial government[25] to administer and control the public works of the province. A chief commissionership of public works was later created.[26] The person chosen for this difficult and responsible post was Hamilton H. Killaly, a civilian engineer who had had considerable experience in the employ of the Welland Canal Company and who enjoyed the respect of the public.

The canals along the St. Lawrence between Lake Ontario and Lachine were six in number, and were built between 1834 and 1848. The Cornwall Canal was constructed in order to enable ships to pass the Long Sault. It was begun in 1834, and although the work had to be suspended in 1838 on account of lack of funds, it was completed in 1843. The Beauharnois Canal which was begun in 1842 and completed in 1845, led from Lake St. Francis to Lake St. Louis. The Williamsburg Canals, of which there were four, were begun in 1843 and completed in 1848, and were situated between Prescott and Dickenson's Landing.[27] The Beauharnois Canal was built in order to overcome a series of rapids immediately below Lake St. Francis. It was here, on the north side of the river, that the small batteau locks already referred to had been built after 1779. The provincial authorities were pressed to construct their canal on the north side also in the interest of military security, and there was a good deal to be said in favor of this, for were not these the "roaring forties" of American history? The military engineers were suspicious of a canal which could not be defended in time of war. Phillpotts preferred the north side of the river in a

25. 4 and 5 Vic., c. 38 (Prov.). 26. 9 Vic., c. 37 (Prov.).

27. The Williamsburg Canals were located at the Galoppes, Point Iroquois, Rapide Plat, and Farren's Point.

lukewarm kind of way. Bonnycastle had no use for any of the St. Lawrence canals, considering them to be vulnerable and unnecessary.[28] Perhaps he would have been prejudiced against anything that was an alternative to his beloved Rideau. The Seigneury of Beauharnois on the other hand, wishing the canal to be on its side of the river, employed two engineers to prove that the south was the better side, and indeed, apart from the question of military security, so it may have been. In the end the canal was built on the south side—on the side where the seigneury and the Americans were—military considerations being entirely sacrificed to economic ones.

Even at an earlier period the government of Lower Canada had undertaken to improve the waterways of that province, though the program was more modest than that of Upper Canada. The Lachine Canal, to which reference has already been made, had been completed in its original dimensions in 1825. It was one of the most important canals in the province, because it was a complementary and necessary part both of the Ottawa-Rideau and of the St. Lawrence routes. The greater dimensions to which the other canals on the St. Lawrence were being built, made it necessary to enlarge the Lachine so as to correspond with them, and this work was completed in 1848. A lock was built at St. Anne's at the western end of the Island of Montreal to overcome the rapids there. In addition a lock and a canal were constructed in order to improve the navigation of the Richelieu, the historic highway to New England both in peace and war.[29]

28. *The Canadas in 1841,* II, 71. Later, however, he changed his mind. "I was at first much opposed to the immense outlay required in constructing the St. Lawrence Canal, when the Rideau answered every purpose for small steamboats; but my mind has since been convinced that the two are perfectly compatible with the best interests of the province, the one as a military, the other as a commercial canal." *Canada, as it was, is, and may be,* II, 251.

29. St. Anne's Lock, between St. Anne's and Isle Perrot, begun 1839, finished 1843. St. Ours Lock, at St. Ours on the Richelieu, begun 1844, finished 1849. Chambly Canal, on the Richelieu between St. John's and Chambly Basin, begun 1831, finished 1843.

The second quarter of the nineteenth century was the Canadian canal age. This period witnessed the end of more than a century of canal development in Great Britain during which time expanding commerce, not yet served by the railway, had sought and found along artificial inland water-routes, the cheap and extensive means of transit so greatly required. Not only Great Britain, but the United States also, had set the precedent, and the Canadians, always an imitative rather than an inventive people, had followed a parallel course. They had been easily convinced of the desirability of improving their waterways. Moreover, since plans for canals are far easier and less expensive to construct than are canals themselves, many and varied had been the suggestions and schemes advanced. In the year 1834 the Port Hope and Rice Lake, and Richmond Canal Companies were formed. Suggestions were made that a canal be built from the Ottawa River to Lake Huron. A certain Charles Shirreff reported very favorably on the project. "It would," he said, "give to upper Canada a body and a shape."[30] Shirreff was urging this scheme on the home government as late as 1843. In 1846 it was announced that "Une souscription a été commencée à Montréal et dans le Haut-Canada pour l'ouverture d'un canal au Saut Sainte-Marie."[31] The idea was deemed of sufficient importance to induce chief commissioner Killaly to go thither on a tour of inspection, and to make an official report on the subject. The possibility of a canal at Sault Ste. Marie had also been suggested by Phillpotts in 1840. A canal to connect the Bay of Fundy with the St. Lawrence was also considered. Nothing, however, came of these proposals.

In the above survey of the Canadian canal problem and its attempted solution down to about 1846, from the point of view of economic conditions in the colony immediately after that date, three things seem to stand out as being of especial importance. The first is that the Canadas, pos-

30. Report dated Jan., 1829. Dom. Arch., Series C., 48, pp. 2–14.
31. *Le Canadien,* Aug. 19, 1846.

sessing a fine waterway to the sea, had every reason to feel that if they only took advantage of their opportunities, their economic future was a bright one. Those who had investigated the potentialities of the St. Lawrence route had returned a unanimous verdict to that effect. An adequate solution of their own transportation problem seemed to present itself. Yet this was not all, for beyond the margin of this measured wish, inquiring and hopeful men saw, or thought they saw, a vision more splendid and spacious by far. It was the vision of numberless great ships, heavy with the grain of all the western land, coming down *their* river to the sea. Was it possible that a people whose lot was fallen to them in so fair a ground, with their feet astride one of the greatest of the world's highways, could live other than prosperously? Moreover, as we shall see, the fiscal policy of the United Kingdom down to the year 1845 served to paint the lily of colonial optimism.

The second point is that having seen what they thought was a golden opportunity, both the authorities in England and the governments and people in the province had acted accordingly. On the whole it may fairly be said that they had left no stone unturned in order to make the most of their advantages. Nearly everyone—not only governments, but business men and the general public—had become convinced that it was necessary to improve the waterways. The difficulties were great, and, scarcity of capital in colonies being remembered, the outlay on canals had been very large. Money was always scarce; but for this purpose at least it had been forthcoming. The imperial and provincial governments were *laissez faire* governments if ever there were any; yet in the matter of canals they had made an exception, and had gone into business on a large scale. Private individuals also had invested considerable sums. The extent of the commitments is reflected in the important place occupied by canals in the political life of the period. The question of public finance was closely interlocked with that of public works.

One commitment led to another, for the building of one canal may create a need for others. As is almost always the case, the actual cost generally exceeded the estimates, and this to an extent which sometimes seems almost grotesque. Engineers did not prove to be infallible, the water in a completed canal being sometimes shallower than the specifications had called for. Many of the canals after completion required to be enlarged, this process occasioning no small amount of waste. Always however the feeling was that the canals were a good investment and would pay their way—perhaps, like the Erie, pay handsomely. The argument ran thus: The greater the outlay the better the canals; the better the canals the heavier the traffic; the heavier the traffic the greater the income. It was reasoning in what might be described as a virtuous circle. Sometimes money was spent in the hope of salvaging previous investments thereby. The province had made very heavy commitments on the strength of its faith in the future of its waterway.

The third fact is that the Canadian waterway was not free from serious competition. For two centuries it had been contending for the trade of the great hinterland. In 1846 the canal program was almost completed, and the waterway was about to stand ready to challenge its formidable rival the Erie. The question as to which would win had been discussed eloquently and endlessly, and was now to be put to the test.

## III

## MONTREAL *VERSUS* NEW YORK

I know, indeed, of no difference in the machinery of government in the old and new world that strikes an European more forcibly than the apparently undue importance which the business of constructing public works appears to occupy in American legislation. LORD DURHAM'S REPORT.

ALONG the Atlantic coast of North America stretches a great chain of mountains, to the westward of which lies one of the most extensive regions of productive country in the world. This whole area shared with the Province of Canada the typical colonial problem of transporting staples to the market, that is to say toward the seaboard; and three great river valleys, breaching the barrier of the mountains or circumventing it, offered themselves as channels for this trade. Far to the westward and southward ran the Mississippi. The other two, the valleys of the Mohawk and Hudson rivers, and of the St. Lawrence, lay to the east of the Great Lakes region and concerned it more particularly. Taken together with the lakes, both valleys reached into the heart of a huge staple-producing area, of which the Province of Canada was but a small part, and they were rivals for the same trade.[1]

For two hundred years they had been rivals. In the seventeenth century the control of the Mohawk–Hudson–New York route had enabled first the Dutch and then the English colonists to compete with the French on the St. Lawrence for the possession of the trade of the interior—furs for the European market coming downstream toward

1. Vide W. A. Mackintosh, "Economic Factors in Canadian History," in the *Canadian Historical Review,* IV, 12–25.

the sea, and a flow of goods moving westward to pay for the furs.

When the frontier pushed westward past the Great Lakes with a broad golden belt of grain behind it, a new era dawned. The hunter gave way to the farmer, and ships in place of canoes came down the water highways, laden with grain instead of furs. All the way from the east end of Lake Ontario to the Mississippi there now stretched a huge plain on which ever-increasing supplies of wheat were being raised. Canada West formed a small part of this huge grain-growing area, which was divided politically by the northern boundary of the United States. Under the leadership of its commercial class the province had undertaken to solve its own transportation problem by constructing a series of ship-canals connecting Lake Erie with the ocean; while it was even hoped, and the hope was supported by the best-informed opinion, that the provincial waterway would also engross the trade of that far larger part of the lake region situated in the United States. A staple crop seeking its distant market tends to obey the law of economic gravitation and go the cheapest way, and when the distance to the market is great, the area served by the cheapest trade-route is likely to be extensive. In such a case therefore, the volume of trade flowing along the most advantageous channel will usually be very great, and the entrepôt is likely to become a large and prosperous city. It was the vaulting ambition of Montreal to become the entrepôt of the western trade.

The State of New York however, as of old had been the case, also enjoyed a key position with respect to the western trade, in that it too possessed a river valley which cut a way through the mountains to the Atlantic. Early in the nineteenth century it had determined to take advantage of this fact by constructing the Erie Canal, a work designed to intercept the western trade coming down the Great Lakes, and to divert it thence southward into the Mohawk Valley, and so down the Hudson to New

York. The Erie was both begun and completed ahead of the Canadian canals, and thus the old rivalry of the Dutch and English with the French for possession of the fur trade, appeared again in a more modern form. In Lord Durham's language, New York State had "made its own St. Lawrence from Lake Erie to the Hudson."

The Erie Canal was begun in 1817 and completed in 1825 at a cost of something over $7,000,000. It ran from a point close to Buffalo on Lake Erie, to Albany on the Hudson. Unlike the works on the St. Lawrence which were ship-canals, the Erie was a barge-canal, suitable only for narrow craft of very shallow draught which can be employed satisfactorily enough in a canal, but are useless on the broader waters outside. Originally it was forty feet wide at the surface and four feet deep, with locks ninety feet long and fifteen feet broad. It was being enlarged in the period, so that by 1849 vessels of a hundred tons could use it, and by 1853 vessels of two hundred tons. It had about ninety locks, and a total lockage of over six hundred and fifty feet. From the main canal several branches led to lake harbors east of Buffalo. The most important of these was one thirty-eight miles long, connecting Oswego on Lake Ontario with the Erie at Syracuse, and another ran northward to Whitehall on Lake Champlain, a distance of sixty-five miles.[2] The recent controversy over the Chicago drainage canal has raised the question of the right to divert the water of the Great Lakes into an outlet other than their natural one. It is therefore worth noticing that in connection with the Erie project a proposal was made "for breaking down the mound of Lake Erie, and letting out the waters to follow the level of the country, so as to form a sloop navigation with the Hudson, and without any aid from any other water."[3] The Erie Canal was

2. See "Report of the Topographical Bureau," in *Senate Ex. Docs.*, No. 4, 30th Congress, 1st Sess., II; and A. Barton Hepburn, *Artificial Waterways and Commercial Development.*

3. De Witt Clinton, "Private Canal Journal," in W. W. Campbell, *Life and Writings of De Witt Clinton* (New York, 1849).

a tremendous success, and was an inspiration to promoters of public works everywhere. So remunerative was it, that ten years after its completion the tolls had repaid the cost of construction. Yet it proved to be much more than a successful business venture. "The decrease in transportation charges brought prosperity and a tide of population into western New York; villages sprang up along the whole line of the canal; the water-power was utilized for manufactures; land values in the western part of the state doubled and in many cases quadrupled; farm produce more than doubled in value. Buffalo and Rochester became cities."[4]

Before the year 1845 the political boundary between Canada and the United States had been a barrier to trade, and Montreal and New York had shared their economic hinterland in accordance with its divided political affiliation. Yet the Erie was capable of serving Canada West as well as the American lake region, and in 1845 and 1846 American legislation authorized a drawback of duty on Canadian trade with other countries by way of the United States. The effect was to open the Erie to the export trade of Canada West. The imposition of an export duty was not a practical economic weapon, consequently the only means in the power of the province for retaining the trade of Canada West for the provincial waterway, was to make the latter a cheaper route to Britain than that by way of the United States. It was already doing everything possible to push forward the mechanical improvement of its waterway, and the American Drawback Laws provided a further stimulus.

The intention had been that the Canadian canal system should be completed by 1846; but the work was delayed and the waterway was not finished until the completion of the Lachine Canal early in 1848. The river was now equipped with a series of canals which an enthusiastic

4. F. J. Turner, *The Rise of the New West* (New York and London, 1906), pp. 33–34.

French Canadian who visited them the following year described as "the most magnificent works of human hands, in the universe." They in fact provided a really splendid waterway reaching all the way from Lake Huron to the ocean. The immensity of the navigable water involved can be realized with the aid of a map, or perhaps by means of the simple statement that the distance from the Straits of Belle Isle to the head of Lake Huron is about two thousand miles.

The enlarged Welland Canal was not as capacious as the St. Lawrence canals. Its locks were big enough to contain a ship a hundred and thirty feet long, twenty-six in beam, and drawing eight feet of water. Such a vessel was of about three hundred and fifty tons burden, and could use the completed provincial waterway all the way from Lake Huron to the ocean. The Welland had not been enlarged to the full size of the St. Lawrence canals below it, apparently because the dimensions given enabled it to deal with the largest ship which could negotiate the passage between Lake Huron and Lake Erie. The St. Lawrence canals, including the one at Lachine, could accommodate a ship a hundred and eighty feet long, with a beam measurement of forty-four feet, and drawing eight and a half feet of water. A ship of this size could carry four hundred and fifty tons of cargo, and could sail by the provincial waterway to the head of Lake Ontario.

The increasing dimensions of the Canadian canals had been due to a desire to avoid trans-shipments, and to the progressive increase in the size of the most economical type of vessel. The canoe had given place to the batteau, "a flat-bottomed, sharp pointed skiff about 5½ feet beam and 35 feet long." Then came the Durham boat, American in origin, "a long-decked barge, square ahead, and square astern." Next came the sailing ship, followed in turn by the paddle-wheel steamer and the propeller.[5] As

5. The batteau could carry about 30 barrels of flour, the Durham boat about 350, and the steamship about 3000.

late as 1851, more than half of the Great Lakes tonnage consisted of sailing vessels, though most of the new ships were propelled by steam. The normal type of steamer was the side-wheeler. The "propeller" as its name implies was a screw-driven steam vessel, those used on the St. Lawrence and the Great Lakes being of the type invented by the great Swedish engineer Ericksson. The propeller was beginning to replace the paddle-wheel ship in the period, as its engines were more efficient and compact, and the screw better in most ways than the wheel. The propeller was also better adapted for use in canals than the side-wheeler was, because the paddles of the latter, projecting outwards on each side, prevented the width of the canal lock from being utilized to the full.

"The Erie Canal and the St. Lawrence are the great leading highways to the ocean," wrote the Toronto *Examiner* in 1847, "and competition between them is now about to commence in earnest." There was no third competitor, for the railways were not quite yet in a position to rival the waterways, and the Mississippi Valley was too remote from that of the St. Lawrence for the two to come into serious economic conflict. Nor was there any rival to the northward, though it is interesting to notice that the American consul, Israel D. Andrews, in one of his well-known and valuable reports on the trade and commerce of the British North American colonies, drew attention to the existence of the Hudson Bay route. "There yet remains one route of importation to be noticed," he stated, "viz: via Hudson's Bay and Lake Superior. Nearly one-half of the imports at Sault Ste. Marie are by this route. It is impossible to say what may yet be done in this quarter. The distance from the shores of Superior to those of Hudson's bay is no greater than that between the Hudson river, at Albany, and Lake Erie, at Buffalo; the sea-route to Britain is shorter this way than by the lakes and Montreal, New York, or Boston."[6]

6. "Report on the Trade of the British North American Colonies." *Senate Ex. Docs.*, No. 112, 32nd Cong., 1st Sess., XV, 430–431.

In 1848 the new provincial waterway was open at last, with the immediate result of greatly reducing the freight rates between the Great Lakes and Montreal,[7] and the competitive efficiency of the route began to be put to a practical test at last. Some in Canada who had given the matter careful attention continued to strike the note of optimism. In the following and very troubled year 1849, a prominent firm of Montreal merchants doing pioneer work in attempting to build up a trade in goods for the western states imported by way of the St. Lawrence instead of through the Erie Canal, reported that "by actual transactions we have done much to disabuse the mercantile mind of the belief, once almost general that the Free Trade policy of England would be injurious to this province, and that, with freedom from impediments, and restrictions on our Commerce we shall be in a better position than ever we have been, and more certain to advance in prosperity. Those views are being daily confirmed by the increasing orders we are receiving for goods from the west."[8] Soon afterwards I. D. Andrews stated that "the basin of the Great Lakes, and of the river St. Lawrence . . . is an American treasure; its value to be estimated less by what it has already accomplished, than by what it must achieve in its progress." More specifically he considered the St. Lawrence to be "the natural outlet of Michigan, a portion of Wisconsin, Illinois, and Indiana, of northern Ohio, of northern Pennsylvania, of northern and western New York, and of the westerly part of Vermont—a district comprising the principal portion of the wheat-growing region of the United States."[9]

7. See D. L. Burn, "Canada and the Repeal of the Corn Laws," in the *Cambridge Historical Journal,* II, 252–272.

8. Messrs. Holmes, Young, and Knapp to Lord Elgin, Montreal, June 1, 1849. Correspondence of the Civil Secretary (Dominion Archives) No. 5185. Holmes shortly afterwards became prominent in the annexation movement, and Young the leader of the anti-annexationists in Montreal.

9. "Second Report," cited above, p. 3; and "First Report," *Senate Ex. Docs.,* No. 23, 31st Cong., 2nd Sess., Vol. IV, 49.

If a physical comparison be made between the St. Lawrence route to Montreal and Quebec, and the Erie-Hudson route to New York as they stood after the opening of the provincial canals in 1848, the Canadian route will be found to have been greatly superior to its American rival. The works on the St. Lawrence were ship-canals: goods could therefore be carried up or down that river in vessels of cargo capacity very much greater than that of the barges on the Erie, and it is a well-known principle of transportation economics that up to a certain point efficiency increases with the size of the unit. Moreover the fact that the Erie was a comparatively narrow and shallow canal carried with it this further very serious disadvantage, that lake vessels which were able to take a cargo up or down the St. Lawrence waterway passing through the canals, were obliged, if their cargo were to go by way of the Erie, to trans-ship it to barges at the entrance to that canal, and there was sometimes a further trans-shipment at Albany. A very much larger proportion too, of the navigation by the St. Lawrence route was in open water as opposed to canals, than in the case of its rival. Indeed the canal mileage on the Erie was about five times as great as that on the provincial waterway. For while the Erie was a canal practically all the way from Buffalo to Albany, ships sailed up the St. Lawrence waterway on the broad surface of a mighty river, save only where for short distances the presence of rapids made canal navigation necessary. It was even possible for ships of five hundred tons burden to go down the river without using the canals at all, and they very often did so; the Williamsburg canals indeed being only designed to handle westward moving traffic. This large proportion of river navigation meant of course much lower expenditure for construction and maintenance, and therefore lower toll charges than would otherwise have been necessary, and had made possible the construction of locks and canals of large size. It also minimized the chances of a stoppage, and enabled ships to travel more swiftly than they could otherwise have done since in open water the friction is diminished and there are no canal walls or locks to injure a vessel or be injured by it. The distance was less too from the Great Lakes to Montreal than to New York, and a cargo could be sent in a much shorter time to the former place than to the latter. A cargo could go from Chicago to New York in about eighteen days, of which twelve were spent in the canal, while the ordinary time from Chicago to Quebec was approximately ten days.[10]

The provincial canals commanded voluminous and dependable supplies of water, for they lay close to the river and on a level with it. In this respect too the Erie was inferior, for it followed an inland route and crossed a height of land. "The canal navigation is still arrested for the want of water," reported a New York newspaper in 1848. "The laden boats from this city and Troy are detained at Schenectady and in that vicinity, and the number is large. . . . Owing to the want of water on the levels east of Rochester, there has been a great accumulation there of boats from the west."[11] Traffic congestion was sometimes a serious problem on the Erie, and in a newspaper in 1847, "A Boat Captain" describing a trip through that canal, bewailed the frequent and long delays. He told of tow-horses standing idle and of bargees playing quoits during what was no doubt an exceptionally protracted delay of three days.[12] Two years later the legislature of Michigan passed a resolution complaining that the Erie was unable "to furnish the necessary means to do and perform, without great delay, the carrying trade between that point [Buffalo] and tide-water."[13] Like the St. Lawrence, the

10. "Report of Commissioners of Public Works, 1848." *Sessional Papers, 1849*, App. B.B. (C.O. 45: 237).

11. *Herald*, May 14, 1848.

12. New York *Tribune*, June 5, 1847.

13. *House Misc. Docs.*, No. 6, 31st Cong., 1st Sess., Vol. I.

COTEAU RAPIDS ON THE ST. LAWRENCE, 1851.

northern part of the Erie was sealed by ice during a large part of each year, though the American route had a slight advantage in this respect.

The St. Lawrence waterway took its course to the sea in the most convenient direction possible, that is to say directly toward Great Britain the principal market for grain exports and the place from which most of the ocean-borne imports came. T. C. Keefer drew attention to this fact both on his map and elsewhere. "Most persons," he wrote, "accustomed to the view of maps and charts upon Mercator's projection, or upon the plane surface of the Atlas, are apt to complain of the great *détour* the St. Lawrence makes to reach the Ocean, and imagine that there is a great additional length of voyage to be made, by a ship starting from Quebec or Montreal for Britain, over one from New York." He affirmed that this was an error, saying that if a thread were stretched out upon the surface of a globe from Lake Ontario to England, the line of the St. Lawrence would be found to lie along it. He went on to point out that the longitudinal lines on a plane map are parallel, whereas in reality "every degree of longitude contains a less number of miles as we approach the poles. Canada has suffered not a little in the estimation of the world, from the conception of Mercator."[14]

As might be expected these decisive advantages were reflected in the cost of carriage, and it was considerably cheaper to send goods from the Great Lakes to Montreal than to New York. Both tolls and freight-rates were lower on the Canadian route than on the Erie. The commissioners of public works presented the following figures for the year 1847, expressing confidence in their accuracy:[15]

14. T. C. Keefer, *The Canals of Canada.* Keefer, who was a government engineer on the canals, and who knew all that there was to know about them, drew a very good map of the waterways for the Paris Exhibition of 1855. On Keefer's map the continent is tilted so as to correct the misrepresentation against which he is protesting here.

15. *Sess. Papers, 1849,* App. B.B. (C.O. 45:237). The barrel of flour is the best unit of comparison for outward cargoes.

| | DOWNWARD (*Per barrel of flour*) | | | UPWARD (*Per hundred lbs. of goods*) | | |
|---|---|---|---|---|---|---|
| | *Tolls* | *Freight* | *Total* | *Tolls* | *Freight* | *Total* |
| Between Buffalo and Albany (Erie). | 31¢ | 46¢ | 77¢ | 24¢ | 15¢ | 39¢ or $7.80 per ton |
| Between Port Maitland and Montreal (St. L.). | 15¢ | 20¢ | 35¢ | 10¢ | 5¢ | 15¢ or $3.00 per ton |

It will be seen that whether coming up or going down, the transportation charges on the Erie were more than twice those on the St. Lawrence, and the difference in favor of the latter would be greater still if the freight-charges between Albany and New York were included.

Nevertheless, a year after the provincial canals were finished, the following was written by a Montreal business man who was thoroughly conversant with the situation. "Business is exceedingly dull both here and in Quebec as a great portion of the Trade of Western Canada now passes thro' New York."[16] In view of all that has been said about the marked superiority of the Canadian waterway this fact, for a fact it was, requires to be explained. Why was business "exceedingly dull" on the St. Lawrence while the less adequate Erie Canal was so crowded that delays were caused by congestion of traffic? The answer is that although the St. Lawrence route was greatly superior to the Erie as a channel connecting the hinterland to a seaport, nevertheless, as an entrepôt for the overseas trade with Great Britain and other countries, Montreal was very inferior to New York. The advantages were almost all on the side of the American port, and they were more

16. Thomas Ryan to Thomas Baring, M.P., June 9, 1849. Baring Papers —Misc. Correspondence.

than sufficient to counterbalance the superior efficiency of the St. Lawrence waterway between the Great Lakes and Montreal.

Ocean freight-rates were very sensitive to varying influences mainly associated with competition and scarcity, and were therefore subject to great and frequent fluctuations; the movement of rates at Montreal and New York however, tended to follow the same course. The rates at New York were usually about two shillings sterling lower, per barrel of flour, than those at Montreal, against which must be offset the saving of about one-and-ninepence in favor of the provincial route above Montreal, leaving a small advantage in favor of New York. In addition, insurance rates were much higher on the Canadian than on the American route, as they still are. A ship is never so safe as when out in the open ocean, and whereas beyond the islands outside New York harbor there is nothing but deep blue sea, on the Montreal route between a quarter and a third of the whole voyage is in narrow waters, in part of which fog and icebergs often form an evil partnership against the safety of ships, the danger being greater early and late in the season than at other times. The factor of relative risk expressed in terms of insurance on a barrel of flour gave New York an advantage of something like sixpence. After the completion of the provincial canals therefore it was usually a little cheaper to send produce to Great Britain from Canada West or the northwestern states through New York than by way of Montreal, and correspondingly cheaper to import goods by the former than by the latter route. Commercial men are influenced by what look like very slight differences in cost expressed in terms of the unit of measurement, because they handle goods in great quantities, and the amount saved by sending the cargo of a lake vessel by way of New York rather than Montreal, might easily amount to a hundred pounds. These facts are like contours on the economic map showing why most of the trade followed the one course rather than the other.

There were many reasons for the higher cost of ocean freight-rates on the Canadian than on the American route. The Canadian harbors, being ice-bound all the winter long, could never become regular ports of call for any ship. Reference has been made to the high insurance rates which prevailed on the northern route. The cargoes were insured separately, but the cost of underwriting the ships had to be added to the freight-rate. Pilotage charges on the St. Lawrence also, for obvious reasons, were greater than at New York, the difference in favor of the latter port, on a typical ship, amounting to about thirty per cent.[17] Between Montreal and Quebec also, expenses were further increased by the necessity of towing freight vessels with tugs in that part of the river, and a witness testifying before a House of Lords committee estimated that the towage and pilotage between Quebec and Montreal, up and down, on a vessel of four hundred tons, would equal at least ten per cent of the freight charge.[18] Apart from pilotage and towage also, the various charges made on a ship coming to either of the St. Lawrence ports were much higher than those at New York. The American genius for simplification had been at work here with striking results in making it relatively inexpensive for a ship to call at New York. A comparison of the respective charges at Quebec and New York in a typical case gives the following result. On a vessel of seven hundred tons drawing fifteen feet of water on the inward voyage and eighteen feet outwards, the public charges including pilotage would have amounted to £47 7*s.* 3*d.* at Quebec, while the corresponding charges at New York would have been £25 5*s.* 0*d.* Wharfage and stevedorage on the same ship would have come to £38 10*s.* at Quebec as against only £11 at New York. There is a difference here of almost £50 in favor of the American port.[19]

17. Appendix to "Report of Commissioners of P.W., 1850." *Sess. Papers, 1851,* App. T. (C.O. 45: 247).

18. *Reports from Committees, 1847–8,* XX, Pt. II, Q's. 3043 ff.

19. Appendixes to *Report of Commissioners of Public Works, 1850.*

The average sailing time too, between Montreal and Liverpool, was a little longer than that between New York and Liverpool. This was because it was possible to make better time in the open sea than in the gulf and the river, and because generally speaking the ships frequenting New York were faster sailers than those which came up the St. Lawrence. A few steamers were already in use and these ran to New York. Commerce at the provincial ports too, was hampered by a frequent scarcity of shipping, a difficulty with which New York was not afflicted, and this lack of competition no doubt tended to increase freight rates. Shipwrecks were fairly frequent in the St. Lawrence River and Gulf, and it is likely that the comparative difficulty and danger attendant upon the navigation there, especially for those not thoroughly familiar with that route, deterred many ships from coming to Quebec or Montreal. A further reason for the scarcity of ships was brought out in the evidence given before the Lords' committee to which reference has already been made:

"I doubt," said a witness, "whether Foreign Vessels or any Vessels would go there in any Numbers without Charters, because they are cut out from all the other Ports of America when they enter the River; and just in proportion as they ascend the River St. Lawrence up to Montreal their Expenses increase, and the Number of Places of loading Decrease."

"(Q) They are in a Cul-de-Sac?"

"(A) Precisely."[20]

From one further disability, too, the Canadian ports and waterway began to suffer at this time. Until the year 1848 the St. Lawrence had been a favorite route for ships carrying emigrants from the United Kingdom to North America. The emigrant trade was a godsend to the shipowners, for it made possible profitable westward voyages for many ships that would otherwise have had to cross in ballast if they crossed at all. After the great Irish famine most of the emigrants sailed to New York, and the vessels

20. *Reports from Committees, 1847–8,* XX, Pt. II, Q's. 3053–54.

which had brought them were loaded with cargoes for the return voyage at that port.

The failure of the provincial waterway to compete successfully with the American route for the trade of the Great Lakes region including Canada West, resulted in the main then from conditions which had always prevailed, but whose existence had only become manifest in the period after 1845. Prior to that time the American tariff, and the policy of colonial preference supplemented at the last by the Canada Corn Act of 1843, had kept the St. Lawrence waterway sheltered behind a political barrier which had enabled it to monopolize the external commerce of the province. During the three years from 1845 to 1847 practically the whole of the barrier was removed leaving the waterway exposed to the vigorous competition of the American route. Just at this time however, a splendid system of ship-canals was being completed on the St. Lawrence, and there was room for hope that the improved Canadian waterway might prove to be more efficient than the Erie-Hudson route. In that event the St. Lawrence seemed destined to obtain not only the external trade of the province but that of the American lake states as well. Such a success in turn appeared to promise a far greater degree of prosperity than the colony had ever known. These hopes however were doomed to disappointment, for under a régime of free competition the greater expense of ocean shipments from Montreal and Quebec as compared with New York, more than offset the advantages of the provincial waterway above Montreal. Consequently, not only nearly all the trade of the American lake region, but also a large part of that of the province itself, followed the path of the Erie and the Hudson to New York.

By the year 1851 the St. Lawrence waterway was not winning in the contest with the Erie and its ability to do so was growing more doubtful; yet hope had not been entirely abandoned. The contest was continued; but the St. Lawrence failed to obtain more than a part of the provincial trade. At the middle of the century the waterway era came to an end, giving place to the first great period of railway construction, which indeed would probably have come sooner than it did had the province been less adequately furnished both by nature and by art with means of communication by water.

In a circular despatch of Jan. 15, 1846, the Colonial Secretary sought to lay down rules for railway legislation. In the earlier part of the period in the province, railways were not as generally popular as they became very soon afterwards. A resident in the colony wrote that "Many people were prejudiced against railways in those days [about 1847] and thought our old roads were best, or at least good enough." Upon one occasion in 1846, Merritt denied that a certain proposed railway would compete with his beloved canals, and asked the legislative assembly scornfully if they would have the presumption to "compare the mighty St. Lawrence to a trumpery Rail Road."

In the year 1845 the first American Drawback Law offered a threat to the trade of Montreal, and in the same year a company was incorporated for the purpose of building a railway to connect Montreal with a salt-water port accessible to ships in the winter time. The harbor was Portland, Maine, and the railway was the St. Lawrence and Atlantic. The line was built, but it did not remedy the defects from which Montreal suffered due to the freezing up of the river in winter. There was also a plan, to which both the imperial and provincial governments gave a good deal of attention, for establishing a railway communication between Canada and the maritime colonies through British territory, "a work," said Lord Grey, "of wh. the construction wd be of such infinite benefit to the whole Empire."[21] Reports on the project were being made in the period, though it was not carried out until many

21. Grey to Elgin, May 3, 1847. Private Correspondence. The underlying idea was very old. In the seventeenth century the intendant Talon had tried unsuccessfully to have a road built from Canada to Acadia. See Parkman, *The Old Régime in Canada,* Ch. XII.

years later. More ambitious still was the idea of a transcontinental line to the Pacific, which was sometimes discussed though not officially.[22] The ingenious and optimistic authors of a contemporary work on the province developed in some detail a plan for such a railway. The latter was to be constructed by means of convict labor, and the more heinous the offense which the convict was expiating, the further west he was to work on the railway.[23]

Unlike the canals, the early railways were privately owned; yet the provincial government played a considerable part in facilitating their construction, and its preoccupation with public works was carried over from the canal age to that of the railways. The middle of the century witnessed the beginning of widespread public interest in the newer form of transportation. The enthusiasm and energy until then devoted to the canals was diverted, and a network of metal roads began to be spread over the inhabited parts of the colony. The railway was destined, partly in conjunction with the waterways, and partly by taking their place, to solve the transportation problem of Canada more or less completely. Ultimately also, by connecting the maritime colonies and the prairies and British Columbia, with the riverine Province of Canada, railways made it possible for the last mentioned colony to become the keystone of that immense arch of provinces which spans the continent from Halifax to Victoria.[24]

22. E.g. in Bonnycastle, *Canada and the Canadians in 1846,* I, 139.

23. F. A. Wilson and A. B. Richards, *Britain Redeemed and Canada Preserved* (London, 1850).

24. Nothing in Canadian economic history is more important or fascinating than the story of the railways. That story begins within the period under discussion; but it is one and indivisible, belongs to a later time, and cannot be dealt with here.

## IV

## THE PUBLIC FINANCES

Set fit interdum vt quod sano consilio vel excellenti mente concipitur intercedente pecunia citius conualescat et quod difficile videbatur per hanc quasi per quandam negotiorum metodum facilem consequatur effectum. Non solum autem hostilitatis set etiam pacis tempore necessaria videtur. DIALOGUS DE SCACCARIO.

THE development of the St. Lawrence waterway had been due to the initiative of Montreal and Upper Canada, and even before the union, as has been seen, the latter had committed itself to an extensive program of canal construction. Lord Durham considered these works to have been "commenced on a very extended scale, and executed in a spirit of great carelessness and profusion." The co-operation of Lower Canada had been difficult to secure; nevertheless Upper Canada, having the greater need and the more lavish ideas, and because most of the work to be done lay within its territory, had spent its money unsparingly on public works.

"The public debt of this Province," wrote the governor of Upper Canada on the eve of the union, ". . . which involves an expenditure in Interest, nearly equal to the whole Revenues of the Colony, has been occasioned, as your Lordship will find noticed in the Earl of Durham's Report, principally by attempts to connect the magnificent inland Waters of the Province with the Sea by means of Canals which if completed, would open a line of inland navigation scarcely equalled in the World. . . . The expectation of a rapid realization of these advantages will at once explain to Your Lordship, the reason why the prudent course of making a provision for the interest of borrowed money from funds immediately available, was not adopted at each successive advance into Debt." The governor thought that the undertaking had been imprudent considering the state of the provincial finances; but that having been begun it ought to be completed. He went on to emphasize that the canals were expected to pay their way, not only indirectly but by the actual payment of interest and profits into the provincial treasury, an idea which had at all times been advanced as one of the strongest arguments on behalf of the waterway scheme. He suggested that the imperial government might perhaps guarantee the interest on a loan for these works, and throughout this long and competent despatch pleaded the cause of "a fine race of people who have been plunged into the deepest political and financial distress by a course of events most awfully calamitous."[1] These arguments he repeated and expanded in a subsequent despatch. His successor, Poulett Thompson, who later became Lord Sydenham, before his departure for the Canadas was informed by the home government of its intention to guarantee the Upper Canada debt.[2] In communicating with the colonial office he rightly took a more cheerful view than his predecessor had done; but agreed with the latter that Great Britain would have to help.[3]

The French Canadians, then as now, expected and received cheap government. They were not given to ambitious public policies which involved large expenditure and increased taxes therewith. Consequently, while Upper Canada entered the union heavily laden with debt, the position of Lower Canada in this respect was much more favorable. The two fiscal systems became one, and the united province assumed the Upper Canadian debt. It had been Lord Durham's opinion that the lower province would also gain by this arrangement in that the customary jobbing of its surplus revenue would cease; but French

1. Sir George Arthur to Lord Normanby, No. 131, of June 8, 1839. Dom. Arch. MS. Room.

2. Lord John Russell to the Treasury, July 24, 1840. Copy enclosed in Russell to Sydenham, No. 282, Jan. 11, 1841. Dom. Arch. MS. Room.

3. Poulett Thompson to Lord John Russell, No. 129, June 27, 1840. Dom. Arch. MS. Room.

Canadians thought differently. The union was consummated however, and a new chapter in Canadian history began. After the union, Lord Sydenham, whose judgment in such matters must have carried great weight, continued the argument in favor of imperial help, which he considered essential. "Nearly all the Canadian Debt," he wrote to the colonial secretary, "has been contracted for public Works which are begun but not completed, from which when completed a revenue will be derived, but which at the same time can only be rendered thus productive by fresh expenditure. The Province is sinking therefore under the weight of Engagements which it can only meet by fresh outlay, whilst that my present inability to meet its engagements, by destroying its credit prevents it from obtaining the means for this expenditure, thro' which it can alone extricate itself permanently from its difficulties." The debt of the province amounted to about a million and a quarter sterling, and Sydenham added to his explanation the following definite suggestion. "I should propose therefore that the Treasury should be authorized to raise a loan to that amount [£1,500,000 sterling], the proceeds to be applied first to the liquidation at par of the Canadian Debt and the residue for the completion of such public Works as might be deemed expedient." He thought that the money could be borrowed at a rate of interest two per cent lower with the imperial guarantee than without it.[4] The principle involved had already been accepted, and in 1842 the home government lent its credit to the Province to the extent that had been suggested, parliament passing a law[5] guaranteeing the interest at four per cent on a provincial loan of £1,500,000. The province was of course to pay the interest, but in the event of its failing to do so the guarantee was to come into effect. This arrangement conferred upon the loan all the prestige of British credit, so far as interest payments were concerned,

4. Sydenham to Russell (Confidential), Feb. 22, 1841. Dom. Arch. MS. Room.

5. 5 and 6 Vic., c. 118.

and the result was that the twenty-year four per cent debentures which were sold from time to time, realized a premium of about twelve per cent. The debentures were sold in London and the proceeds credited to the provincial account at the Bank of England. The provincial government undertook to create and build up a sinking fund, and to spend the money on certain specified public works. So stimulated, the construction of the canals proceeded apace, and by the summer of 1846 the province had drawn and spent practically the whole amount of the loan. A request for a similar guarantee on a further loan of £250,000 sterling, was refused.[6]

The action of the imperial government in guaranteeing this large provincial loan was exceedingly generous. The colony was largely a free agent in financial matters, influenced but not effectively controlled. Colonial governments were inclined to be irresponsible in financial affairs, at least if judged by the very rigid standards of London. The liability resulting from the guarantee might remain passive and thus incur not a penny of expense. On the other hand, were the province to default, an obligation would result from the guarantee, for an unpredictable amount up to more than a million sterling over a period of twenty years. Most of the proceeds of the loan moreover, were to be used for the improvement of the St. Lawrence waterway, a competitor with the Ottawa-Rideau line of canals which the imperial government itself owned and operated. The help afforded to Canada was a precedent. It was likely to lead to further requests from the same source or from other colonies for a wider extension of the pleasant policy of imperial guarantees.

After the union, work on the canals was pushed forward more quickly than before, and the provincial debt continued to grow with great rapidity. The increase was especially marked between the years 1843 and 1847, since the proceeds of the guaranteed loan were then available,

6. Cathcart to Gladstone, No. 84, June 27, 1846; and Grey to Cathcart, No. 20, Aug. 18, 1846. Dom. Arch. MS. Room.

and possibly also because the Canada Corn Act of 1843 had increased the existing confidence in the future of the St. Lawrence waterway. In 1846 the debt was more than twice as large as it had been in 1843, and although the province was growing both in population and wealth, this was very lavish public expenditure.

Lord Durham was not the only one who charged the province with extravagance. It does not seem however that money for public works was corruptly spent, nor were public charges of dishonesty made. In seeking a verdict on the question of extravagance it must be realized that the provincial finances were so tightly interwoven with the development of the waterway that the two are one. Attention has already been drawn to the formidable array of prophets major and minor who had promised success to the improved waterway. Once the canals were completed however, it would be possible to measure the accuracy of these prophecies by a reference to the account-books of the government, and from the point of view of the public finances it seemed to be of the utmost importance that the canals should prove to be a financial success. If they were, the waterway project would be high statesmanship that had sown its seed in fertile ground; while in the opposite event the expenditure, though not necessarily to be denounced, would be vastly more difficult to justify. In 1846 the inspector-general, speaking in the legislative assembly, defended the expenditure on public works, on the ground that these were necessary and that the St. Lawrence could be made a cheaper route than that by way of New York. He also said that "one thing is evident that when they [the public works] were commenced, what would be their actual cost, was not known . . . the actual cost had gone far beyond the estimates."[7] "A consideration of what the debt has been expended on," said the *Examiner*, "should raise the credit of the Province higher than if she did not owe a farthing."[8]

7. *Mirror of Parliament of the Province of Canada* (Montreal, 1846), p. 41.

8. *Examiner,* Mar. 21, 1849.

Canals are very costly and relatively permanent structures. Though the expense of their maintenance is usually low in proportion to the amount of capital invested in them, the annual revenue derived from them is also as a rule low in relation to their cost. Neither within the period nor later did the Canadian canals succeed in paying the interest on their capital cost,[9] and this fact imposed a heavy burden upon the public revenue. The St. Lawrence canals only began to yield an appreciable revenue as they approached completion in 1846. In 1848, the year when they were opened, there was a decrease to less than half the revenue of the preceding year. The Welland was much the most profitable of all the provincial canals, because it was part of the Erie system and tended to prosper with the latter. It was often better for American cargoes, instead of entering the Erie at Buffalo, to be sent through the Welland, and thence to Oswego and Syracuse. This had the effect of substituting about a hundred miles of open water navigation in large ships, for a corresponding amount of slow and toll-paying navigation on the Erie. Yet even the Welland was unable to pay more than a part of the interest on the cost of its construction. As late as 1851, the revenue from the public works merely sufficed to pay the interest on the guaranteed loan, which was the smaller half of the debt, and much the less burdensome part thereof on account of the low rate of interest. Thus the hopes of so many years found no fulfilment.

9. Net Revenues, etc., on the St. Lawrence and Welland Canals respectively, 1845–1849 inclusive:

| | *St. Lawrence* £ | *Welland* £ |
|---|---|---|
| Net revenue 1845 | 1175 | 13,926 |
| 1846 | 2967 | 24,669 |
| 1847 | 7309 | 18,394 |
| 1848 | 3069 | 13,932 |
| 1849 | 8729 | 28,492 |
| Percentage of net revenue on cost for 1849 | 3/5 | 2 1/5 |

Above table from figures on pp. 46–47 of the *Report of the Commissioners of Public Works* for 1849.

A generation later, Sir John A. Macdonald was destined to establish a strong claim to statesmanlike foresight and faith by his support of the Canadian Pacific Railway, even though that great undertaking scarcely possessed such fine prospects as the waterway of an earlier day had done. Indeed a colony is very likely to be obliged—the freedom of choice being only apparent—to construct expensive public works with but slender resources; and if in the process it escapes serious financial embarrassment it is to be reckoned highly fortunate.

The net cost of the canals had to be met out of the public revenues of the province. "In colonies," says Gibbon Wakefield, "as compared with old countries, the landlord and the tax-gatherer get but a small share of the produce of industry."[10] An immature colony, even though its inhabitants maintain a high standard of living, is exceedingly difficult to tax. There are no great accretions of wealth, since these are generally the product of long periods of settled social life, or of industrial development. Moreover such capital as does appear, whether home-grown or imported, tends to assume a form not too easily taxable, by investment in land or improvements to the same. Nor must capital be taxed to discouragement, for it is scarce and urgently needed, requiring therefore to be humored and enticed. The inhabitants of colonies are anarchists at heart, and resent any form of direct taxation. Nor, even if they did not, would such taxes be easy to collect, because the population is not sufficiently static. Indirect taxes therefore seem to be more suitable, being relatively painless and simple. Also a community of this type, since it does almost no manufacturing, and because it produces a surplus of raw materials, is certain to import a large quantity of goods. It is therefore not surprising, that the main resource of any Canadian inspector-general of the period, was a tariff on imports. In the five-year period from 1846 to 1850 inclusive, customs

10. Edward Gibbon Wakefield, *A View of the Art of Colonization* (London, 1849), pp. 82–83.

duties provided almost eighty per cent of the provincial revenue. Next in importance came the revenue from public works, followed by that derived from lands, and excise. Such a community as the province was, will not even consider the imposition of high import duties however, because its producers are exporters and its business men are merchants, and also because almost all manufactured articles being imported it is perfectly evident to all that protection will raise the cost of living. Moreover since there are practically no industries to protect, there are no vested interests dependent upon high tariffs for their existence and growth, or thinking themselves to be so. Nationalism, to which protectionists appeal so successfully, is as yet only an embryo. A self-sufficient protectionist policy therefore is likely to find little support whether among producers, merchants, or consumers. In such circumstances as these the expression "tariff for revenue only" will be used sincerely.

The outlay on provincial public works had been large, and the ratio of the amount required for the service of the debt to other expenditure was therefore very high for a colony. Thus for the year 1851 the total expenditure of Canada was £634,666 6*s.* 8*d.* of which £225,350 3*s.* 11*d.* was interest on the public debt; while the total expenditure of Nova Scotia for the same year was £84,748 8*s.* 6*d.* of which only £1951 2*s.* 6*d.* was interest, and that of New Brunswick £112,655 16*s.* 6*d.* of which £3828 9*s.* 0*d.* was interest.[11] The real annual outlay for public works was represented by the sum of the expenditures under the headings of Interest on Public Debt, Public Works, and Sinking Fund. During the previously mentioned five-year period, 1846–1850, the total expenditure under these three heads amounted to more than forty per cent of the entire annual expenditure. In the same period however, the annual payments to the sinking fund for the extinction of the guaranteed loan, which had been fixed first at £91,250, and later at £73,000 were allowed to fall into

11. *Sess. Papers, 1855–6,* App. D.D.D.D. (C.O. 45:284).

arrears. Otherwise the entire amount spent for the service of the debt would have been about half the total expenditure. Yet if the public works were exacting, in other respects the colony required comparatively little government; though that little was not cheap largely because the population was small and scattered and the "overhead" expenditure high. The financial position of the province however, though very difficult was by no means desperate, and had it not been for the direct expenditure on canals there would have been an annual surplus except in the very bad year 1848. Unfavorable economic conditions reacted in that year with tremendous effect upon the provincial treasury, the public revenue diminishing by about a quarter as compared with the previous slightly subnormal year.

The sums of money mentioned in this chapter and elsewhere, whenever sterling is not specified, are Halifax Currency, or simply "Currency" as it was called in the province. Here a brief description of the provincial monetary system is necessary.[12] From the earliest times the various North American colonies had found it impossible to retain and use the coinage of the parent state, since such money when brought into a colony invariably and immediately returned to the place whence it had come. Spanish coinage from the south however proved to be a less tender exotic, and the British colonies soon found themselves using Spanish dollars whether they liked it or not. Competition between the various colonies for these coins, increased their local value measured in pounds, shillings, and pence. Payments were made in dollars; but calculated and recorded in pounds. This curious hybrid monetary system was introduced into Canada at the conquest.

The monetary arrangements found in the Province after the union were very unsystematic and complex.[13]

12. See Robert Chalmers, *A History of Currency in the British Colonies* (London), Chs. I and XV.

13. See William Draper's evidence before the Decimal Coinage Commission, in *Reports from Commissioners, 1860,* XXX, [2591], pp. 45–52.

The official standard of value was the Halifax currency already referred to, the units of which were divided, as in the case of sterling, into twenty shillings of twelve pence each. It was a slightly degenerate offspring of sterling, and it had depreciated in relation to the latter because of the high valuation which had been given to the Spanish dollars. It was represented by no special coins, being merely a standard of value and a system of reckoning. The soul of the pound sterling had as it were entered into the body of the dollar, becoming slightly shrunk in the process. This shrinkage is measured by a provincial law of the year 1841 which fixed the value of the pound sterling in terms of currency at £1 4*s.* 4*d.*, and by an American law passed in 1846 which for the purpose of customs computations valued the pound of the British North American colonies at four dollars.[14] The United States dollars which circulated in the colony were therefore equivalent to five shillings currency each. Government accounts and those of the banks were kept in currency: business and family accounts either in currency or in dollars and cents. There were a number of chartered banks doing business in the province, of which the Bank of Montreal and the Bank of British North America are still in existence. These issued bank notes up to a limited amount, carrying on their face a promise to pay so much in currency, and having usually a dollar valuation also. Cash payments were made either by means of these notes or in coins of many nationalities, a bewildering assortment of which were in circulation.[15] There were British coins, and various ones of the prolific dollar family, from Spain, the United States, Mexico and elsewhere. In Lower Canada French coins found favor, and there may even have been some *louis d'or* of the old régime still circulating there. The

14. 4 and 5 Vic., c. 93. (Prov.). U.S. Statutes, 29th Cong., 1st Sess., c. 23.

15. "But the currency of a small state, . . . can seldom consist altogether in its own coin, but must be made up, in a great measure, of the coins of all the neighbouring states with which its inhabitants have a continual intercourse." *Wealth of Nations.*

British shilling was rated at 1*s.* 3*d.* currency, or a quarter of a dollar. To complicate matters still further the monetary arrangements of the various British North American colonies were not entirely uniform.

It had long been recognized that the colonial monetary situation was unsatisfactory, and in 1825 the imperial government began a policy of trying to replace existing colonial currencies with sterling. The attempt succeeded in the West Indies; but not in British North America, although colonial opinion appears to have been favorable. Official opinion in England therefore began to change, Lord Grey being one of the early converts. In 1850 he wrote to Lord Elgin: "At the same time I have a long standing controversy with the Treasury (i.e. in fact with C. Wood) on the whole subject of Colonial Currency wh. seems to me in a most unsatisfactory state. What I shd. like to do wd. be to adopt what was Ellice's recommendation to poor Lord Althorp many years ago & coin dollars wh. shd be the only legal tender over the whole of the Bsh Colonies & in wh. all Colonial paper shd be made payable. The circulation of Bsh. silver I believe to be the greatest of all absurdities."[16] It was consistent of Grey to apply the *laissez faire* principle here also, and there can be little doubt that it was wise counsel as well. Canada never had a satisfactory monetary system until she overcame her sentimental preference for something which looked like the English system, and recognizing that the dollar standard existed in fact, permitted it to exist in name also.

In 1850 the provincial legislature passed a law[17] authorizing the government to strike gold and silver coins representing convenient amounts of currency. The following year the introduction of a decimal system was provided for.[18] Accounts were to be kept in dollars and cents, and a coinage based on the dollar was authorized. The new unit of value was to be the equivalent of five shillings currency, and this in fact meant the full naturalization of

16. Grey to Elgin, Oct. 25, 1850. Private Correspondence.
17. 13 and 14 Vic., c. 8. (Prov.)
18. 14 and 15 Vic., c. 17. (Prov.)

the American dollar in the province. The treasury authorities and the government in London objected to this provincial legislation on several grounds. They admitted the seriousness of the problem; but desired that an attempt should be made to solve it in a much broader way, by introducing sterling currency into all British North America. A uniform currency throughout the various colonies at that time, would have been very advantageous. In view however of the increasingly intimate economic relations with the United States which the future held for all the colonies concerned, sterling money, even if practicable, would have proved inconvenient. The home government's plan was not adopted. The monetary revolution which began in the year 1850, was completed soon after confederation, and may be regarded as one of the numerous by-products of the new commercial policy.

The state of the provincial credit was a problem that faced one inspector-general after another. It was not rated very highly in London financial circles, a tribunal from which there was no appeal. Hence the interest rate which the province had to pay on its borrowings was high, and sometimes money could not be procured at all. There were many reasons for this weakness of credit, and two of them have been dealt with already—a swollen debt and a limited revenue. The viewpoint of the colonist must also be considered. The colonial status seems to have made for a diminished sense of financial responsibility, since it sometimes happened, as in the case of the guaranteed loan, that if the need were sufficient the imperial government would come to the rescue. It also seems probable that in a young colony the general level of business integrity is lower than in a more mature society. The public moreover is very apt to exhibit an unfriendly attitude toward the money-powers that be, and this is probably due to the absence in these communities of a wealthy middle class, and to lack of indigenous capital. Investors are thus strangers and seem to be parasitical, while the constant sending of interest payments out of the country looks to the colonial like absentee landlordism. Accordingly we find in the colonial viewpoint a hostility to the outside investor which in some ways resembles socialist class-consciousness, but which unlike the latter is founded upon no philosophy. Yet this feeling is not entirely unrestrained, since imported capital is a sheer necessity.

The attitude just described sometimes results in an inordinate desire for increased credit facilities without recourse to the distant capitalist. This statement could be plentifully illustrated from the history of the United States. The colonist is apt to feel that an economic millennium might easily be brought into being by means of increased amounts of money—by more banks, each of them issuing more paper. In a mild form this feeling was present in the Canada of the forties, and found expression in legislation at the beginning of the following decade.[19] This measure had been framed and sponsored by Merritt, and was an almost exact copy of a law in force in New York State. It was designed to facilitate the formation of small, note-issuing banks, and at the same time to provide adequate legislative safeguards in the interest of sound banking. These two objectives lie in opposite directions, and a step toward one is a step away from the other. Neither the inspector-general nor the colonial secretary liked the measure. The former foresaw great difficulty in refusing charters, even to small and weak banks and to those in the less prosperous communities, consequently he thought that the law would result in too many banks and bank failures. Lord Grey stated privately that he was "quite prepared to allow the Colony to make what I think very foolish laws if it is determined to do so."[20] The point is that there were certain ingredients in colonial opinion not altogether palatable to the investor.

Upper Canada had once defaulted. On occasion too the

19. 13 and 14 Vic., c. 21. (Prov.) "An Act to establish freedom of Banking in this Province, and for other purposes relative to Banks and Banking."

20. Memorandum by Hincks in Correspondence of the Civ. Sec., No. 5488; and Grey to Elgin, June 13, 1851. Private Correspondence.

province after the union had been dilatory in making payments to its creditors, and this, no matter what the cause, is injurious to credit. In the autumn of 1847 the colonial secretary thought it necessary to make the following remarks in a despatch. "In the mean time, I have to suggest that you should, in concert with your Executive Council, take without delay the necessary measures for meeting the payment of interest on the debt of the Province, which will shortly become due, remembering that a failure to meet that payment with punctuality would probably have the effect of rendering it impossible for the Province hereafter, for any objects, however important, to resort for assistance to the money market of this Country, except upon terms of great disadvantage."[21] The following year the Bank of England sent this communication to the provincial receiver-general, regarding a sum of £140,000 sterling which had been lent by the Bank in August 1846, supposedly for a period of nine months: "No remittance having yet been made, either for the repayment of the advance referred to, or for the interest which has accrued thereon, although the period for which the amount was borrowed has long since expired, I am directed to call the attention of the Canada Government to the circumstance."[22]

Certain other considerations, some of them political in character, must also have weighed with the British capitalist. American investments in general were looked upon as relatively insecure by the European investor, who had had a good deal of experience with them. A defeatist attitude toward colonies and colonization prevailed in England at that time. Among colonies Canada had the reputation of being politically unstable to an unusual extent. Armed rebellion had been seen there a few years before. Annexation to the United States seemed possible

21. Grey to Elgin, No. 135, Nov. 3, 1847. *Accounts and Papers, 1847–8*, XLVII, [50].

22. Enclosure in Elgin to Grey, No. 36, of Mar. 27, 1848. Dom. Arch. MS. Room. The letter is dated Feb. 25, 1848.

or even probable, especially during and after the year 1849. The Oregon boundary difficulty was too recent to have been forgotten, and war with the United States would have placed the province in a very precarious position.

For these many reasons therefore, Canadian Government securities did not attract the *rentier* type of investor who is content to forego a high rate of interest and that prospect of increase in the value of his holding which the speculator seeks. To the prospective purchaser of government securities, certainty and safety are the paramount consideration, and the *rentier* was distrustful of the ability and willingness of the province to pay promptly and in full. Nor was there much to attract the less cautious type of investor. Thus in the London market the securities of the province were often passed by unwanted.

A primary cause also of the financial difficulties of the province in the period, was the severe commercial and financial depression that existed everywhere. This affected the public finances in two ways. In the first place it reduced the volume of imports, and diminished therewith the all-important revenue from import duties, while the same commercial conditions had a similar effect upon other important sources of revenue, as for example canal-tolls, land-sales, and excise. In the second place, during the depression money was scarce and loans difficult to obtain either for public or for private purposes.

Among those who played a part in the economic life of Canada at the middle of last century, no one is more important than Francis Hincks.[23] In 1848 with the accession to power of the Baldwin-Lafontaine Ministry, he became inspector-general and made the improvement of the provincial credit the corner-stone of his financial policy, laboring unceasingly to achieve it. In respect of the prompt meeting of provincial obligations he maintained a higher

23. "Sir Francis Hincks was our greatest economist and financier. I always read him with respect and profit." Goldwin Smith, *Reminiscences*, p. 437.

standard than some of his predecessors had done, and ultimately this scrupulousness bore the desired fruit of increased confidence; yet a reputation once lost is not easily nor instantly regained. A provincial law of April 1849,[24] was an expression of Hincks' policy, as it stipulated that the entire net revenue from the public works in excess of £20,000, should be devoted to the sinking fund in addition to the annual payment already provided for. Any unappropriated revenue might also be transferred to the sinking fund by the governor-in-council. The law was probably designed for the double purpose of reducing the debt and of looking as though it would reduce the debt. The government was also empowered to appoint "one or more fiscal Agents of the Province in the City of London."[25]

As a general rule, in the period, the province paid six per cent on its loans. The debentures bearing this rate of interest were sold sometimes at par and occasionally below it, and there were times when it was difficult or impossible to dispose of them at any price that the province was prepared to accept. In glaring contrast to all this stood the terms and acceptability of the guaranteed loan, which, paying only four per cent, had been disposed of at a premium. The difference between these two interest rates, which in fact amounted to between two and three per cent, kept the relatively low state of their credit constantly before provincial eyes. There was heartburning also because the United States got their money more cheaply and easily than Canada did, and the credit of certain American states, and even of one or two cities, was better than that of the province. In 1849 W. H. Merritt "met Mr Bates one of the firm of Baring Brothers and Co. in Boston . . . [and] endeavoured to convince him that Canadian Securities were equal to U.S. and better

24. 12 Vic., c. 5. (Prov.) "An Act for the better management of the Public Debt, Accounts, Revenue and Property."

25. The Province had for some time been transacting its financial business in London through the two firms of Baring Bros., and Glyn, Hallifax, and Mills. Hincks continued the connection with both firms.

than the State of N.Y. . . . —but he draws a wide distinction between U.S. and Can. Secty."[26] The Canadian argument was that the province possessed a power to raise revenue by a tariff and in other ways, equal to the corresponding power of the United States, and far greater than that of any state or city. "It is mortifying to know," wrote Hincks to the Barings in 1848, "that at this very time that the Province of Canada is unable to obtain a small temporary loan [£20,000 sterling], debentures of the United States, as well as of the City of Boston, have been disposed of to a large amount, in London."[27] To this the Barings replied: "We can assure you that we regret as much as yourself that the securities of the Province do not rank as high as the most favorite stocks with Capitalists here & which credit [*sic*] is only permanently maintained by the knowledge of ample powers and constant regularity in meeting all money engagements. The debt of a colony always labors under some disadvantage in this respect and the stock of the federal Government of the United States is certainly more valued & finds readily purchasers on both sides of the Atlantic. We were not aware that the City of Boston had made a loan here, but the Bonds of Canada without the guarantee of Great Britain would be considered here much in the same light as the Bonds of separate states of the United States of America many of which even with a surplus revenue are not quoted higher than or so high as Canada Bonds."[28]

Hincks replied at considerable length.[29] He argued that the province was financially sound, saying that: "Canada then has 'ample powers' of meeting her engagements; in fact, precisely the same powers as the Federal Government of the United States: both raise by duties on imports the

26. Copy of Merritt to Elgin, June 20, 1849. Enclosed with Elgin to Grey, June 25, 1849. Private Correspondence.

27. Hincks to Baring Bros., Nov. 8, 1848. Baring Papers—Misc. Correspondence.

28. Baring Bros. to Hincks, Dec. 1, 1848. Baring Papers—Letter Books.

29. The Hon. Francis Hincks, *Canada: its Financial Position and Resources,* pp. 6–12.

revenues which they require." He claimed too that the province had the will as well as the means to meet all its obligations. "The fact is," he went on, "that our bonds are not recommended as an investment, while those of the United States are; indeed, I have felt mortified to find that the price of Canada bonds is never quoted in the list of stocks, although those of each of the United States, as well as of all other foreign governments, are kept constantly before the public." He then made the inevitable reference to the canals, "on the success of which, as a source of immense revenue, we have every confidence: every effort and sacrifice must be made to complete these works. Since the creation of our Sinking Fund, we have saved from actual surplus of revenue half a million currency, or one-eighth of our whole debt."

There was a large deficit in the year 1848 and for a while the province was unable to borrow. So difficult did the situation become that for a time the salaries of public officials had to be paid in small short-time debentures which could only be negotiated at less than their face value. The credit of the province at this time was adversely affected too by the whole series of disquieting occurrences which culminated in the annexation movement, and Hincks publicly charged the Tory press with the intention to injure the provincial credit. In 1849 he was faced with the necessity of borrowing the large sum of £500,000 sterling, and in the summer of that year he set out for London with the double purpose of defending the policy of the provincial government in connection with the Rebellion Losses Bill, and of doing everything possible to improve the credit of the colony and so get the money that was so greatly needed. On his arrival he obtained some moral support from Lord Grey, and tried to create a more favorable opinion of Canada in the minds of business houses and investors by publishing a pamphlet presenting with a good deal of ability the case on behalf of the resources and integrity of the colony.[30] He prophesied

30. Hincks, *Canada: its Financial Position and Resources.*

that the canals would pay, emphasized the loyalty of the colony to the British connection, and made light of the annexation movement. His long letter to Messrs. Baring of Dec. 20, 1848, was reproduced in full. He asked the imperial government to help in the construction of the proposed railway from Quebec to Halifax. So far as obtaining the loan was concerned Hincks' mission was not immediately successful; but by the following spring conditions were becoming normal once more—the tide of depression having turned—and the half-million pounds were forthcoming.

Public opinion was affected by the financial troubles of the province while they lasted. Wistful comparisons were often made between the finances, particularly the expenditure, of Canada and of the American union, or individual states thereof more especially New York. Thus, according to the Toronto *Examiner*, "The fiscal extravagance of one government can best be shown by a comparison with the expense of other governments similarly situated." The cost of government in Canada was then unfavorably compared with that of New York and Ohio.[31] The comparison however was unfair, for it failed to include the expense of their Federal Government to the people of those two States. It should be noted too that the whole cost of defending Canada was paid by the imperial government.[32] The salary of the representative of the crown however, which amounted to £7000 sterling, was paid by the province, and so was the rent of Monklands near Montreal, the official home of the governor-general while that city remained the seat of government, the rent amounting to £450 a year. As so often in the history of British colonies, the amount of the governor's salary was the subject of much criticism. Indeed official salaries on this scale are for many reasons not in consonance with colonial ideas,

31. *Examiner,* Sept. 19, 1849.

32. In the year 1846–47 the amount was about £475,000 sterling. This money came from the taxpayer in Great Britain, and nearly all of it was spent in the colony.

and Merritt wanted to have the amount reduced though Hincks did not. Considering the obligations involved the salary was barely sufficient unless the governor concerned had private means.[33] The argument in favor of large salaries for colonial governors seems to outweigh that of mere economy. The office requires men of first-rate standing and ability, and if such men are to be obtained they must be paid on a scale commensurate with that which they could obtain at home. The Jacksonian theory that anyone can do everything well is unsound, and has been weighed and found wanting even in the land where it originated. Lord Grey thought that for political reasons colonial governors ought to be paid by Great Britain, and that the colonies ought to contribute substantially toward the cost of their own defense. Lord Elgin thoroughly approved of the former idea; but was very doubtful that the colonists could be induced to assume any part of the defense burden. Many suggestions were made for retrenchment in public expenditure, and a very strong and probably overlarge committee, representative of many shades of political opinion, was appointed in 1850 to consider the question, and issued two reports.[34] The recommendations contained in these reports however, revealed no far-reaching program of economy in public expenditure.

We might perhaps expect that thenceforth, for a time at least, the provincial government would have drawn the purse-strings very tight, so far as transportation schemes were concerned. The day of the railway however had dawned, and the Canadian State was now to begin that peculiarly intimate association with railways which it has ever since maintained. In 1849 the province inaugurated the policy of guaranteeing in certain circumstances the

33. Lord Elgin's salary was paid in currency. Though not an extravagant man, he had great difficulty in making both ends meet. He was practically without private means, being the son of that Lord Elgin who had discovered an inverted alchemy for turning gold into marble and transmuted all the gold he had.

34. *Sess. Papers, 1850,* App. B.B. (C.O. 45:243).

interest on railway investments. The Barings were suspicious of railway projects, and exercised as great a restraining influence on the province as they could. "We may think it improvident on the part of the legislature," they wrote, "to have engaged in such extensive guarantees before the credit of the Colony was firmly established, but we are aware of the state reasons for the promotion of public works & especially railroads."[35] The provincial government did not abandon its policy of guarantees; but pledged itself not to make grants of public money for railway construction. Thus the principle of state ownership which had been followed in the case of the canals was abandoned from the outset so far as the railways were concerned, and only of recent years has the Canadian government been compelled by circumstances to undertake the public ownership of railways on an extensive scale.

The colony had thus entered the critical period between 1845 and 1850 burdened by heavy financial commitments and impaired credit; consequently after 1846 the situation became very difficult, remaining so until 1850 when things took a turn for the better. The financial condition of the province in this period follows very closely the trend of world commerce and finance, and it is plain that the relation is one of cause and effect. Large investments in public works which are very characteristic of young colonies, are especially so of this particular one. The weakness of provincial credit made the lot of inspectors-general a hard one, and tended to aggravate the other problems with which the colony had to contend. Yet the economic life of a society possesses automatic powers of readjustment and self-preservation not unlike those of a living organism, and it is probable that the low state of its credit exercised a salutary influence upon the financial policy of the province.

In finance as in so many other ways Canada was sub-

35. Baring Bros. to Hon. F. Hincks, Dec. 27, 1850. Baring Papers—Letter Books.

ject to two very powerful external influences. Great Britain was the financial centre of the Empire whence continual streams of fructifying capital flowed forth. The current normally responded only to the law of supply and demand; but at times it was affected by political action as in the case of the guaranteed loan. In the calculations of the business men however political considerations played no part at all, and not even Cobden himself could have been more detached in this respect than they. An important influence also was exercised by the United States, that country being in direct competition with the province for British capital. It fulfilled moreover the function of what biologists term a "control," for the Canadians had in their neighbors to the southward an ever-present criterion of financial success.

The story of the public finances of the province in the period bears unmistakable witness to the fact that agricultural communities are comparatively immune to financial crises of the most acute type. The situation though very embarrassing was never fundamentally serious, and although Hincks was a business-like finance minister and did much to restore confidence, the return of general prosperity was far more effective than all his efforts. We take our leave of Hincks, his big half-million-pound loan successfully floated, bargaining with Messrs. Baring for terms on guaranteed railway bonds, and announcing to the legislative assembly that "in England our 5 per cents are worth nearly par, our Agents being unable to purchase them, on account of the Sinking Fund, as rapidly as we could wish."[36] The weight of the debt incurred in developing the St. Lawrence waterway did not in the long run prove difficult to carry. For a number of years the revenue derived from canal-tolls sufficed to defray a part of the interest charges: the province too was growing rapidly in population and wealth. Nor was the debt at any time, when considered in relation to population, of really formidable dimensions. Eighty years later the per capita

36. Quebec *Gazette,* July 28, 1851.

debt of the Dominion, measured in dollars, was about nineteen times as large as that of the province in 1851.[37]

37. Table showing the Revenue, Expenditure, and Public Debt of the province, 1843–1852 inclusive. (Shillings and pence omitted). The outlay on the canals reveals itself in the increasing debt; but not under the second heading, which merely shows the annual expenditure for ordinary purposes.

| | 1843 | 1844 | 1845 | 1846 | 1847 |
|---|---|---|---|---|---|
| | £ | £ | £ | £ | £ |
| Revenue, | 320,987 | 515,783 | 524,366 | 512,993 | 506,826 |
| Expenditure, | 284,829 | 448,091 | 523,453 | 505,228 | 458,021 |
| Debt, | 1,588,212 | 2,179,050 | 2,944,004 | 3,341,173 | 3,595,432 |

| | 1848 | 1849 | 1850 | 1851 | 1852 |
|---|---|---|---|---|---|
| | £ | £ | £ | £ | £ |
| Revenue, | 379,645 | 513,431 | 704,234 | 842,184 | 880,531 |
| Expenditure, | 474,491 | 450,913 | 532,063 | 634,666 | 797,125 |
| Debt, | 3,751,818 | 3,873,314 | 4,085,634 | 4,512,468 | 4,451,961 |

Figures from the Annual Reports on the Public Accounts of Canada.

# V

## TARIFFS

The history of modern colonization does not show a single case where a newly settled country has enjoyed any considerable economic prosperity, or made notable social progress, without a flourishing commerce with other communities. This dominance of foreign commerce in economic affairs may be considered the most characteristic feature of colonial economy. G. S. CALLENDER, *Selections from the Economic History of the United States, 1765–1860.*

PRIOR to the year 1846, British colonies were surrounded by a double wall of tariffs. There was an imperial customs law,[1] which together with the British tariff and the Navigation Laws made up the colonial system on its economic side. In addition there were colonial tariffs which might supplement but might not conflict with the imperial law.

In 1825 preferential treatment was accorded to colonial breadstuffs in the British market, this policy being expressed also in the Act of 1828.[2] Not long afterwards Canada was singled out for special favors, for the British Possessions Act of 1833,[3] which placed a duty of five shillings a barrel on foreign wheat flour, and of twelve shillings a hundredweight on foreign preserved meat entering the other colonies in America, permitted these articles to enter Canada duty free. "The object of granting this Exemption to Canada, was to draw this species of produce from the North Western States of the Union down the River St Lawrence to the Atlantic."[4] In 1842

1. The current act was 8 and 9 Vic., c. 93. "An Act to regulate the Trade of *British* Possessions abroad." Aug. 4, 1845.

2. 9 Geo. IV, c. 60.

3. 3 and 4 William IV, c. 59.

4. Stanley to Bagot, No. 227, Aug. 17, 1842. Dom. Arch. MS. Room.

however the concession was withdrawn,[5] on the ground that the result had been to favor the St. Lawrence at the expense of other colonies especially the West Indies. The Corn Law of the same year[6] was revolutionary in character. "The general plan . . . was, to remit the duties upon articles of raw material, constituting the elements of manufacture in this country."[7] It is obvious that such a policy could not be combined with the old colonial system, and that one or the other would have to be abandoned.

Canada was far in the lead as a wheat-growing colony, and had more than once requested the imperial authorities to remove the duty on its wheat. A despatch from the Colonial Office in 1842 was construed in the province to mean that if Canada would put a duty of three shillings a quarter on American grain imports, parliament would be asked to reduce the duty on Canadian grain and flour to a nominal amount. The provincial parliament made haste to pass the necessary legislation,[8] and the British government responded by introducing the Canada Corn Bill into parliament.[9] Under the existing Corn Law, which imposed differential sliding-scale duties, the rate on colonial wheat varied from one to five shillings a quarter, while that on the foreign product varied from a shilling to a pound. Exact comparisons cannot be made because the sliding-scale duties fluctuated continually, both actually and in relation to each other. In general however the law gave colonial wheat a substantial preference except when the price of wheat was high. The duty on flour was proportioned to that on wheat and varied with it in both the colonial and the foreign scales.

The Canada Corn Act which took effect on October 11, 1843, admitted wheat and wheat flour "the Produce of the said Province of *Canada*" to the British market at a fixed duty of a shilling per quarter of wheat, and a pro-

5. By 5 and 6 Vic., c. 49.

6. 5 and 6 Vic., c. 14.

7. Peel in the House of Commons, *Hansard,* 3rd Ser., LXXXIII, 241–242.

8. 6 Vic., c. 31. (Prov.)

9. 6 and 7 Vic., c. 29. For the debates see *Hansard,* 3rd Ser., LXIX.

portionate amount on a barrel of flour. This was equivalent to stabilizing the duty at the lowest rate possible under the previous law. It had been customary for many years to admit American wheat milled in Canada into the British market at the colonial rate,[10] on the general principle that the process of manufacture "naturalized" any raw material, and though the text of the law of 1843 omitted all reference to the subject, it was passed on the distinct understanding that the former precedent should hold good. "Flour the produce of American wheat ground in Canada was, he [the Colonial Secretary] repeated, to be considered as if it had been grown in Canada."[11]

The Canada Corn Act, supplemented by the provincial three-shilling tariff law, brought about a situation the results of which are exceedingly difficult to estimate. Taken in conjunction with the larger protective system of which it formed a part, it might or might not have resulted in bringing large quantities of American grain down the St. Lawrence; but the conditions which it created lasted for so short a time that no pragmatic judgment can be formed. The law took effect too late in 1843 to have much influence on the grain trade of that year, while after 1845 everything was changed. A statistical solution therefore is not possible. Moreover the general Corn Law, equipped as it was with sliding scales, was so complicated and unstable that economic theory affords no certain solution to the problem. Yet there are a number of relevant considerations which assist in establishing the probabilities of the matter. The law must in the long run have conferred a considerable advantage upon the Canadian wheat-grower, for the duty on his grain and flour was "pegged" at the lowest rate possible under the existing foreign and colonial scales, while the three-shilling law protected him against the competition of American grain in his domestic market. Yet the law did not necessarily

10. The Canada Corn Act of 1843 is often incorrectly regarded as having established a precedent in this respect.

11. *Hansard,* 3rd Ser., LXIX, 805–806.

throw the British market open to Canadian-milled flour of American origin, and it is not certain what its effect would have been over a series of years on the trade in United States breadstuffs down the St. Lawrence. American grain coming into the province to be milled would have had to surmount the barrier of the three-shilling duty, except in the unlikely event that smuggling had been resorted to on a large scale. Whether it would cross that barrier at any given time, or go by way of New York, would have been largely dependent upon the probable rate of the British duty on foreign grain in the immediate future, and that in turn was contingent upon the actual and prospective price of grain in the English market. Were grain prices in Britain to reach a low enough level, the differential duty would almost certainly bring large quantities of American grain into the St. Lawrence, but not otherwise. There was always the possibility however that under the Canada Corn Act the St. Lawrence grain trade might have imitated the action of the column of water in a siphon, which continues to flow once it has been properly started. For a voluminous stream of breadstuffs flowing into the British market by way of the St. Lawrence, might have been able to maintain its own movement by keeping the price in that market depressed and the protection high against competitive routes. Merchants exporting through Canada were unlikely to reap much advantage from the fact that the duty which they had to pay was fixed and therefore determinable in advance, since the duty which would have to be paid by their competitors exporting by alternative routes was a sliding-scale duty. Indeed it is the vagaries of the sliding scale that are largely responsible for the fact that it is impossible to estimate the probable effects of the Canada Corn Act with any accuracy. Yet had other things been equal, it seems possible or probable that the law would in time have conferred a decisive advantage upon the St. Lawrence route. Other things however were not equal because of the fact that the St. Lawrence was not a competitive route. It is unlikely that the price of wheat in Britain would have remained low enough to maintain a differential duty which would have offset not only the three-shilling provincial duty, but also the relative cost of the St. Lawrence route. Consequently it seems probable that the bulk of the American grain shipments to Britain would have continued going by way of New York.

Until a considerable time after the completion of the canals however, it was not known that the St. Lawrence would prove to be the more expensive route for shipments, and many business men both in Canada and the United States thought that the Canada Corn Act, if it remained in force, would cause much of the western trade to use the provincial waterway. On this point Grinnell, Minturn and Co. of New York sought the opinion of correspondents in Oswego, which was a key position in the American grain trade, and received a very interesting reply dated December 31, 1843, of which the following is a part. It will be noted that the opinion expressed in this letter rests entirely upon the "siphon" argument which has already been explained:

"In relation to the Corn Laws of England and Canada as at present modified we are of opinion if they are suffered to remain permanently (which now looks doubtful) they will induce a large, a constant & regular supply of Western Lake Country Wheat from the States to pass through the Canadies [*sic*] to England, to the entire exclusion of all direct shipments from the States.

"Our reasons for this opinion are, that it now costs about the same price to transport Wheat from the Western Lakes to Quebec, as to New York, and when the Canadian improvements are made—say two years hence—in their inland navigation the cost in that direction will be reduced till a trifle more [*sic*]. While on the other hand, New York has an advantage of perhaps 2/6d. sterling per Bbl in freight & Insurance, and the further advantage of 5 or 6 mos more open Navigation. But Canada will hold an advantage more than equivalent in the rate of

Duties, which to her are fixed and low, or rather nominal, while to the States by the sliding scale they will hereafter be high with few or no intervals of low duty as heretofore, & for the plain reason that Canada or rather the North Western States through Canada will permit a regular and steady supply, and thus prevent a high price and a consequent reduction of Duty or opening of ports to Provisions as heretofore."[12]

As a result of the apparently promising features of the Canada Corn Act and the legislation supplementary to it, the promoters of the provincial waterway were encouraged to push forward their scheme with greater vigor than before, and an uncertain amount of capital was invested in the business of handling grain along the St. Lawrence, particularly in mills. These seem to have increased in size rather than in number, which probably means that comparatively few people not already millers went into the business. A writer on the subject thinks that investments in mills actually decreased in 1843 and 1844 as compared with those of the immediately preceding years, and such statistics as there are, which are very unsatisfactory, seem to support his contention.[13] During the six years previous to the opening of the St. Lawrence canals the milling equipment of the province was greatly increased. The provincial board of registration and statistics gives the number of mills, based on census returns, as 414 with 584 pairs of mill-stones in the year 1842, while by 1848 the number had been increased to 548 mills with 1200 pairs

12. The firm of Baring Bros., extensively interested in the wheat trade, had asked for information as to the probable effects of the Canada Corn Act from Grinnell, Minturn and Co., their agents in New York. The latter firm "wrote to our friends at Oswego as presenting the best channel through which the desired intelligence could be procured," receiving in reply the letter from which the extract is taken. A copy was enclosed with Grinnell, Minturn and Co. to Baring Bros., Jan. 10, 1844 (incorrectly dated 1843). The name of the Oswego firm does not appear. Baring Papers, Official correspondence—Grinnell, Minturn and Co., 1841–1855.

13. D. L. Burn, "Canada and the Repeal of the Corn Laws," in the *Cambridge Historical Journal*, II, 252–274. The official mill statistics are criticized in the *Appendix to the First Report of the Board of Registration and Statistics*.

of stones. According to these figures the milling capacity of the province had been increased more than a hundred per cent in six years. Yet immediately after the passage of the Canada Corn Act, the investments in mills seem to have diminished. It is probable that although most people in the province thought that the Canada Corn Act would stimulate the St. Lawrence trade, the governing motive in the minds of investors down to 1848 was faith in the future of the St. Lawrence waterway, and in the resulting progress of the colony with or without the help of the Canada Corn Act. When that confidence began to seem misplaced, they regarded themselves as having been more seriously misled than was really the case. A number of investors in mills must have been actually deceived by the legislation of 1843, while others afterwards complained, and probably believed, that they had been. A certain Jacob Keefer of the village of Thorold near the Welland Canal claimed that he had invested £8000 in mills on the strength of the situation which existed before 1846: "—but my mill has *done nothing since it was finished*," he wrote, ". . . I embarked *all* in my enterprize with now the almost certain prospect that *all* will be a loss."[14] This letter got into print, and has been quoted in overemphasis on the sufferings of that rather nebulous body of millers who were misled by the legislation of 1843. It is interesting to notice that the year after his letter was written Keefer became an enthusiastic supporter of the annexation movement.[15]

During the short time that they remained in force the Canada Corn Act and its supplementary legislation do not seem to have increased the St. Lawrence transit trade in breadstuffs. From the imperial point of view it was unsound legislation, resting upon no principle whatever, unfair to the consumers, and discriminating grossly in

14. J. Keefer to W. H. Merritt, April 19, 1848. Copy enclosed with Elgin to Grey, No. 65, May 24, 1848. Dom. Arch. MS. Room.

15. J. Keefer to Robert McKay, Dec. 4, 1849. *Can. Hist. Review,* V, 240–241.

favor of one particular colony. As might have been expected, the Montreal Board of Trade wanted flour and meal made from other grains to be put upon the same favorable basis as wheat flour, and colonists in South Australia petitioned to have their wheat admitted on the Canadian terms.[16] Whatever may have been the merits or defects of the Canada Corn Act, the responsibility for its enactment rested with the provincial legislature, on whose initiative it was passed. The imperial government presented that measure to parliament reluctantly, and only did so in order to keep faith with the provincial authorities.

Generally speaking the policy of Great Britain has been strikingly consistent; but her corn legislation during these years was a noticeable exception to this rule. The reason for this was that the whole foundation of her protective system had been methodically undermined, and the edifice was swaying uncertainly to and fro. The story of the extraordinary achievement of the Anti-Corn Law League in educating English public opinion, and of the gradual conversion of Sir Robert Peel and the consequent repeal of the Corn Laws, needs no repetition.

On January 27, 1846, Peel made his eagerly awaited pronouncement on tariff policy, and referring to the Corn Laws, he said: "I propose, therefore, that there shall be at once a considerable reduction in the existing amount of protection. And I also propose that the continuance of such duties so reduced shall be limited to a period of three years."[17] Meanwhile in Canada the situation had been arousing great anxiety, which was reflected in a despatch written the day after Peel's speech, wherein Lord Cathcart at the earnest request of the members of his executive council urged upon the imperial government the necessity of continued protection for the colonial trade in wheat and flour. As usual the waterway scheme was ad-

16. Board of Trade Minutes, No. 267, Feb. 22, 1843; and No. 1828, Dec. 11, 1844, (B.T. 5: 51).

17. *Hansard,* 3rd Ser., LXXXIII, 260–261.

vanced as an argument. Along with this went an intimation that if free trade were to divert traffic from the St. Lawrence route to New York, and otherwise injure the province, future payments of interest on the guaranteed loan might prove to be impossible. The despatch added that if there were to be a relaxation of colonial protection, "it is of infinite consequence that it should not be sudden."[18] In reply the colonial secretary announced the new policy, which he defended, saying that "there are matters in which considerations immediately connected with the supply of food for the People of this Country, and with the employment of its population, must be paramount." He urged that the province should follow the example of the mother country by introducing as far as possible the policy of unrestricted trade, and confidently repeated the free trade credo. He also enumerated the natural advantages possessed by the colony, which a mere legislative change would be powerless to affect. This interesting but pedantic despatch contained a final word of encouragement in this very Gladstonian sentence. "I trust, therefore, that the Agricultural Population of Canada will look forward, without fear, to a change, of which it is probable that the effects will be far less violent, either for good or for the partial evils which may accompany such good, than many, prompted either by their hopes or their fears, have been forward to anticipate."[19] The colonial secretary wrote several subsequent despatches in the same tone, and to the political argument against free trade he replied, somewhat smugly perhaps, that "it would indeed be a source of the greatest pain to Her Majesty's Government if they could share in the impression that the connection between this Country and Canada derived its vitality from no other source than from the Exchange of Commercial preferences."[20]

18. Cathcart to Gladstone, No. 7, Jan. 28, 1846. See this and other relevant documents in *Accounts and Papers, 1846,* XXVII, Nos. 321 and 374.
19. Gladstone to Cathcart, No. 32, Mar. 3, 1846. Dom. Arch. MS. Room.
20. Gladstone to Cathcart, No. 83, June 3, 1846. Dom. Arch. MS. Room.

When the provincial legislature opened, on March 20, 1846, the official announcement and the details of the new policy had not yet been received, and in the speech from the throne it was stated that until the arrival of fuller information "it would be premature to anticipate that the claims of this Province to a just measure of protection had been overlooked." On March 26 the assembly debated in a very calm frame of mind the contents of Gladstone's despatch of March 3. In the course of debate on April 17 however there was an extreme expression of opinion by the member for Quebec, his speech being reported as follows: "The question was one that interested all; if we are to be deprived of the benefit we enjoy as a colony, then we are not prepared to bear its evils, and he thought that if England took away its protection from them, that she should be required to pay the vast amount they had expended upon their canals. The hon. member's speech was received throughout with marked applause."[21] The same day attorney-general Draper drew attention to the problem confronting the colony. "Protection had ceased to be a principle of Colonial policy," he said, "and we should consequently look a-head. Three years notice was given, and as we could not avert certain consequences, we should see at once to the means of neutralizing them." Draper's speech was rather vague: he expressed confidence in the efficiency of the St. Lawrence route, and advocated the removal of the three-shilling duty on grain imported for re-export, such a duty being no longer necessary.[22] Provincial ideas crystallized considerably during the weeks which followed, and in May the assembly passed an address to the Queen, voicing the fears aroused in the province by the new commercial policy.[23] The address stated that "we view with serious apprehension and alarm, as detrimental to the best interests of this Colony, the adoption of the proposed principle of commercial intercourse, now under the consideration of the Imperial Parliament." The sug-

21. *Mirror of Parl.*, p. 83. 22. *Ibid.*, pp. 82–83.
23. *Assembly Journal, 1846*, pp. 229–230. (C.O. 45:224.)

gestion was put forward that Canadian products might be admitted to Britain entirely free of duty; the assembly also asked that negotiations be opened looking to some reciprocal tariff arrangements between the province and the United States. This is the beginning of the movement in favor of reciprocity which will be described in due time.

Soon afterwards in England the corn duties received actual sentence of death.[24] After the end of January 1849 only nominal duties of a shilling a quarter on grain, and four-pence half-penny a hundredweight on meal and flour were to be levied, no distinction being made between foreign and colonial produce. In the interim colonial breadstuffs were to be admitted at the rate mentioned above, while those from foreign countries were to pay sliding-scale duties with a very much lower maximum than before. The period of transition was justified by Peel as a means to enable all those interested to adjust their affairs to the requirements of the new order. Referring to the province, he thought that "considering that Canada has now an advantage as to the admission of her corn, compared with the corn of foreigners, it would be more acceptable to Canada, and more for the interest of that Colony, that some time should elapse before Canada corn came into direct competition with that of the United States. It was on this account, believing that the arrangement we proposed was more likely to prevent panic, and on the whole better for the agriculturalists, that on the part of the Government I made the proposal."[25]

No sooner had Great Britain made her economic declaration of independence, than the question arose of the control by each colony of its own tariff, and even partial economic autonomy involved a radical change in imperial tariff arrangements. The provincial government brought this point forward, suggesting that the imperial tariff was primarily for the furtherance of commercial policy, while the colonial one was for revenue. "So far as revenue

24. By 9 and 10 Vic., c. 22, June 26, 1846.
25. *Hansard,* 3rd Ser., LXXXIII, 1027.

merely is concerned," wrote Lord Cathcart, "I submit to your Lordship that it would be far more convenient that the duties should be imposed by one set of enactments only, and that as they would affect Colonial interests only, or at least as far as that would be the case, they should be imposed by Colonial Enactments. . . . While a tariff is on the one hand indispensable to Canada as a source of Revenue, until Canal tolls or other present or future sources yield an amount equal to the public exigencies—it is most desirable that its character should be such as will be least burdensome to the agriculturalists the principal consumers, and least discouraging to the Commercial portion of the Province. The experience of her Majesty's Ministers on such important points would be a safe & desirable guide for any measure that the Provincial Government might bring before the Legislature."[26] Before this request had been received however, parliament had given it an unequivocally favorable legislative answer.[27] Wide authority was conferred upon colonies affected by the British Possessions Act to reduce or repeal any or all of the imperial tariff in so far as it affected the imports of the particular colony concerned, such legislation to be subject to the usual royal assent. Actually however the Corn Laws disappeared before their appointed time, because the Irish famine led to their absolute suspension from January 26, 1847, to March 1, 1848.[28] Thus in the space of less than a year did the British Empire commit itself to a largely negative commercial policy of decentralized authority.

The story of the timber trade in the period is simpler and less important. Certain areas in the colony, lying chiefly in the Ottawa Valley, where the trees grew near to the rivers and were easy to remove, were the scene of a very extensive timber industry, which was the second great

26. Cathcart to Grey, No. 117, Aug. 27, 1846. Dom. Arch. MS. Room.

27. 9 and 10 Vic., c. 94. "An Act to enable the Legislatures of certain *British* Possessions to reduce or repeal certain Duties of Customs." Aug. 28, 1846.

28. By 10 and 11 Vic., cc. 1, 3, and 64.

staple of the colony. White pine was the principal wood, and accounted for a good deal more than half the total amount. Red pine came next, and there was a considerable quantity of oak, elm, and larch, which last was used for building ships. The principal port of shipment was Quebec, and the destination was the British market. As the British tariff favored unmilled timber, most of it was exported in that form, though a limited number of staves and deals were also sent over, as well as timber in the form of ships. The industry employed thirty to thirty-five thousand men, chiefly French Canadians, and it was a seasonal occupation, most of the work being done in the winter when farm work was at a standstill. This trade enabled Lower Canada to pay for such imports as it needed; but that part of the province was not dependent on its staple, and much of the capital of the lumber industry was owned in Britain. Some of the Ottawa Valley timber was sent out through the Rideau; but most of it went down the Ottawa to Quebec where it was loaded and shipped. The industry was often regarded as very demoralizing to the workers engaged in it, and so no doubt to a certain extent it was; yet too much can easily be made of this in the case of a community like Lower Canada.

"The bearing of the lumbering business on the settlement of the country is a point well worthy of notice. The farmer who undertakes to cultivate unreclaimed land in new countries generally finds that not only does every step of advance which he makes in the wilderness, by removing him from the centres of trade and civilization, enhance the cost of all he has to purchase, but that, moreover, it diminishes the value of what he has to sell. It is not so, however, with the farmer who follows in the wake of the lumberman. He finds, on the contrary, in the wants of the latter a ready demand for all that he produces, at a price not only equal to that procurable in the ordinary marts, but increased by the cost of transport from them to the scene of the lumbering operations. This circumstance, no doubt, powerfully contributes to promote the settlement of those districts, and attracts population to sections of the country which, in the absence of any such inducement, would probably remain for long periods uninhabited."[29]

This hitherto protected trade was subjected to marked reductions in its tariff preference in 1842, so that after 1843 the foreign duty was twenty-five shillings a load of fifty cubic feet, as against a shilling for the colonial wood.[30] The great Canadian rivers afforded an excellent means of transporting the timber to the sea. Yet wood is probably the bulkiest of all products, and timber from the Baltic, which was the strongest competitor, had a comparatively short distance to go to reach the British market. The differential duty was therefore less protective to Canadian timber than it appeared to be. To a great extent however, the various types of wood had specialized uses, and were complementary to each other rather than mutually exclusive, while owing to the very extensive railway construction in Britain during the forties, the market had a keen appetite for wooden sleepers. As a result, the Canadian trade was not injured by the legislation of 1842, and the year 1845 was one of the most prosperous that it had known. The industry was ill-regulated on its productive side, and in consequence of the high profits of the preceding year a serious over-production followed in 1846 to the extent of some thirteen millions of feet. Following upon this came a pronounced contraction of the markets with the trade depression. Now the imperial government, although it intended to apply its raw material policy to timber, felt the need of greater caution in dealing with that trade than in the case of breadstuffs, and intended to proceed more gradually toward the same goal.[31] Nor did the famine of 1846 and 1847 unexpectedly hasten the process as it did in the case of grain. In the free trade

29. Elgin to Newcastle, No. 58, Aug. 16, 1853. *Accounts and Papers, 1852–53,* LXII.

30. 5 and 6 Vic., c. 47.

31. See Peel's speech, *Hansard,* 3rd Ser., LXXXIII, 243–244.

orgy of 1846 a considerable reduction in the colonial preference was provided for, to take place in two stages in the spring of the years 1847 and 1848.[32] The remaining colonial preference was slight; after April 5, 1848, the duty on foreign unmilled timber per load of fifty cubic feet was fifteen shillings, while that on the colonial article was a shilling per load. During the depression supply continued to exceed demand, and there were numerous failures among the timber merchants at Quebec. So in January 1849 the provincial legislative assembly appointed a select committee to inquire into the timber industry and the causes of its depression. The two reports of this committee,[33] with minutes of evidence, throw much light on the situation. The committee found the problem to result from overproduction which occasioned a permanent surplus of timber at Quebec. They considered that this overproduction had been caused partly by the high prices of 1845 and partly by a recently discarded regulation of the crown lands department which had required a certain quantity of timber to be taken annually off each "limit," whether conditions in the market warranted it or not. They expressed the opinion that the uncertain tenure of timber-limits had tended toward overproduction on the analogy of the hay and the sunshine. The reports contained no thorough-going remedy; but suggested a number of administrative changes. It is interesting to find that these reports made no mention of the recent change in commercial policy, which omission was probably due to political considerations. Some of the witnesses stressed the importance of Baltic competition, and one of them asked, among other things, for "a recognition by the Government, both imperial and colonial, and a portion of their fostering care." Free trade sentiment was probably widespread among those interested in the Ottawa Valley timber industry.

The nearest market for Canadian timber lay in the

32. 9 and 10 Vic., c. 23.

33. *Sess. Papers, 1849,* App. P.P.P.P. (C.O. 45:238).

northeastern states, where much wood was consumed, and where the native supplies had become depleted. Had economic law been free to operate, it is likely that those states would have absorbed the entire production of the Ottawa Valley, for the water communication by way of the Richelieu and Lake Champlain was very good, or was capable of being made so. The American tariff laws of 1842 and 1846[34] however, imposed a twenty per cent *ad valorem* duty on unmanufactured wood, that is to say logs or boards, and this protection continued until 1854. In 1851 the remnant of the preference in the British market was withdrawn from colonial wood,[35] though the British domestic product retained a protection of seven-and-sixpence a load. On the whole the timber exports from Quebec followed the general trade cycle fairly closely; we are therefore entitled to say that changes in the tariff policy of Great Britain influenced them only slightly in the period.[36]

It has already been stated that in providing for the practical dissolution of the imperial customs system, parliament had made provision for the establishment of local tariffs, without however desiring that the colonies should embark upon a policy of protection. Before 1842 raw materials had been admitted to Canada free of duty, while a low import duty on manufactured articles gave a preference to British goods. The provincial law of 1842 which imposed an import duty of three shillings a quarter on

34. 27th Cong., 2nd Sess., c. 270; and 29th Cong., 1st Sess., c. 74.

35. By 14 and 15 Vic., c. 62.

36. The exports from Quebec of white pine, the principal wood, 1844–1851, inclusive, were as given: From table in I. D. Andrews' *Second Report,* p. 419.

| *Year* | *Cubic Feet* |
|---|---|
| 1844 | 11,950,438 |
| 1845 | 15,828,880 |
| 1846 | 14,392,220 |
| 1847 | 9,626,440 |
| 1848 | 10,709,680 |
| 1849 | 11,621,920 |
| 1850 | 13,040,520 |
| 1851 | 15,941,600 |

American grain, was, so far as the province was concerned, founded on no principle of protection or revenue, being merely a prerequisite to the Canada Corn Act; but it inaugurated a shortlived régime of low duties on agricultural products.[37] This was a temporary measure which was repealed early in 1845. Yet the news of the impending repeal of the Corn Laws was known in advance, and it served to raise the whole question of future provincial tariff policy. In May 1846 a law was passed which would permit foreign grain, including grain milled in Canada, to pass through the province without paying duty, should parliament repeal the Corn Laws. This act provided for the repeal of the three-shilling duty of 1842; but imposed the same amount of duty on grain imported for domestic consumption.[38]

The question of colonial differential duties, discriminating against foreign goods or routes, was one that involved the relations of the empire with foreign powers, and in 1843 Lord Stanley had issued a warning in regard to it, in a circular despatch to the various colonial governments.[39] "The imposition of discriminating Duties," he wrote, "on Goods imported into the British Colonies, when the discrimination is made for the protection of some branch of British or Colonial Industry, is an office of great difficulty. To the right discharge of it, an intimate acquaintance with the Commercial Treaties and Political Relations between this Kingdom and Foreign States is indispensable." He considered the colonial legislatures to be unfitted to deal with this type of problem; but made an exception covering the Canadian three-shilling duty law of 1842, and any similar legislation. On the eve of Corn Law repeal the province prepared to impose a discriminating duty against goods imported other than by sea, that is to say other than by way of the St. Lawrence. Gladstone objected to this, and to any other discrimina-

37. See 7 Vic., c. 1. (Prov.), and several subsequent provincial acts.
38. 9 Vic., c. 1. (Prov.)
39. June 28, 1843. *Accounts and Papers, 1846,* XXVII, No. 263.

tory or protective colonial legislation, admitting however that his general principle was "more strictly applicable to maritime commerce than to the case of a Colony having direct and extended relations along a frontier of many hundred miles with a foreign Country."[40]

Actual Corn Law repeal, and the passage of its corollary the British Possessions Act, which conferred a liberal measure of tariff autonomy on the colonies, simplified matters by removing much of the uncertainty which had previously existed. On June 1, 1846, near the end of the session of the provincial legislature, Merritt re-introduced the question of repealing the British preference. "If the productions of Canada," he said, "are to receive no advantage over the productions of foreign countries, when admitted into Britain, the manufactures of Britain are not entitled to any advantage over the manufactures of foreign countries when admitted into Canada."[41] The following spring the speech from the throne at the opening of the legislature contained these words: "By a Statute passed during the last Session of the Imperial Parliament, the Colonial Legislatures are empowered to repeal differential Duties, heretofore imposed in the Colonies in favor of British produce. It is probable that by exercising this power you may be enabled to benefit the consumer without injury to the Revenue."[42] This declaration of policy was implemented by a law which marks a decisive step in both Canadian and imperial tariff history.[43] This law set up a new system of import duties, "in lieu and instead of all other Duties of Customs whether Imperial or Provincial, upon goods, Wares and Merchandize imported into this Province." It was a revenue tariff pure and simple, and, speaking approximately for the sake of simplicity, it lowered the average rate of the duties on Ameri-

40. Gladstone to Cathcart, No. 17, Feb. 3, 1846. Dom. Arch. MS. Room. See also Grey to Cathcart, No. 46, Nov. 2, 1846. *Sess. Papers, 1847,* App. W. (C.O. 45: 231).

41. *Mirror of Parl.,* p. 209.

42. *Council Journal, 1847,* p. 15. (C.O. 45: 228.)

43. 10 and 11 Vic., c. 31. (Prov.), July 28, 1847.

can manufactures from twelve and a half to seven and a half per cent, and raised that on British manufactures from five to seven and a half per cent. It also made conditional provision for reciprocal free trade with the other British North American colonies.

This act, though it was not disallowed, caused concern to the authorities in England, and in the opinion of the Board of Trade it was a measure "which may be described in general terms as an adaptation of all Customs Laws to the circumstances of the Colony."[44] The board objected to the new law on two grounds, and the first of these was that the imperial tariff had only been modified, not repealed, and that the imperial customs officials had still to enforce its active provisions—its prohibitions for example—and that the enforcement of the Navigation Laws devolved upon them also. Yet the province had set up another set of officials and of regulations, and a conflict was feared, for the sovereignty had been divided. The Canadian government on the other hand took a decided stand in the matter, desiring to control all the customs machinery in the province. The second objection was that the new duties on British imports were high enough to be regarded as protective, and this point was reinforced by protests from several groups of British manufacturers. As a matter of fact the Canadian tariff of 1847 was hardly high enough to be called protective, nor was it intended to be so. It did however, within its terms of reference, abolish the imperial preference; yet in doing so it effected no more than the repeal of the Corn Laws had done. Nor did the imperial government raise any objection to this; but it took the ground that there must be no discrimination against Great Britain or the rest of the empire, and that quite apart from discrimination, the colonial duties on British goods ought not to be prohibitively high. "I think," said the prime minister a few years later, "we have a right to ask this in return for the protection

44. This Board of Trade Minute, and other relevant papers are printed in *Sess. Papers, 1849,* App. N. (C.O. 45: 236).

which we afford to the colonies."[45] In regard to the policy of placing Great Britain on a commercial equality with foreigners, I. D. Andrews expressed this opinion: "The commercial interest of the lower province yielded to this policy from sympathy with the free trade movements in England; while it is probable that the western province supported the measure as a means of emancipation from the monopoly of their imports by Montreal and Quebec."[46]

Throughout the period there were occasional complaints from the imperial authorities that duties were being levied on supplies imported into the province for the use of the military forces, more particularly on wine for the officers' messes. It was obviously unreasonable and parasitical that provincial duties should be collected on supplies paid for by the British treasury, imported for the use of soldiers who were maintained in the colony for its defense. Eventually Lord Elgin was able to state that this particular difficulty had been satisfactorily overcome, and he added sarcastically, the events of the year 1849 being still fresh in his mind, "It is gratifying to reflect that henceforward the Gentlemen of H. M.'s army will be able to drink confusion to the Gov Genl and his administration in untaxed liquor."[47]

The Reform Party was returned to power in the winter of 1847–48; but the change had no perceptible effect upon the provincial tariff policy. A new law was passed in 1849, which like its predecessor imposed a strictly revenue tariff.[48] The attitude of the provincial political parties toward tariff policy is neither clearcut nor obvious, and requires explanation. That the Reformers came to power when they did, and were able to establish their political claims, is a fact of great importance quite apart from its bearing on the evolution of responsible government. The principles of the Reform Party were those of English lib-

45. Lord John Russell in the House of Commons. *Hansard,* 3rd Ser., CVIII, 549.

46. *Second Report,* p. 412.

47. Elgin to Grey, Aug. 2, 1850. Private Correspondence.

48. 12 Vic., c. 1. (Prov.)

eralism, including free trade. Thus the Reform *Examiner* had been ready to admit in 1845 that "when the oppression is removed from the heart and lungs of trade, manufactures and commerce, at the centre of the empire, the life-blood of a healthy prosperity must flow to its remotest ramifications."[49] Francis Hincks, the economic expert of the party, on one occasion warned the assembly against protection in these words. "You cannot protect any class of labourers, except at the expense of the great body of consumers; and the error into which persons reasoning on this point are apt to fall, is that of considering themselves only in the light of producers, instead of consumers, which all persons are. He did not believe that it was desirable to attempt to raise up in Canada a protected manufacturing interest."[50] As liberals the Reformers were predisposed to co-operate with a Liberal government in Britain. The party had an overwhelming majority in the assembly after 1847, and enjoyed the undivided support of French Canada, a part of the colony but little affected by changes in imperial commercial policy, and where satisfaction with political triumphs outweighed economic considerations. The party leaders worked throughout in complete harmony with the greatest of Canadian governors-general, at whose hands as well as at those of the imperial government they considered themselves to be receiving an ample measure of justice. These factors made very strongly for cordial relations between the imperial and provincial governments during the difficult and even dangerous period of transition.

Free trade did not however become a political issue in the province, though it might conceivably have done so after 1846. The Reformers neither advocated it while in opposition, though Elgin at one time thought that they might do so,[51] nor tried to apply it when they came to power. Indeed they could only have done so with great

49. *Examiner,* Mar. 19, 1845.
50. Legislative Council, June 6, 1851. *Globe,* June 10, 1851.
51. Elgin to Grey, May 27, 1847. Private Correspondence.

difficulty, for there was little prospect of wide support for a free trade program, and the public revenues were largely dependent upon import duties. In practice therefore the Reformers were a revenue-tariff party, and indeed the extremely modest provincial tariffs of that day were unlikely to offend any but the most dogmatic free trader. Even the *Canadian Economist*, the short-lived organ of the Montreal free trade association, was content to preach the empirical gospel. "Of course our readers are aware that we set our faces in toto against duties of every kind whatsoever, except such as are imposed *for the mere purpose of raising revenue.*"[52]

Nor on the other hand did there develop at this time a purely Canadian protectionist movement, aiming at industrial development and self-sufficiency. It is true that among the annexationists, inconsistently enough, there were a few forerunners of the National Policy; but they obtained almost no support. Agriculture was in part a staple industry, and, as has been said before, most of the business men were merchants, not producers.[53] Furthermore the St. Lawrence waterway exercised an influence on this as on almost every other phase of economic life. For the colony was, or rather wanted to be, a link in a great commercial chain, and protection is unfriendly to such an ambition. Moreover these were the days when the free trade movement was young, vigorous, and on the offensive, and it had made many converts in Canada as elsewhere. Indeed anyone who is familiar with the language and ideas of the province at this time, will realize how grotesque the idea of self-sufficiency inside a tariff wall must have seemed. So futile did the policy of protection appear that the Tory party did not seriously attempt to make an issue of it. As for the *Rouges* in Lower Canada, they were free traders, and extremists in this as in all else. Papineau proclaimed himself to be "Disciple dès ma

52. *Canadian Economist,* Oct. 17, 1846.

53. See the petition of the Toronto Board of Trade against duties on agricultural imports. *Assembly Journal, 1848,* p. 65. (C.O. 45:233.)

première jeunesse de l'école d'Adam Smith, et de tout temps ennemi de tout monopole et privilège."[54]

The fact is that very few Canadians were either unconditional free traders, or protectionists in the modern sense, and the practical result of this was a stable tariff policy except in so far as changes over which they had no control made adjustments necessary to them. The province was thoroughly accustomed to regard itself as an adjunct of a larger economic unit, and had been satisfied with the situation which existed before 1846—a time of economic security which in the uncertain years between that date and 1851 came to be regarded as a golden age. "We should like," said the Tory *Courier* in January 1849, "with reference to the Mother Country, to be in the same situation as one of her own counties; we should like to see our productions received in England without one farthing of duty paid thereon, and we should like to receive her manufactures in the same way."[55] Many conservatives advocated a return to the old order of imperial preferences, and this was in a half-hearted and hopeless kind of way the attitude of the Tory party for several years. They had been in power in 1846, and had opposed the repeal of the Corn Laws with all the means at their disposal: they had also passed the autonomous tariff law of 1847, the thoroughgoing nature of that law being to some extent perhaps a reflection of their bitter feelings. In 1849 Sir Allan MacNab spoke of colonial preference as something to which the province was entitled, and he even laid claim to a belief that a return to the old order was likely.[56] This yearning after the dear dead day of colonial preferences however came to be identified with the annexation movement, and to be discredited accordingly. One of the most

54. Address to the electors of Huntingdon County, reported in *La Revue Canadienne*, Dec. 21, 1847.

55. *Courier* (Montreal), Jan. 9, 1849. The "county" argument often appeared in parliamentary debates and elsewhere; but it would not bear analysis.

56. Legislative Assembly, Jan. 26, 1849. *Globe*, Feb. 3, 1849.

stubborn advocates of the *status quo* was Cayley, who as late as June 1851 supported the introduction into the assembly of an address to the Queen asking that the old commercial system might be restored.[57] At no time however did this policy become an effective party issue, for Britain was evidently becoming more attached every day to the *laissez faire* policy, consequently a reversion to the former state of affairs was too remote and unlikely a contingency to appeal to more than an optimistic or stubborn minority as a practical plan of campaign. Its advocates were left to ransack the printed utterances of English parliamentary leaders for signs of relenting which were not there.

Yet the Canadians wanted, and indeed they had to have, a market for their staples, and they were accustomed to having that market preferentially protected in their favor. They preferred to carry on the largest possible proportion of their external trade with Great Britain, both for reasons of sentiment, and because, to most people, an existing situation, provided that it be reasonably satisfactory, is preferable to that which is unfamiliar and uncertain. It seemed improbable to many Canadians, however, that the preponderance of their intra-imperial trade could be maintained under the new commercial régime, and ultimately, though not by any means as rapidly as most of them supposed, this forecast proved to have been correct. Now the province was within the sphere of influence of two great nations, and no sooner had the intentions of the mother country become quite certain, than an alternative suggestion was made—that the United States should be persuaded to enter into a reciprocal agreement whereby Canadian raw materials would obtain entry into the American market on preferential terms. Under the American tariff of 1842 wheat had to pay a duty of twenty-five cents a bushel, and wheat flour one of fourteen

57. Cayley was later to become the leader of the first real protectionist movement in the province.

dollars a ton, while the act of 1846 imposed a twenty per cent *ad valorem* duty on grain, flour, and timber. To many it seemed that the lowering or removal of this barrier would bring certain prosperity to the province, and this view was not only widely held, but became an important part of the policy of the Baldwin-Lafontaine government. The Tories did not oppose it, nevertheless reciprocity was essentially a Reform measure, while a return to the old order was advocated almost entirely by Tories. It is clear then that in the matter of practical policy Canadians were neither complete free traders, nor yet protectionists in the modern sense, but preferentialists. They had as yet no aspirations after commercial self-sufficiency and only desired reciprocal arrangements with some larger and more mature community, preferably Great Britain. When they had lost apparently irrevocably their old preferential relationship with that country, they tried to establish a similar arrangement with the United States, and after much effort they were successful. They were not able however, to maintain permanently their preferential access to the American market, and when it also was denied to them they turned to national protection as a last resort.

In Britain the free traders entered upon the new policy without much misgiving on the score of its probable effect on the empire. "Nothing could be more to be deprecated," said one of them in the House of Commons, "than that we should attempt to continue our connection with the Colonies by a system of inflicting on each other mutual injury."[58] With others, cheap food for the British working man, which was one way of saying low production costs, was the paramount consideration. At this point, so far as free traders were concerned, the interests of Britain as the workshop of the world had to take precedence over those of Britain as the metropolis of colonies, and the choice was not difficult for them, since the two interests did not seem to them to clash, but on the contrary to

58. *Hansard,* 3rd Ser., LXXXIII, 989.

march together.[59] The theory held by Turgot that a mature colony of settlement was bound to fall like ripe fruit from the imperial tree,[60] was also widely held, and the result was a good deal of indifference to the subject of colonies in general.

In 1849 Grey wrote to Elgin that "unfortunately there begins to prevail in the H. of Commons & I am sorry to say in the highest quarters, an opinion (wh. I believe to be utterly erroneous) that we have no interest in preserving our Colonies & ought therefore to make no sacrifice for that purpose. Peel, Graham, & Gladstone if they do not avow this opinion as openly as Cobden & his friends, yet betray very clearly that they entertain it, nor do I find some members of the Cabinet free from it."[61] Lord Elgin constantly criticized and expressed his resentment of this attitude of indifference in his letters to Grey, while Wakefield and his friends splintered many a lance upon it also. When the new colonial policy was under attack, it was occasionally argued that it might involve the dismemberment of the empire. On one occasion the House of Commons had been told that: "For the first time, in our history you avow, or at least you act upon, an anti-colonial policy."[62] This type of argument however was rare.[63]

Lord Elgin's opinion of the probable effect of the new commercial policy on the imperial structure, underwent a decided and interesting change as time passed by. Soon after his arrival in Canada he had expressed regret that the commercial ties of empire had been loosened. Nearly two years later however he wrote, it may be with greater wis-

59. It is perfectly true that free traders were anything but enthusiasts for colonies. Yet they did not leave them out of the reckoning as is so often stated. Free trade was a panacea.

60. "Les colonies sont comme des fruits qui tiennent à l'arbre jusqu'à ce qu'ils en aient reçu une nourriture suffisante; alors ils s'en détachent." Turgot, *Oeuvres* (Ed. Schelle), I, 141.

61. Grey to Elgin, May 18, 1849. Private Correspondence.

62. Sir William Heathcote in the House of Commons, *Hansard,* 3rd Ser., LXXXIII, 562.

63. For public opinion on the subject in Britain, and the colonies, see C. A. Bodelsen, *Studies in Mid-Victorian Imperialism,* pp. 13–59.

dom born of fuller experience: "I am sure also that when Free Trade is fairly in operation it will be found that more has been gained by removing the causes of irritation which were furnished by the constant tinkerings incident to a protective system, than has been lost by severing the bonds by which it tied the Mother Country and the Colonies together."[64]

64. Elgin to Grey, Jan. 14, 1850. Private Correspondence.

# VI

# THE NAVIGATION LAWS, AND THE OPENING OF THE ST. LAWRENCE

As defence, however, is of much more importance than opulence, the act of navigation is, perhaps, the wisest of all the commercial regulations of England. ADAM SMITH.

Il [Turgot] pensait que la prospérité des Colonies exigeait qu'elles jouissent de la liberté du Commerce. DUPONT DE NEMOURS.

IT is customary to trace the Navigation Laws of England back to the legislation of the Commonwealth.[1] At that time directed against the commerce of Holland, they worked, or seemed to work, extraordinarily well, and came to form a considerable part of the restrictive code of mercantilism, which was to a great extent a theory of colonial policy. Adam Smith, in that famous sentence of his which no writer on the Navigation Laws ever fails to quote, had given these laws his blessing, restrictive though they were, and all other colony-owning nations had imitated them. The English-American colonists, prior to 1776, disliked them, and broke them continually, although afterwards as an independent nation they enacted similar laws for their own use.

Natural causes had combined with legislation and long-established habits to make the old empire an economic unit. The political independence of the United States therefore exposed the British Navigation Laws to new strains of great intensity, since the system was then no longer reinforcing existing economic tendencies, but tending to thwart them. The Navigation Laws had never been so entirely consistent as to exclude all exceptions; but

1. Their lineage however is even longer than this, going back to 5 Richard II, c. 3.

after 1776 and especially after 1815 when the Americans adopted a navigation law of their own, the British system became less logical and more opportunist than had previously been the case. This process was furthered by the growth of free trade sentiment, which was reflected in Huskisson's reciprocity treaties. Indeed with the age of *laissez faire*, the Navigation Laws were exposed to salvoes of arguments hitherto unknown, and might even suffer condemnation on moral grounds. Yet so generally popular were they, and so basic a part of imperial policy, that they remained essentially intact throughout the earlier free trade period, and survived their less vital partner the Corn Law.

The British navigation code of the period under consideration was embodied almost wholly in two statutes passed in the year 1845.[2] The coastwise trade of any country seems naturally to belong to its citizens, and the navigation laws of the various countries sought, if not to abolish the ocean, at least to confer upon the trade between each country and its colonies, or between various colonies forming part of the same empire, the monopolistic character of coastwise traffic. Economically as well as politically the colonies were to be an extension of the metropolis, and this theory of colonial policy, although in the long run it did not work, was logically the soundest that has yet been devised.

So far as Canada was concerned, the laws of 1845 placed these restrictions on trade. The direct trade between Canada and Great Britain, or between Canada and any other British colony, or between two Canadian ports, had to be carried in British ships. Goods might not be sent from Canada to Britain by way of the continent of Europe. The only Canadian port from which ocean-borne trade might be carried on with foreign countries was Quebec. On the other hand, goods from a foreign country, the produce of that country, might be imported in the ships of that country. American ships on the Great Lakes might

2. 8 and 9 Vic., cc. 88 and 93.

trade between United States and Canadian ports; but not from one colonial port to another. Nor were they allowed, though this prohibition was not contained in the Navigation Laws, to use the St. Lawrence between Montreal and Quebec. Goods not forbidden other than by the Navigation Laws might be warehoused for re-export at Quebec. Also such goods "brought by Land or Inland Navigation, or imported in *British* ships," might be similarly warehoused at Kingston, Toronto, Hamilton, and Montreal. A British ship, within the meaning of the law, was any British-built and owned vessel, with a British master, and a crew three-quarters of whom were British. The definition included colonial ships, while very small vessels engaged in the coastwise trade were recognized as British ships without the formality of registration.

It has already been said that Quebec had special privileges in regard to foreign trade. It was a free port. It was enacted by 8 and 9 Vic., c. 93: "That no Goods shall be imported into, nor shall any Goods, except the Produce of the Fisheries in *British* Ships, be exported from any of the *British* Possessions in *America* by Sea from or to any Place other than the United Kingdom, or some other of such Possessions, except into or from the several Ports in such Possessions, called 'Free Ports.'" These last had originated in the 18th century in an attempt to cope with illegal trading in the West Indies. The first so-called "Free Port Act" had gone into effect in 1766,[3] and the policy had afterwards been extended. The only free port in Canada was Quebec, and this was something of a grievance in Montreal and the subject of several petitions. It was not however the hardship that at first sight it appears to have been, since the bulk of the Canadian trade was with Great Britain, and in respect of this trade Montreal enjoyed the same status as did Quebec.

Unlike the colonists of the earlier empire, the Canadians of the Corn Law period did not dislike the Navigation Laws. It is true that there were protests from Canada

3. 6 Geo. III, c. 49.

concerning them; but these were protests to the effect that they were not inclusive enough. Objection had been raised to clause 31 of the Act of 1833.[4] It provided "That it shall be lawful to bring or import by Land or by Inland Navigation into any of the *British* Possessions in *America* from any adjoining Foreign Country any Goods which might be lawfully imported by Sea into such Possession from such Country, and so to bring or import such Goods in the Vessels, Boats, or Carriages of such Country, as well as in *British* Vessels, Boats or Carriages." This clause had been interpreted by the authorities as giving the right to American vessels to bring into Canada across the lakes, any goods whether the produce of the United States or not. In time there came to be a considerable and increasing colonial mercantile marine on the lakes, particularly on Lake Ontario, and in 1843 and 1844 owners of lake shipping were expressing anxiety lest American ships should get too much of the lake trade. "May we hope," wrote one of them, "that the british Government will extend to us on the Lakes so much of the british navigation laws as shall prevent foreign Vessels from bringing to our ports other than the growth, produce or manufacture of their own country."[5] There was more anxiety after the passage of the American law of March 3, 1845,[6] which permitted a tariff drawback on foreign goods re-exported to British North America. From the point of view of the provincial ship-owner, this meant that a lucrative trade was being established across rather than down the lakes, and that American ships were being allowed to share it on terms which were thought to be less than fair. In support of this last point Canadian shipping interests urged that American ships had relatively small dues to pay, and that American merchants and shippers favored their own ships. The fear was expressed that "the right of trading

4. 3 and 4 William IV, c. 59.

5. Captain Hugh Richardson to the Civil Secretary, Jan. 24, 1844. Correspondence of the Civ. Sec., No. 3097. See also D. Bethune to W. H. Draper, of Dec. 30, 1843, *ibid.*

6. 28th Cong., 2nd Sess., c. 70.

with the British Possessions on the Inland Waters, enjoyed by the Americans, with their own vessels, together with the want of the Registry Laws of Great Britain, has, in itself, a most pernicious effect on the Commerce of the Country; but the addition of the mischievous tendency of the drawback bill, in opening up a new source of Commercial enterprise will, if not counteracted, destroy all hope of the Colonies ever possessing a Commercial Navy on the great Inland Waters of America."[7]

With the tidings that the Corn Laws were to be repealed however, colonial opinion of the Navigation Laws changed, and this was true of the colonies in general. When the Canadians saw that colonial preferences in England had gone by the board and were unlikely to be recovered, they unwillingly accepted the situation since it might no better be, and began to clamor loudly for repeal of the Navigation Laws, in the names of logic and of justice. In so doing, it is necessary to concede as the British parliament very shortly did, that they had right on their side. The old colonial system was a *system*, and it did not lend itself to a partial application or a limited repeal. So when once the decision had been reached to adopt free trade, the Navigation Laws became indefensible, whether on grounds of precedent, equity, or expediency. The old system had stood, like an arch, on two supports—preferential tariffs and navigation laws—and the structure could not stand on one alone. The colonists were therefore on very strong ground in demanding repeal. Taking the now discarded system as a whole, mother country and colonies had alike obtained a preferred market, a shipping monopoly, and perhaps an increased defensive power. Yet to the colonists it was the British market that was chiefly important, for they had few ships of their own, and in the matter of imperial defense they felt no concern. The problem of inducing a colony that was not directly, immediately, and obviously threatened, to take

7. The Attorney-General to the Civil Secretary, April 26, 1845. Correspondence of the Civ. Sec., No. 4062.

any practical interest in imperial defense was never solved in the nineteenth century, and in the twentieth has found only a very partial solution. So to colonial eyes Navigation Laws plus duty-free imports looked like all pill and no sugar-coating. The colonies moreover found themselves in the morally strong position of urging a further removal of restrictions upon a government to which restrictions were very abhorrent, and nothing was easier than to say to the imperial government: "Thou hast appealed unto Cobden: unto Cobden shalt thou go." So Montreal preached the pure gospel of Manchester, arguing that the removal of impediments to trade would increase competition, and efficiency therewith. For once the provincials found themselves in possession of a theory.

No matter how obstructive a law may be in principle, it must at least seem to restrict in practice also, or it ceases to have any real vitality as a grievance. Was not the British merchant marine the largest and most efficient in the world, and thus more than able to handle the Canadian trade, and to do so competitively, ship against ship? It is necessary to avoid being misled by the conditions of a later day. The steam ship was just in its beginnings, the metal ship as yet unknown, and the superiority of the British merchant marine far less decisive than it afterwards became. English-built ships were the strongest and the most long-lived in the world, and were especially well adapted to carrying heavy cargoes; but they sailed comparatively slowly and were exceedingly expensive to build. The North American colonies had, it is true, ships of their own. Yet these were chiefly noted for the extreme cheapness of their construction, and possessing neither durability nor first-rate sailing qualities could hardly hope to solve the problem of competition on the Atlantic. Some foreign countries had the advantage of cheap labor and cheap ships. The most serious competition however came from the American ships which were the fastest on the sea, and in sailing days speed was economy. Perhaps not generally more efficient than English vessels, they appear to have been so for the purpose of the direct trade between North America and Great Britain, for more than half the unrestricted part of that trade was carried in American bottoms.[8] So that by preventing these fine vessels from competing in Canadian ports, the Navigation Laws appeared to be excluding a competitive factor of the greatest importance. Moreover a large proportion of the ships which entered the St. Lawrence ports came thither in ballast, which of course meant that the level of the freight-rates outward had to be high enough to take care of the unprofitable inward voyages. It was a recognized defect of the Navigation Laws that they increased the proportion of voyages in ballast,[9] and the tendency for ships to come up the St. Lawrence empty, seemed to result from the restrictions imposed by those laws.

In and after the year 1846, a cloud of petitions, addresses, and memorials appeared, asking that the Navigation Laws be repealed, or be not repealed, and variously addressed to the Queen, the governor, Lords and Commons. They came from many sources—from shipping interests opposed to repeal, and from business men of the *laissez faire* persuasion who favored it. Many came from the colonies, for instance from South Australia, from some of the West Indies, and from Ceylon. Colonial petitions nearly all asked for repeal, though an exceptional one in this respect was received from New Brunswick. These petitions are scattered broadcast through the parliamentary papers of the time which deal with the question of the Navigation Laws. Canada had a particularly strong case against those laws, and was the spear-head of the opposition to them so far as the colonies were concerned. The legislature and executive of the province repeatedly pressed for repeal. There were petitions and memorials, some of them oft-repeated, from the boards of

8. The evidence given before the Lords and Commons committees contains much interesting information about ships.

9. J. H. Clapham, "The Last Years of the Navigation Laws, II," *English Historical Review,* XXV, 703.

trade of Montreal, Quebec, Toronto, and Hamilton.[10] Public meetings were also held, as for example, one in the Bonsecours Market in Montreal, reported, probably with some exaggeration, by *La Minerve* of June 15, 1848. The Ottawa lumbermen too gathered in Bytown and passed resolutions in favor of repeal. Special interests in Quebec and Hamilton however defended the Navigation Laws, for a time at least. The Board of Trade of Quebec petitioned for repeal in the usual manner; but a counter-petition was got up "because they deem it incompatible for Colonists seeking protection to ask for the abrogation of a Law, which may severely injure the shipping interests of the Mother Country and the Colonies." The motive here was in part due to the favored position occupied by Quebec under the existing laws. This may also help to account for the fact that the anti-Navigation Law fervor reached its climax in Montreal. The Hamilton Board of Trade in 1846 desired the retention of the Navigation Laws. They stated quite frankly that a large part of Canada West was so situated that it could best export its wheat by the Erie–New York route, and desired every facility for that trade. Hamilton undoubtedly stood to gain by the development of the Erie trade, which the Navigation Laws were generally supposed to favor. Two subsequent petitions from the same source however asked for repeal in the orthodox way. The temporary suspension of the Navigation Laws in 1847, encouraged attempts to have the change made permanent, and as the end of Peel's transitional period approached with the year 1849, opposition to the Navigation Laws became more intense. So the stream of petitions flows on undiminished in volume right down to the date of the repeal. The arguments used were numerous, the following being the more important of them.

Canada ought to be released from "restrictions for the benefit of the British shipowner." "A great reduction of freight [rates] at Montreal might safely be calculated

10. For a typical anti-Navigation Laws petition, see Appendix A.

upon as an effect which would necessarily result from their repeal." Canada's great canal investments are endangered by the existing situation. One memorial concluded thus: "it is obvious the Question simply amounts to this,—Will the British Shipowner allow the Foreigner to compete with him in the St. Lawrence, or will he compel himself to compete with the Foreigner in the Ports of the United States."[11] It was sometimes pointed out that the colony had been entirely content with the old system, the implication being that those who had tilted the boat ought to bail out the water. The provincial executive council in a memorandum of May 12, 1848,[12] said this: "The advantage and disadvantage of this system of protection and monopoly alternated according to circumstances, but on the whole, the colony, while her products were protected in the British market, did not complain of the monopoly in favour of British shipping, which seemed to be an essential point in the policy of the trade of the empire." A Montreal petition took what looked like high ground, though the language was much more lofty than the idea which it adorned. "In nations," it said, "there are interests infinitely transcending those of a mere pecuniary nature; and your petitioners would regard the integrity of the British dominions, the preservation of Britain's political power and influence, as cheaply puchased by any pecuniary loss the colonies might occasion her."

In the later period the petitions from Montreal became less measured in tone. One from the Board of Trade, of December 14, 1848, expressed a fear of certain changes that might result from England's new commercial policy, and that "the most prominent of the changes referred to is a growing commercial intercourse with the United States, giving rise to an opinion which is daily gaining ground on both sides of the boundary Line, that the interests of the two Countries under the changed policy of

11. Memorial from the Montreal Board of Trade, May 26, 1848. *Reports from Committees, 1847–8,* XX, Part II, App. FF.

12. *Accounts and Papers, 1847–8,* LIX.

the Imperial Government are german to each other, and under that System, must sooner or later be politically interwoven." The petitioners added that being loyal they did not desire this, and made several suggestions to avert it. These were that the Navigation Laws should be repealed, the St. Lawrence opened, and a moderate fixed duty of say five shillings a quarter imposed on foreign wheat entering Great Britain, while the colonial article should be admitted free. They argued that such a duty would be paid not by the consumer but by the producer, and that it would be a tariff for revenue and therefore not protection. They also wanted the free admission of breadstuffs of whatever origin, shipped from Canadian ports.

This bold forecast of separation, and union with the United States, even though uttered as a warning and not as a wish, was strong language for use in a petition to the crown, and thirteen members of the board wrote to the president, Peter McGill, a few days later, taking exception to what had been done.[13] They protested that the implication that annexation was imminent, was neither suitable nor true.[14] They objected to the suggestion of a five-shilling duty on foreign wheat, as the latter would be a violation of the new commercial principles of the British government, "and one which, as colonists, we have no right to petition for." They claimed that customs duties are paid by the consumers, and that the English people ought not to be taxed for the benefit of the colonies. They prophesied that the St. Lawrence route might be made successful by the entire repeal of the Navigation Laws in so far as these affected Canada, and admitted the likelihood of dissatisfaction against England were those laws to remain on the statute book.

An analysis of Canadian opinion after 1846 in regard to the Navigation Laws, gives the following result. The Reform Party, true to its *laissez faire* principles, strongly

13. *Accounts and Papers, 1849,* LI, No. 1016.

14. Less than a year later seven of these men signed the annexation manifesto.

favored repeal, the Reform government did everything in its power to bring this about, and the party press advocated it with fervor. The *Pilot*, for example, while admitting as nearly everyone did that under the old régime the Navigation Laws had worked well enough, went on to inquire: "If a barrel of flour shipped at New York in an American ship is admitted on the same terms as one shipped at Montreal in a British one, what Canadian miller will pay the latter a higher freight in order to maintain a British commercial marine? It is clear to us as the sun at noon-day that without a repeal of the navigation laws the commerce of Quebec and Montreal is doomed."[15] The French liberal press also supported repeal with enthusiasm, though its primary interests were not economic ones. The Reformers were in a stronger position in advocating Navigation Law repeal than they had been in acquiescing in the repeal of the Corn Laws, for the former attitude was much more generally popular than the latter. The Tory party and press on the other hand gave the Navigation Laws some support, yet they were at a disadvantage, because it was exceedingly difficult to justify the continued existence of those laws to a colonial public after the Corn Laws had been abandoned, and it was hard to convince any but the most stupid or the most optimistic that there was any likelihood whatever that the Corn Law would be re-enacted. Consequently they were not united on this issue, and many of them thought with the Tory member for Ottawa that the old commercial system was preferable to free trade, but that the adoption by Great Britain of the latter policy had rendered it desirable that the Navigation Laws should be repealed.[16] In January 1849 when a resolution for repeal was before the legislative assembly, Cayley moved an amendment which declared the general opinion of the province to be in favor of a British preference on Canadian breadstuffs; but this amendment was defeated by forty-eight votes to four-

15. *Pilot,* Sept. 18, 1846.
16. John Egan in the legislative assembly. *Globe,* Feb. 7, 1849.

teen.[17] There were a few die-hards however who continued to demand the old colonial system, the whole of it, and nothing else.

As a whole therefore, public opinion in the colony on the subject of the Navigation Laws was about as clearly defined and unanimous as it ever is anywhere except perhaps in time of war. It required no skilled politician, highly sensitized to the movements of public sentiment, to know what a large majority of the colonists wanted, and throughout the whole period here discussed the governors-general had been urging the desired policy on the authorities at home. In 1844 Lord Metcalfe drew Lord Stanley's attention to the desirability of extending the ordinary provisions of the navigation code to the Great Lakes. Cathcart two years later urged that the St. Lawrence should be thrown wide open to foreign ships, and still later Lord Elgin advocated the adoption of practically the same policy.[18] In a despatch written late in the spring of 1848, he pressed strongly the case for repeal. "The Canadian farmer," he wrote, "is a supplicant at present to the Imperial Legislature, not for favour, but for justice." He urged as they all did the claims of the river, and expressed fear of the political results of the existing situation. The most enlightened and profitable treatment of this subject by Elgin, however, is to be found in a private letter to Lord Grey which deserves to be quoted at some length:

"I am glad to see yr. bold measure on the Navigation Laws. You have no other course now open to you if you intend to keep yr. colonies. You cannot halt between two opinions. Free trade in all things or general Protection. There was something captivating in the project of forming all the parts of this vast British Empire into one huge Zollverein with free interchange of commodities between

17. *Globe,* Feb. 7, 1849.

18. Metcalfe to Stanley, No. 29, Feb. 3, 1844. Cathcart to Grey, No. 117, Aug. 27, 1846. Elgin to Grey, No. 81, June 15, 1848. Dom. Arch. MS. Room.

its members, and uniform duties against the World without. Though perhaps without some federal legislation it might have been impossible to carry it out. Undoubtedly under such a system the component parts of the Empire would have been united by bonds which cannot be supplied under that on which we are now entering. Though it may be fairly urged on the other side that the variety of conflicting interests which would under this arrangement have been brought into presence would have led to collisions which we may now hope to escape. But as it is the die is cast. As regards these colonies you must allow them to turn to the best possible account their contiguity to the States that they may not have cause for dissatisfaction when they contrast their own condition with that of their neighbours."[19] This letter is Lord Elgin at his very best. Hincks, whose advice in matters of this sort Lord Elgin rightly valued very highly, referred to "the repeal of the Navigation Laws the only boon which the Free traders of Canada have to ask, and which would remove every just cause of Complaint on the part of the Colonists."[20]

In the old land however conditions were very different, where a more complicated economic structure included interests far more divergent. The Navigation Laws were popular in many quarters in England to the very last. Business interests were divided; yet generally speaking the shipping interests, supported by naval opinion and by patriotic torydom, saw in repeal that "national destruction" for which conservatives have always so keen an eye. After 1846, nevertheless, the navigation code was continually under fire as the star of Manchester moved more and more into the ascendant. Moreover, comment and debate on the subject gave scope for expressing sentiments of the sort which Elgin so often deprecated and deplored. Thus a good mercantilist, speaking on the Navigation

19. Elgin to Grey, June 6, 1848. Private Correspondence. Printed in Theodore Walrond (Ed.), *Letters and Journals of James, Eighth Earl of Elgin.* (London, 1873), p. 61.

20. Enclosure with Elgin to Grey, Jan. 4, 1849. Private Correspondence.

Laws in the House of Commons in 1848, said that "The only use of the colonies was to contribute to the strength and commerce of the country; but when they ceased to be effective in that way, the sooner they were got rid of the better."[21]

In February 1847 a select committee of the Commons was appointed to investigate the whole question of the Navigation Laws. Sir Robert Peel, I. L. Ricardo, Bright, Hume, and Thomas Baring were on this committee, which collected voluminous evidence of extraordinary interest. A similar investigation was made by a committee of the Lords, and the resulting reports are a mine of information.[22] Meanwhile the crisis caused by the famine of 1846–47 demanded instant action, and the question of a temporary and partial suspension of the Navigation Laws arose. They were suspended soon afterwards,[23] at first from January 26 to September 1, 1847, and later until March 1, 1848. The suspending acts permitted the importation into the United Kingdom, for home use, of any breadstuffs and potatoes, in the ships of any country. These arrangements might have put Montreal at a further disadvantage, because not being a free port foreign ships were prohibited from doing business there, whereas for the time being they might engage in the trade between New York and Great Britain. To meet this difficulty the treasury authorized foreign ships to go in ballast to Montreal, and thence to bring down breadstuffs destined for the United Kingdom. The suspension was hailed with joy in Canada, and undoubtedly diminished the prestige of the Navigation Laws. For it could be said effectively if speciously, that "Temporary suspension of the operation of monopoly laws, arising from their admitted incompatibility with the general interests of the country amount to an acknowledgment of their injustice, and forbode their ultimate abolition."[24]

21. *Hansard,* 3rd Ser., XCVIII, 1029.
22. *Reports from Committees, 1847–8,* XX, Parts I and II.
23. By 10 and 11 Vic., cc. 2 and 86.
24. *Examiner,* July 14, 1847.

So far as the colonial secretary was concerned, arguments from the colony on behalf of repeal could only convince the already convinced, for Lord Grey loathed trade restrictions in every form. The British government also was favorable to repeal, and bills to that end were unsuccessfully introduced in two separate sessions, the stumbling-block being the House of Lords. Nevertheless it was recognized by both parties in parliament that Canada had a particularly strong case for repeal, and the question of opening the St. Lawrence without a general repeal was seriously considered. By the spring of 1849 many members of the government including Lord Grey, were prepared to resign unless the repeal went through.[25] Lord John Russell informed Lord Palmerston that both he and Lord Lansdowne were agreed "that after having brought forward the Navigation Bill in so solemn a manner for two sessions we ought to resign if we are beaten by a considerable majority in the Lords. . . . But the probable case is that we shall carry the Bill if we show ourselves in earnest upon it. . . . There is one part of the Bill respecting the navigation of the St. Lawrence which it is absolutely necessary to carry this year. Whether in the event of the rejection of the Bill it could be separated from the other parts will deserve instant attention."[26]

The "opening of the St. Lawrence," might mean either of two things. The Navigation Laws forbade foreign ships to trade at Montreal, and restricted them at Quebec. Another type of prohibition, too, prevented the carrying on of another sort of trade—that in American vessels between the lakes and the ocean. Below Montreal the St. Lawrence was a British river, and it had long been closed between that city and Quebec, to American vessels,[27] the only foreign ships at all likely to engage in that trade. Occasionally individual American ships obtained special

25. Grey to Elgin, April 20, 1849. Private Correspondence.

26. G. P. Gooch, *The Later Correspondence of Lord John Russell, 1840–1878* (London, 1925), I, 194–195.

27. By Section 3 of the Jay Treaty of 1794.

permission to make a single trip, but such exceptions were not numerous. Opinion in Canada was far less decided on this matter than it was in regard to the Navigation Laws. On the one hand it seemed desirable to allow a monopoly of that trade to provincial and other British shipping; but against this it was urged that the prohibition debarred United States vessels from using the St. Lawrence canals to the financial benefit of the latter, and helped to drive the American trade out by way of the Erie. Merritt strongly advocated this change in the legislative assembly, in June 1846. He argued that "by refusing this you retain no advantage to our shipping interest—the effect is merely to force their products through their canals and deprive us of the toll and trade which their increased transit would create."[28] The debate however developed some opposition to this, and "Mr. Viger was decidedly opposed to admitting American vessels to enter into competition with Canadian. He considered that the man who would allow a foreign power to exercise the sovereignty of its waters would be a traitor to his country."[29]

The St. Lawrence was closed to American ships by executive action in assertion of a right which rested on an agreement by treaty. This prohibition then was entirely distinct from any contained in the Navigation Laws, and was capable of being retained or done away with independently of them. To the lake states of the union, then as now, the outlet to the sea by the St. Lawrence was very important. The Americans never attempted to disguise this fact, and after 1849 it occupied their serious attention. A petition to congress in 1850, signed by certain inhabitants of the lake states,[30] drew attention to the extensive trade of their part of the continent, and complained: "That this immense trade has hitherto been, from necessity, forced to market through the Erie canal, four feet in depth and forty feet in width, . . ." that this was unsatisfactory, and that additional transit facilities were

28. *Mirror of Parl.*, p. 209. 29. *Ibid.*, p. 210.
30. *Senate Misc. Docs.*, No. 111, 31st Cong., 1st Sess., I.

needed. "As a remedy for this great and growing difficulty," the petition continued, "the undersigned beg leave to call the attention of your honorable body to the river St. Lawrence. This great and natural outlet of the lakes seems designed by Providence as the great commercial channel by which the immense commerce of the lakes should find its way to the Atlantic ocean and the world." They feared however that it would remain unavailable unless Congress took some action.

I. D. Andrews expressed the same opinion in 1850, in his first report to the United States Senate on the trade of the British American colonies, saying that "the navigation interests of those States bordering on the lakes, . . . require the free use of this river without any restrictions whatever." The report also went on to predict that "the peaceful acquisition of this important navigation will more than compensate for all the partial evils which might follow from reciprocal free trade with Canada."[31] There is also a report to the House of Representatives, of the same year, dealing with the same subject.[32] This report considered that an open St. Lawrence would be most beneficial to the United States, and would harm no British interest. It based the American case mainly on "natural right," developing the idea at some length. This argument led up to the idea that if Great Britain should claim absolutely untrammelled sovereignty over the lower part of the river, then the United States might claim the right to divert unlimited quantities of water from Lake Michigan into the Mississippi or Ohio. For, according to such a doctrine of sovereignty, the United States would possess absolute control over Lake Michigan and the water in it. A glowing picture was presented of the probable future expansion of the northwestern states and of their trade, and on this a plea of commercial necessity rested. The report envisaged the possibility that an open St. Lawrence might enable American lake shipping to ply on the ocean during

31. *First Report,* pp. 35 and 50.
32. *Reports of Committees,* No. 295, 31st Cong., 1st Sess., II.

the winter months instead of being laid up. The practical suggestion was made that "if England will not acknowledge the right, as conferred upon us by the hand of nature, she should acknowledge it by treaty." It was admitted that some *quid pro quo* might have to be given. Interest in the St. Lawrence as a possible channel for commerce was of course strongest in the lake states. New York, with its special interests, was less enthusiastic; yet the New York *Tribune* admitted that "it is right that the great West should be enabled freely to choose between these routes, using the cheapest, which, after all, may prove to be the Erie and Oswego Canals."[33]

There was a means whereby, for all practical purposes, the Canadian disabilities, real or alleged, as well as those of the lake states, might have been removed without a general repeal of the Navigation Laws, or an opening of the St. Lawrence to all foreign shipping—namely a mutual suspension of their respective laws and orders restricting navigation by Great Britain and the United States in each other's favor. This would have thrown open the trade between Canada and Britain to American ships, which provided nearly all the potential competition. By the Convention of London of 1815 the United Kingdom had relaxed her navigation laws in favor of American ships; but had retained monopoly rights for her ships in British America. The law was not popular with foreign nations and many complaints had been made, for instance by Russia, Prussia, and Denmark. A report to the United States Congress in 1842 had stigmatized the law as very unfair to American shipping, and recommended an adjustment by negotiation or retaliation. In 1847 the American minister in London suggested to the foreign secretary a mutual abrogation of existing restrictions, and received a generally favorable answer;[34] but nothing was done.

Yet in spite of its numerous defenders, the days of the

33. Issue of July 31, 1847.

34. *Accounts and Papers, 1847–8,* LIX, No. 901.

navigation code were numbered, and in June 1849 parliament passed a law[35] repealing it excepting in so far as it protected the strictly coastwise trade of Great Britain or of each individual colony. The repeal was to go into effect on January 1, 1850. The imperial government was authorized, on the application of the legislature of any colony, to throw open by order in council the coastwise trade of that colony; while any two colonies might in the same way have the water-borne trade between them protected. So far as Canada was concerned, the new law allowed any foreign vessels to load or unload cargoes in Montreal or elsewhere, irrespective of their previous port of call or subsequent destination. It is evident that this removed all the restrictive features of the old law to which the Canadians had objected.

The actual use of the St. Lawrence by American ships sailing to or from the Great Lakes, began in a very limited way. It happened that the cheapest means of transportation between Fort Covington on the Salmon River in New York State, and Lake Champlain, was by way of the Salmon, St. Lawrence, and Richelieu Rivers. This trade promised to increase the diminutive amount of the tolls collected on the Chambly Canal; but it involved the use by American vessels of the St. Lawrence between Montreal and Sorel, which, it has already been stated, was denied to them. In May 1846[36] the province asked that the prohibition be lifted so far as this trade was concerned. The commissioners of customs in England objected that the proposal was inconsistent with the general policy of the government in regard to the navigation of the St. Lawrence by foreign ships, and that it would encourage extensive smuggling. The necessary permission was given, nevertheless, by an order in council of May 8, 1847. The opening of the St. Lawrence throughout its entire length to all American ships, however, was a larger question, and

35. 12 and 13 Vic., c. 29.

36. Cathcart to Gladstone, No. 51, May 12, 1846. Dom. Arch. MS. Room. See also *Reports from Committees, 1847–8,* XX, Part II, App. K.

one on which as has been seen, provincial opinion was not uniform. Early in 1850, in response to an inquiry from the imperial customs authorities in the province, it was officially laid down that the repeal of the Navigation Laws had not opened the river to foreign ships going to or from the Great Lakes.[37] Now the northwestern states of the Union wanted an open river, and their government had more than once approached Great Britain with a view to obtaining that privilege. There were therefore good reasons for believing that Canada had here an asset which the Americans would be very glad to share, and for which they would be willing to give something in return. This came to be the opinion of Lord Elgin, Baldwin, and many others. The question very soon became merged in the larger one of reciprocity with the United States, the province taking up the position that the right to use the river must form part of a preferential trade agreement, and this, after much negotiation and delay, it eventually did.[38]

Before the year 1850 the Navigation Laws forced the shipping that came into the St. Lawrence to pass through a political sieve, and in the colony it was quite generally held that this sifting process was responsible for the high level of the ocean freight-rates prevailing on that route. This however was only an assumption, though a plausible one. Was it or was it not correct? Professor Clapham says of the navigation code in its last phase that "like most of the offspring of mercantilism, its complexity excludes confident estimates of its achievement."[39] Yet to the limited question just put forward a reasonably definite answer can be made, for it is contained in the statistics of shipping in the St. Lawrence before and after repeal, and it is in the negative. The repeal of the Navigation Laws did not augment the shipping resources of the St. Lawrence; indeed the total tonnage in 1850 was less than it had been

37. Merivale to Trevelyan, Mar. 6, 1850. (C.O. 43: 112.)

38. Elgin-Marcy Treaty, 1854, Article IV. The concession was withdrawn in 1866, and granted again in 1871.

39. *English Historical Review,* XXV, p. 687.

the year before. Taking the series of years between 1846 and 1855, the total tonnage figures correspond fairly closely with the downward and upward movements of world trade. Free competition demonstrated that the St. Lawrence route as a whole, mainly for reasons of geography, was economically inferior to that by way of New York. The Navigation Laws therefore were not responsible for the lack of success of the St. Lawrence route between the years 1845 and 1850. They constituted a grievance which so far as the province was concerned was apparent rather than real, and their repeal proved to be an entirely inadequate remedy for the failure of the waterway.

## VII

## RECIPROCITY

Sie haben die Gegenden verlassen, wo es hart war zu leben: denn man braucht Wärme. Man liebt noch den Nachbar und reibt sich an ihm: denn man braucht Wärme. ALSO SPRACH ZARATHUSTRA.

THE importance of a market for the staples of the colony has been emphasized: it has also been pointed out that Canadians felt themselves to require in their external market some sort of legislative monopoly. When therefore the British market ceased to be a preferential one, the colony began to covet a privileged position in that of the United States. The idea was very natural in view of the contiguity of the two countries, and it seemed especially attractive during the years of depression, because prices in general were higher in the United States than in Britain, or than in the province itself where there was a widely prevalent impression that the American farmer always received considerably more for his grain than his Canadian neighbor did. The American tariff rates, too, seemed to Canadians to be inordinately high.

The question of protection had been for many years a controversial one in American politics. In 1833 as a concession to the South, a tariff had gone into effect which provided for an automatic reduction of duties step by step to a general twenty-per-cent rate. Yet no sooner had this level been reached in 1842, than there was a reversal of policy toward higher protection. In 1846 a new tariff law was passed which remained in force until 1857.[1] This was a very simple and straightforward protective instrument, imposing *ad valorem* duties only. It levied a twenty per cent duty on breadstuffs and on unmanufactured wood

1. Statutes of the United States, 29th Cong., 1st Sess., c. 74.

including boards and other milled timber. The rate on manufactured wood was thirty per cent. Professor Taussig says that "the act of 1846 is often spoken of as an instance of the application of free-trade principles. In fact, however, it effected no more than a moderation in the application of protection."[2] Yet it goes without saying that there was far less sentiment in favor of protection in the United States ninety years ago than there has been in recent times, in spite of the fact that the infant industries argument, probably the strongest which can be advanced on behalf of protection, was perfectly valid as applied to the United States of that day. The free-trade gospel, however, had made its appeal there, the tariff of 1846 was less protective than its predecessors, and there were many free traders in the country. In 1845 one of the Barings' correspondents in Boston expressed pleasure at seeing the British government "setting an example of acting on sound principles & on a liberal scale."[3]

In 1848 a very prominent New York merchant giving evidence before the Lords' committee on the Navigation Laws, considered that "the Tendency of Opinion in America is now in favour of the Removal of Restrictions on Commerce."[4] In 1853 a circular letter was addressed by the secretary of the treasury to a large number of business men and others, asking for their opinions in regard to protection. Some of the very numerous replies[5] were in favor of complete free trade, and on the whole they pointed to a fairly widespread sentiment supporting free trade in raw products with moderate protection for manufactures. One reply concluded by referring to "the time, doubtlessly now not far off, when customs duties will be

2. F. W. Taussig, *The Tariff History of the United States* (6th Ed., London and New York, 1914), Pt. I, Ch. III.

3. T. W. Ward to Baring Bros., Mar. 21, 1845. Baring Papers—Official.

4. *Reports from Committees, 1847–8,* XX, Pt. II. Evidence of Robert B. Minturn.

5. Letters printed in *House Ex. Docs.,* No. 74, 33rd Cong., 1st Sess., X. It is of course possible that the recipients of this circular letter had been carefully selected with a view to their known opinions. There is no evidence that this was so, nor would there be any.

things that were." It is likely that reciprocity was not an absolute impossibility after 1845, so far as American public opinion was concerned.

No sooner did the abolition of the imperial preference become probable, than a movement began in Canada in favor of freer trade with the United States. In 1845 the Gore District agricultural society petitioned the imperial government to negotiate with the government of the United States for lower duties on Canadian wheat; but the authorities in Britain declined to move in the matter on the ground that such an attempt would be futile.[6] Nevertheless, even before free trade had actually gone into effect, the establishment of reciprocal tariff preferences with the United States had become part of the commercial policy of the provincial government. The objective was not unrestricted free trade between the two countries, which was out of the question, but free trade in a selected group of raw materials. Six weeks before the Corn Laws were actually repealed the provincial assembly passed an address to the Queen stating that although Canada had repealed its duties on American produce entering for re-export, the Americans continued to levy very heavy duties on imports from Canada.[7] It asked that a negotiation should be opened with the American government "for the admission of our products into their Ports, on the same terms that theirs are admitted into those of *Great Britain* and this Colony."[8] Gladstone replied that the government would willingly direct the minister in Washington to begin the necessary negotiations which he hoped would be successful. He added however that previous attempts on the part of Great Britain and other countries to negotiate such treaties gave little encourage-

6. Stanley to Metcalfe, No. 472, Dec. 6, 1845. Dom. Arch. MS. Room.

7. By 9 Vic., c. 1, the province had provisionally repealed the three-shilling import duty on American grain intended for re-export. This was a partial repeal of the three-shilling duty which, it will be remembered, had been imposed as a means to obtaining the Canada Corn Act. The address was passed a few weeks before the American tariff law of 1846.

8. *Assembly Journal, 1846,* p. 230. (C.O. 45:224.)

ment; but that Canada would in any case derive great benefit from having a tariff lower than that of the United States.[9] The minister in Washington, Sir Richard Pakenham, received the necessary instructions, in which the foreign minister represented that "the eventual benefits to be derived from relaxed commercial intercourse between the United States, and a territory of such vast dimensions as Canada lying on their extended frontier are so obvious and lie so completely on the surface that they can scarcely fail to strike everyone who duly reflects upon the subject."[10] He was asked to choose a suitable opportunity for opening the negotiation, and in view of what he rightly regarded as an unfavorable political situation in the United States, he decided to wait.[11] The tariff bill of 1846 had been passed by the House of Representatives and was about to enter the Senate where its fortunes seemed to be uncertain. Its supporters who were low-tariff men were not at all averse to Canadian reciprocity in itself, yet they feared that it might wreck their general bill on the rocks of sectional interest. Pakenham went to Canada in the autumn of 1846 and was documented for his negotiations in Washington; but in May of the following year he left the United States, and the business of the legation remained in the hands of John F. Crampton the *chargé d'affaires*.

In Canada, opinion in favor of reciprocity strengthened as the commercial depression became more acute, and Merritt, that most enthusiastic of advocates, made the cause his own, mainly perhaps because he thought that reciprocity would assist the provincial waterway to obtain the western trade. In December, 1847, the Hamilton Board of Trade memorialized the governor-general in favor of

9. Gladstone to Cathcart, No. 83, June 3, 1846. *Assembly Journal, 1847* (C.O. 45:229), pp. 51 ff.

10. Aberdeen to Pakenham, June 18, 1846. Enclosed in Gladstone to Cathcart, No. 94, June 27, 1846. Dom. Arch. MS. Room.

11. Pakenham to Aberdeen, July 13, 1846. Enclosed in Grey to Cathcart, No. 14, Aug. 11, 1846. Dom. Arch. MS. Room.

closer trade relations with the United States—a policy which was even more popular in that part of the province than elsewhere. The memorial was careful to assert that the proposed reciprocal agreement would not diminish the trade of Montreal or Quebec. A number of the merchants and millers who had been injured by the success of the Erie Canal, also were ardent advocates of reciprocity.[12] On its accession to power in 1848 the Baldwin-Lafontaine government took the matter up energetically, its opinion on the subject being expressed in a memorandum by the inspector-general.[13] The argument was that under the new commercial policy of Great Britain, the manufacturing districts of the United States would often be the best market for Canadian agricultural products, and that no friend of the British connection would wish to see Canada excluded from that market by high if not prohibitive duties. "As no injury can be inflicted on British interests by such an arrangement, if may be hoped that Her Majesty's Government will endeavour to carry out the wishes of the entire Canadian population." Reciprocity was believed to be an attainable objective, since the province was strongly in favor of it, and since it would not be without influential support in the United States. It was added that a desirable basis for such an arrangement would be the free navigation of the St. Lawrence and reciprocal free admission of all articles of food. Moreover, since the provincial government possessed no diplomatic machinery of its own, it was necessary that the imperial government should understand clearly why reciprocity was desirable. The memorandum stated very emphatically that the provincial administration would have to be able to show the legislature at the next session that everything possible had been done to secure reciprocity, or great popular dissatisfaction would result. It was suggested that the minister in Washington might be empowered to communicate freely on the subject with the

12. Letters in Correspondence of the Civ. Sec., No. 4995.
13. *Ibid.*, No. 4957.

governor-general, "which is the more necessary as the consent of the Canadian Parliament to any measures determined on would be required." In May 1848, Merritt who at that time was president of the council in the Baldwin-Lafontaine government, went to Washington to supplement the efforts of the legation. He notified Crampton of his presence there and offered his help, asserting that there was talk of annexation in the province, and insisting that reciprocity was essential. Lord Elgin also lent to the movement his wholehearted support, not merely as the official mouthpiece of the government, but also as a convinced believer in the absolute necessity of reciprocity, and, in season and out of season, he reiterated its importance in his private letters to Grey. In May 1848, he referred to the extreme desirability of a treaty with the United States, granting to that country the navigation of the St. Lawrence in return for the free admission of Canadian produce, and expressed the opinion that such an arrangement might be made without affecting the Navigation Laws. "I confess," he wrote, "that I dread the effect of the continuance of the present state of things on the loyalty of our farmers. Surely the admission of the Yankees into the St Lawrence wd be a great boon to them and we ought to exact a 'quid pro quo.' "[14] In subsequent letters Elgin continued to press upon his chief what was his main argument for reciprocity—that it was absolutely necessary to make some arrangement whereby Canadians would not be at an economic disadvantage by remaining within the empire.

A commercial agreement such as the province desired may be effected either by means of a treaty or convention, or by concurrent legislation. The former alternative was the normal and obvious method; but it was subject to the disadvantage common to all such proposed arrangements with the United States, that it required a two-thirds majority in the Senate, that lethal chamber of treaties. The disadvantage was the more serious in this particular case,

14. Elgin to Grey, May 4, 1848. Private Correspondence.

in that the Senate was that branch of Congress in which most of the opposition to reciprocity was to be expected. Lord Palmerston, who was foreign minister, favored an attempt to obtain a treaty. The secretary of state however declined to enter upon such a negotiation, on the ground that President Taylor preferred concurrent legislation since reciprocity involved questions affecting domestic policy and revenue, and was therefore clearly a matter for Congress as a whole to decide.[15] The entire first phase of the actual negotiations therefore was given over to an attempt to obtain reciprocity by concurrent legislation.

In the spring of 1848 a bill was introduced into Congress, by the terms of which a number of important Canadian raw products including grain and lumber were to be put on the free list whenever similar benefits should be conferred upon American produce by the provincial legislature. The bill was of a nature entirely satisfactory to the province. "Commercially, this measure will 'annex' us to the United States," was the comment of the *Examiner*, "but it will render the contingency of political annexation more remote and uncertain. Retaining our isolated position it will give us the commercial advantages of annexation, and leave us nothing to hope for in actual annexation beyond a change in our condition wholly political."[16] Congress however did not pass the bill.

The imperial government did not reject the idea of concurrent legislation, but agreed to approve any provincial measure for the purpose, provided that differential duties were not thereby established against Britain or the other colonies in favor of the United States. As the proposal for reciprocity embraced raw materials only, and since British imports to the province consisted almost entirely of manufactured articles, while reciprocity with the

15. Clayton to Crampton, June 26, 1849. *House Ex. Docs.*, No. 64, 31st Cong., 1st Sess., VIII. The letter reads like an essay in American constitutional law.

16. *Examiner,* May 24, 1848.

other British North American colonies had been provided for by the provincial tariff law of 1847, it was quite possible to establish reciprocity without such differential duties. The Colonial Office pointed out, however, that ores of metals had been included in the schedule of the American bill, and that a certain amount of ore on which a duty was levied was customarily imported by the province from Britain. It also desired that the articles included in any Canadian reciprocity act should be admitted free of duty from all countries.

Scarcely anything had been achieved before the year 1848 came to a close, and the following year negotiations were renewed. The St. Lawrence navigation was once more offered as an inducement. Retaliation too began to be considered, and even so staunch an advocate of free trade as the *Globe* suggested it as a last resort. Great Britain was to be induced to threaten tariff retaliation, and if this failed the province was advised to levy heavy but not prohibitive duties on manufactured articles made of such materials as wool, linen, leather, iron, and wood—in the manufacture of which it was suggested that Canada could soon excel because she had the raw materials—while on other manufactures, in the production of which the province might hardly hope to compete in the immediate future, duties for revenue only were to be imposed. "It is a miserable affair at this time of day," the *Globe* concluded, "to build up walls between people of the same origin and language, and inhabiting the same country, and fain would we hope it may not be necessary to resort to it."[17] The provincial agricultural association of Canada West petitioned the assembly to do all in its power to establish reciprocity, bringing forward Lord Elgin's favorite argument with the prophecy that "we shall look in vain for a spirit of enterprise for content or prosperity among the Farmers of Canada West until their products shall be free to command the price (minus freight) which is obtained

17. *Globe,* Jan. 24, 1849.

for products of a like description and quality by the Farmers of the State of New York."[18]

A law to give effect to reciprocity as far as it was in the power of the province to do so, had been under discussion for some time, and on February 6, 1849, the assembly passed a resolution in favor of such a law by a majority of fifty-eight to twelve. A few weeks later a bill was passed, similar to the one which the American Congress had rejected, to go into effect by proclamation should a corresponding law be passed in the United States.[19] The annexation movement greatly increased the desire of the provincial government to obtain reciprocity, which would destroy almost every one of the arguments which the annexationists were accustomed to use. Merritt, who was anything but easy to discourage, and whom Elgin considered to be "overzealous for a negotiator," set forth in the month of June on another pilgrimage to Washington. Before leaving he explained his view of the matter in a letter to Lord Elgin,[20] laying great stress upon the apparent tendency of grain prices to rule higher in the United States than in Canada. "Dissatisfaction has increased rapidly and widely from this cause. Annexation is openly and freely discussed and believed by many to be the only remedy for restoring the prosperity of Canada. It therefore behooves us to lose no time in obtaining justice." He advocated reciprocity as the only remedy, and was willing to concede the St. Lawrence navigation in exchange; but wanted the coasting trade of the United States to be thrown open to the shipping of the province. If retaliation proved to be necessary he wanted Great Britain to impose a discriminating duty against maize

18. Correspondence of the Civ. Sec., No. 5180.

19. 12 Vic., c. 3. (Prov.), April 25, 1849. The following products were to be admitted free of duty from the United States: "Grain and Breadstuffs, of all kinds, Vegetables, Fruits, Seeds, Animals, Hides, Wool, Butter, Cheese, Tallow, Horns, salted and fresh Meats, Ores of all kinds of Metals, Ashes, Timber, Staves, Wood and Lumber of all kinds."

20. Merritt to Elgin, June 8, 1849. Correspondence of the Civ. Sec., No. 5180.

from the United States except when shipped by way of the St. Lawrence, and he argued that this would not increase the price to the British consumer because the St. Lawrence route was cheaper than any other.

For the most part the usual free-trade arguments were advanced in negotiation with the Americans. It was asserted that the United States would benefit by reciprocity, since it would enable Americans to buy in Canada whenever it was in their interest to do so, and because it would enable the Canadians to buy more goods from the United States. Reciprocity was represented as likely to benefit the American canals. It was also demanded as a matter of justice, this claim resting upon a threefold foundation. Goods from the United States entering the province paid a much lower rate of duty than did Canadian goods entering the United States. The provincial tariff of 1847 had placed American imports on terms of entire equality with those of Great Britain. The latter country moreover had thrown her market wide open to many of the unmanufactured products of the United States. In addition it was argued that reciprocity would further the comity of nations. The American negotiators on the other hand, asking for better terms, claimed that reciprocity would lower the price of American wheat, that reciprocal arrangements would of necessity include other countries with whom the United States had most-favored-nation agreements and that reciprocity ought to include manufactured goods. They claimed too that the Canadian market for raw materials was not a fair equivalent for that of the United States, and this was true inasmuch as the latter country was partially industrialized. On the other hand the Canadians were offering more than merely free access to their market. As is usual however in the case of such negotiations, the issue did not primarily depend upon the merits of the case, real or alleged.

Meanwhile Sir Henry Bulwer, a diplomat of more than usual talent, had taken over the duties of minister to the United States, with instructions to press strongly for reciprocity. In the other British North American colonies also, movements had been started similar to the one in Canada, in favor of reciprocity with the United States. As early as May 1848, a meeting had been held in St. John, New Brunswick, at which resolutions had been passed advocating a reciprocal agreement and any steps necessary to obtain it. The wish expressed earlier by the Canadian government that direct communication might be established between the minister in Washington and the governor-general, was carried out, Bulwer being told to keep in direct touch with Lord Elgin. The other colonial governments were instructed to communicate with Bulwer only through Elgin, who would represent all the colonies in the negotiations.

In September 1849, a meeting of colonial delegates was held in Halifax, at which measures for common action were discussed. With the manifestation of a desire on the part of the maritime colonies to be included in any reciprocity agreement, the old question of the fisheries at once became involved. The United States wished to obtain for her citizens the right to fish in British waters off the Atlantic coast, in return for the concession of reciprocity to the colonies off whose shores the fisheries lay. To the maritime colonies however, the fisheries were all-important, wherefore the lieutenant-governor of Nova Scotia on getting into communication with Lord Elgin requested that no final action be taken about them until the legislature of Nova Scotia had been consulted. He was however friendly to the idea of reciprocity, "in favor of which a very strong feeling exists in this Colony," and was ready to co-operate and to furnish any information which might be desired.[21] The lieutenant-governor of Prince Edward Island reported that the unconditional concession of the fishery rights was strongly favored in that colony, for it was thought that the American fishermen would cure their fish on the island, besides buying supplies there and pos-

21. Sir John Harvey to Elgin (Confidential), Dec. 13, 1849. Correspondence of the Civ. Sec., No. 5271.

sibly ships also. He stated that the colony had already enacted a law authorizing the free importation of certain raw materials from the United States, which would go into force whenever the latter country should pass a corresponding measure.[22] In a very cautious despatch the governor of Newfoundland expressed the opinion that on the whole that colony was disposed to favor the concession to the Americans of those fishing rights not already possessed by them, in exchange for a measure of reciprocity. The principal question was whether a free American market for their fish would compensate them for the fish taken by Americans in their waters. He thought that it would do so, partly because the presence of American vessels would benefit Newfoundland, but more especially because of the depressed state of the colony's fishing industry, which was due not to unproductive fisheries but to lack of markets.[23] Sir John Harvey subsequently stated that Nova Scotia would support such concessions as might be prerequisite to reciprocity. A belated despatch announced that New Brunswick too favored any necessary concessions.[24] All the colonies therefore desired reciprocity and were willing to concede the fishing rights in exchange for it. Three of them wished the United States to concede American registry to British-built ships, on the ground that British registry had recently been granted to ships built in the United States.[25] The maritime colonies insisted that fish should be on the list of free commodities in any reciprocal agreement. In this way the question of reciprocity broadened out and became more complicated. Bulwer was of course supplied with copies of these despatches; but he took the view that it would be inadvisable at that time to seek a treaty embracing all the colonies. He considered that the introduction to Congress of a bill

22. Sir Donald Campbell to Elgin, Dec. 17, 1849. *Ibid.*, No. 5277.

23. Sir Gaspard Le Marchant to Earl Grey, Dec. 31, 1849. Copy marked Private and Confidential enclosed with Le Marchant to Elgin of the same date. *Ibid.*, No. 5273.

24. Sir Edmund Head to Elgin, Feb. 27, 1850. *Ibid.*, No. 5299.

25. By 12 and 13 Vic., c. 29.

similar to the previous ones, and having reference only to Canada, would be the most favorable initial step. If such a bill became law its scope might afterwards be broadened; while attempts to extend its terms of reference before its passage through Congress might prevent its being passed at all. If on the other hand the more limited aim were not realized, a comprehensive reciprocity treaty might be tried. Bulwer's opinion was that a treaty might be made if the Newfoundland fisheries were included, but not otherwise.[26]

The Canadians meanwhile were chafing at their inability to obtain what they wanted. Memorials were drawn up and the question was discussed at length in Upper Canada, though for a considerable time it was overshadowed by that of annexation. The year 1850 saw another reciprocity bill introduced into Congress, and strenuous efforts for its passage were made by its champions. At various times during that year, Merritt, the Hon. Malcolm Cameron, and Hincks were in Washington. During this time too, Elgin was eloquently and persistently emphasizing to Grey, both in despatches and in their private correspondence, the absolute necessity of obtaining reciprocity. He regarded it as the best and indeed the only solution for the difficulties of the province, and had set his heart upon obtaining it. "I cannot too often repeat it," he wrote in June 1849, "either this or annexation. It is of no use to preach patience to the Canadians."[27] Soon after the publication of the annexation manifesto in the autumn he wrote: "I cannot conceal from you my belief that on the establishment of reciprocity of trade with the United States the peace of this Colony and the permanence of the connection with Great Britain in a great measure depend."[28] Grey however thought that the importance of reciprocity was exaggerated in Canada, for

26. Bulwer to Elgin, Feb. 25, and April 5, 1850. Correspondence of the Civ. Sec., Nos. 5309, and 5344.

27. Elgin to Grey, June 11, 1849. Private Correspondence.

28. Elgin to Grey (Confidential), Nov. 8, 1849. (C.O. 42: 560.)

his unqualified free trade principles convinced him that the essential thing was for the province to keep its own import duties at the lowest possible level, and that the American protecting duties were chiefly injurious to the country which had imposed them. Nevertheless he caused the Foreign Office to be informed "that Lord Grey considers it a matter of great importance to obtain from the Govt of the U. States, if possible, a compliance with the wishes so generally entertained by the people of Canada on this subject."[29] At intervals Grey repeated the request that everything possible should be done.

In Washington the negotiations were continued, but without avail, for in the autumn of 1850 a reciprocity bill was again rejected by Congress. "Fortunately," wrote Elgin, "the desire for the measure has very much abated on this side.—so that I do not apprehend any great mischief from their refusal at present."[30] Indeed with the increasing prosperity which characterized that year, economic remedies in general became less important than before. Yet the province was still very anxious to obtain reciprocity, and the advisability of retaliation was receiving further consideration. Merritt again brought forward his impracticable plan of getting Great Britain to retaliate by means of discriminating duties, and in May 1851 he introduced into the assembly a series of resolutions[31] which he had constructed as the groundwork of an address to the throne, asking that Great Britain should impose on certain raw materials from foreign countries the same rates of duty as were imposed by those countries on like goods the product of Great Britain or her dependencies. One of these resolutions stated that reciprocity "is essential to the maintenance of its [Canada's] connexion with Great Britain." Merritt however was no longer a member of the government, and these proposed resolutions did not necessarily express any official policy.

29. Merivale to Addington, July 9, 1849. (C.O. 43: 112.)
30. Elgin to Grey, Oct. 6, 1850. Private Correspondence.
31. *Globe,* May 29, 1851.

The main official proposal for retaliation was that the provincial canals should be closed to foreign ships. The refusal of the government to open the St. Lawrence between Quebec and Montreal to American vessels was also largely a measure of retaliation, the position being stated in the assembly by Hincks when he said that "there was no difference of opinion in that House that the opening of the St. Lawrence would be a great boon; but at the same time, he was not prepared to grant the Americans what they look upon as the most valuable concession that could be made by this country."[32] A duty of twenty per cent on goods from the United States was also proposed. The Colonial Office however was strongly opposed to retaliation by means of discriminating provincial duties, and Grey informed Elgin privately that he would probably recommend the disallowance of any act embodying such duties. Retaliation was discussed in the province not perhaps so much with a view to carrying it out as in order to influence American opinion, and Merritt afterwards admitted that this had been the intention of his resolutions. Hints were occasionally dropped into the midst of the negotiations at Washington, to the effect that reprisals were conceivable, as when Hincks said in a letter to the chairman of the House committee of commerce: "I have no hesitation in stating that the advocates of a retaliative policy are rapidly gaining ground."[33]

The possibility of having the St. Lawrence opened to American ships interested the American government, because the idea was very popular in the northwest. Early in 1850 Bulwer was asked whether in the event that Congress passed a Canadian reciprocity law the British government would or would not be willing to open the St.

32. Legislative Assembly, July 30, 1851. *Globe,* Aug. 2, 1851.

33. Hincks to the Hon. R. M. McLane, Jan. 6, 1851. *Senate Ex. Docs.,* No. 1, 32nd Cong., 1st Sess., I, 87. Hincks had this letter printed as a pamphlet "for convenience of reading and not for circulation." See also enclosures in Bulwer to Daniel Webster, June 24, 1851, *ibid.*

Lawrence, and he replied in the affirmative.[34] A year later the hands of the supporters of reciprocity were strengthened by the publication of the first of I. D. Andrews' two reports which have so often been referred to in other connections. In view of the fact that the British North American colonies seemed to be going through something like a commercial revolution after 1846—a fact of no little importance to the United States—Andrews had been commissioned to report upon the economic conditions prevailing in those colonies. He was a free trader, and the report returned an unequivocal verdict in favor of reciprocal free trade in natural products between the United States and Canada, on the ground that "this measure recommends itself strongly to American interests and magnanimity."[35] It was stated that the two countries were economically complementary to each other, and that protection in the United States was directed mainly against the maturer productive power of Europe. So far as Canadian breadstuffs were concerned, Andrews denied that their free admission would lower the price of grain in the United States. He advanced the theory which the subsequent history of American protection has shown to be valid, that a product of which there is a large exportable surplus cannot be effectively protected by means of a tariff. "Canada and the United States," he wrote, "export a surplus of wheat to the same foreign market. The prices at Mark-lane, to a great extent, fix the prices of the American market."[36] He maintained that the colonies already imported as great a quantity of American goods as they could consume and pay for, and that their purchases from the United States would increase with their prosperity.

In 1851 Bulwer again proposed to open the St. Lawrence in return for reciprocity, and also offered to concede the fishing rights subject to certain limitations. American

34. Bulwer to Clayton, Mar. 27, 1850. Copy in Correspondence of the Civ. Sec., No. 5341.

35. *First Report,* p. 43.

36. *Ibid.,* p. 46.

fishermen would be admitted to the Atlantic-coast fishing grounds excluding those of Newfoundland; but only on the condition, which could not be withdrawn, that all British North American fish should be admitted free of duty into the American market.[37] Yet it was all of no avail for Congress would not pass the necessary law, and after nearly four years of failure the period of attempts to secure reciprocity by concurrent legislation was brought to a close.

Bulwer had done his best, and he had enjoyed the advantage of possessing the unenthusiastic good will of the administration; yet there had been great difficulties to contend with, and his failure is not surprising. Protection did not lack defenders in the United States, and even though the government was favorable, tariff policy lay at the very centre of political controversy. Moreover in the South where free-trade opinions prevailed more strongly than in any other part of the union, the question of reciprocity with Canada involved a consideration beside which that of tariff policy was insignificant. Over the whole political life of the United States lay the slavery issue—an ominous black cloud charged with the thunder and lightning of guns near Gettysburg. In the South it was feared that reciprocity would lead to the annexation of Canada and the other colonies, with a consequent accretion of states which would always be free soil. Before the Civil War the southern states could usually command enough votes in the Senate to block the path of any piece of legislation to which they were strongly opposed, and senators from the South had been the insurmountable obstacle to reciprocity. At Washington therefore, political rather than economic considerations had proved decisive. Moreover both Great Britain and the province had come on to the field of negotiation stripped of their armor. For the former country was discarding protection as fast as possible, and the latter had lowered its duties on Ameri-

37. Bulwer to Webster, June 24, 1851, and enclosures. *Senate Ex. Docs.*, No. 1, 32nd Cong., 1st Sess., I.

can goods to the level of revenue requirements. Neither had used the concession as a means to obtaining reciprocal favors from the United States, and both were thus placed at a disadvantage. The peculiar limitations which the American constitution of government places upon international action had made it impossible for Bulwer to exercise any decisive influence on the fate of reciprocity without going beyond the limits of orthodox diplomatic procedure. Free admission of American raw materials into the Canadian market, too, was a much smaller concession than it sounds. As a result, extraneous makeweights like the St. Lawrence navigation and the fisheries had been introduced; Bulwer was therefore obliged to negotiate in such a way as to meet the requirements not only of the Foreign Office and the government of Canada, but of the four other colonies as well. Also the United States was less dependent upon a foreign market than the province was; and it is always difficult to negotiate on behalf of that party which needs, or thinks it needs, a successful issue, while to the other party it is a matter of comparative indifference. Nor had the Canadians been restrained and silent; on the contrary their impatient desire to have reciprocity and to have it at once, had been entirely undisguised. Threats to retaliate were not very impressive, because it was obvious that the United Kingdom would not reimpose import duties on grain, and that any effective form of reprisal undertaken by Canada would be likely to do more harm to the province itself than to the United States.

Reciprocity was the most important, and with the possible exception of the repeal of the Navigation Laws, the most generally popular of all the proposals for restoring prosperity to the colony; yet within the period it was not destined to be tried. Only as a belated yet practical and useful stimulus to trade was it put into effect when Lord Elgin, about to bring his tenure of office in Canada to a close, went to Washington and by an extraordinary exercise of those arts whereby politicians sometimes gain their ends, brought low the mountains and hills of senatorial opposition, and presented the province with a reciprocity treaty as a parting and royal gift.[38]

38. Lord Elgin's secretary explains the success of the mission. "At last, after several days of uninterrupted festivity, I began to perceive what we were driving at. To make quite sure, I said one day to my chief,

'I find all my most intimate friends are Democratic senators.'

'So do I,' he replied dryly; and, indeed, his popularity among them at the end of a week had become unbounded." Laurence Oliphant, *Episodes in a Life of Adventure* (New York, 1887), p. 40.

# VIII

## THE FAMINE MIGRATION OF 1847

Nous sommes la pauvre famille
Emigrant vers d'autres climats:
Nous n'emportons pour pacotille
Que notre courage et nos bras.

HENRI MURGER.

DURING the first half of the nineteenth century, as everyone knows, an increasing stream of migrants flowed outward from the British Islands toward the United States and various British colonies. Of the latter, those in North America were the most accessible to the emigrant, and in several other ways the most attractive. Not only could they be reached with comparative cheapness and speed, but the return home at some more or less distant date seemed to be relatively easy. If the colony selected should prove to be uncongenial, El Dorado would be close at hand in the United States, and the British American colonies were free from the stigma of convict transportation. In the eighteen-forties the bulk of the migration to British America was coming to Canada. When the decade was two-thirds over, circumstances arose which for the time being converted this normal and healthful infusion of population into a menace and a curse.

What is well-known need not be labored. The European harvests were a partial failure in the growing seasons of 1845 and 1846, and the dearth had a particularly disastrous effect in Ireland. In the summer of 1846 a devastating blight descended upon the potato plants. "The first appearance is a little brown spot on the leaf, which is hardly perceptible, and which gradually increases in number, and then affects the stem, assuming by degrees a darker colour until it presents to you an appearance as if it had been burnt. . . . After this blight has seized the leaves and stem, it communicates with the potato, which ceases to grow, and the whole plant above ground withers away rapidly. . . . In less than a week the whole process is accomplished."[1] The potatoes were destroyed, and on that crop Ireland depended to an extent that is proverbial. Considering its resources the Irish population was large, and therefore poor, and a situation thus arose as serious as can well be imagined.[2] Starvation stared a large proportion of the inhabitants of the island in the face. Under the existing law no outdoor poor relief might be given, and the workhouses soon became full to overflowing.[3] Contemporary descriptions of conditions in Ireland could easily be multiplied—one or two will suffice. An observer wrote: "The future prospect is frightful, . . . Our Union Workhouse has 160 beyond its number compressed within its walls."[4] There were people who subsisted for two years on such food as turnips and nettle tops, with sometimes a little maize. The latter had been shipped into Ireland as an emergency ration, and was by no means popular. The government was far from being indifferent to Ireland's plight. Anyone seeking information on this point should look at the statute books for the years 1846, 1847, and 1848, which are full of Irish famine legislation. The calamity was mitigated by official action; but was very far from being wholly relieved. In these critical circumstances many victims of the famine began to think of flight from the ills which beset them. In the winter of 1846 an official in Ireland wrote: "One thing is certain, the whole face of the Country is waste and the people, those

1. Sir R. Routh to Mr. Trevelyan, Aug. 11, 1846. *Accounts and Papers, 1847,* XI.

2. See George O'Brien, *The Economic History of Ireland from the Union to the Famine* (London, 1921), Pt. I, Ch. 7.

3. *Transactions of the Central Relief Committee of the Society of Friends during the Famine in Ireland, in 1846 and 1847* (Dublin and London, 1852), pp. 13–14.

4. Undated extract from a letter from Mr. Herd, a magistrate of County Cork, to Capt. Stawell. Grey Emigration Papers, 1823–50.

that can, are preparing, as soon as the Spring opens, to emigrate to America." Another official wrote as follows: "I can state from authority, that 700 persons from this district would gladly embark for Canada, if they had the most trifling encouragement. I have no doubt, if they had 3 l. each, they would most cheerfully go."[5]

So there began a *sauve qui peut*—a wholesale emigration which was eventually to reduce the population of Ireland by about forty per cent. More than half of this emergency migration went to the United States. Most of the remainder went to the British North American colonies, especially Canada, and it is this last portion that must now be dealt with. Statistics,[6] such as they are, show that

5. These letters are printed in *Accounts and Papers, 1847,* XI and IX.

6. Table I. Migration from Great Britain and Ireland, in the period from 1844 to 1849 inclusive.

DESTINATION

| *Year* | *British North America* | *United States* | *Australia and New Zealand* | *All Other Places* | *Total* |
|---|---|---|---|---|---|
| 1844 | 22,924 | 43,660 | 2,229 | 1,873 | 70,686 |
| 1845 | 31,803 | 58,538 | 830 | 2,330 | 93,501 |
| 1846 | 43,439 | 82,239 | 2,347 | 1,826 | 129,851 |
| 1847 | 109,680 | 142,154 | 4,949 | 1,487 | 258,270 |
| 1848 | 31,065 | 188,233 | 23,904 | 4,887 | 248,089 |
| 1849 | 41,367 | 219,450 | 32,191 | 6,490 | 299,498 |
| TOTAL | 280,278 | 734,274 | 66,450 | 18,893 | 1,099,895 |

These figures from the *Census of the Canadas, 1851–1852,* II, 7.

Table II. The number of migrants arriving at Quebec, in the period from 1844 to 1849 inclusive.

ORIGIN

| *Year* | *England* | *Ireland* | *Scotland* | *Germany* | *Lower Ports, etc.* | *Total* |
|---|---|---|---|---|---|---|
| 1844 | 7,698 | 9,993 | 2,234 | .... | 217 | 20,142 |
| 1845 | 8,833 | 14,208 | 2,174 | .... | 160 | 25,375 |
| 1846 | 9,163 | 21,409 | 1,645 | 896 | ... | 32,753 |
| 1847 | 28,725 | 50,360 | 3,628 | 7,437 | ... | 90,150 |
| 1848 | 6,034 | 16,582 | 3,086 | 1,395 | 842 | 27,939 |
| 1849 | 8,980 | 23,126 | 4,984 | 436 | 968 | 38,494 |
| TOTAL | 69,433 | 135,678 | 17,751 | 10,164 | 2,187 | 234,853 |

These figures from the *Journal of the Statistical Society,* XIII, 364. The statistics of migration at this time are not accurate. Nevertheless they afford a reliable general picture of what was happening.

nearly all the excess emigration from the British Islands in the year 1847 went to North America. Of these migrants some forty-five per cent went to British colonies, approximately thirty-five per cent going to Canada. Excepting in the case of British North America, emigration steadily increased after 1847. The North American colonies experienced a high tide of immigration in the year 1847, followed by greatly diminished totals in subsequent years. The Canadian total for 1847 was prodigious considering the size of the colony; nor was the problem quantitative only, since the immigrants of the year 1847 were probably the most diseased, destitute, and shiftless that Canada has ever received. In one important respect the statistics are misleading. Of the total number of immigrants shown as coming from England in 1847, more than twenty-one thousand, or roughly three-quarters, were from Liverpool. Nearly all of these, that is to say about twenty thousand, were Irish. This increases the Irish total to about seventy thousand, or approximately seventy-eight per cent of the whole. The fact is important as the Irish emigrants at that time had very special characteristics.

At the time the charge was widely made that poor law unions and landlords in Ireland, actuated by wholly selfish motives, forced great numbers of people to leave the country. It may be supposed that landlords and others sometimes found it cheaper to "shovel out" some of their excess dependents than to assume responsibility for them at home, and acted accordingly. In the very well-informed opinion of the colonial land and emigration commissioners, such action was exceptional. "No emigration," they reported, "could have been more thoroughly spontaneous."[7] There is evidence that some landlords, with the best intentions, desired to find a home beyond the sea for obviously redundant laborers. The government, as will be

7. "Report of the Colonial Land and Emigration Commissioners," *Accounts and Papers, 1847–8,* XLVII.

seen, did practically nothing to encourage or assist the exodus from Ireland.

As a rule, a proportion of migrants to the New World receive the wherewithal to make the journey from members of their own race, and usually of their own family, who emigrated earlier. The emigrant who has settled in the new country and is earning money, sends some of it to the wife or children, relations or friends, whom he has left behind, to enable them to join him. This particular form of generosity has been especially characteristic of the Irish. In the period immediately following the great famine, very large sums were sent to the old country by expatriated Irishmen. A few years after 1847 an amount of money was being sent annually from America to Ireland, partly for this purpose, which greatly exceeded the total cost of the contemporary Irish emigration. It may be conjectured that during the year of the great famine remittances from North America played a large part in financing the exodus from Ireland. Yet it seems unlikely that more than a minority of the famine emigrants were assisted by this means, because their number was so great, and because the habit of sending remittances for that purpose was not then as well-established among the Irish as it soon afterwards became.

Conditions on the emigrant ships were bad at the best, and at the worst were horrible. Vessels were bound by law to furnish a pound of bread daily to each passenger; but emigrants were supposed to provide themselves with food to supplement this, and in ordinary years they appear to have done so. Destitute people, however, fleeing from famine, often had little or no food to bring on board with them. Many of the emigrant ships were overcrowded, and of some of them sordid tales could be told. The existing legislation to regulate conditions on emigrant vessels proved to be inadequate in the time of stress. It must of course be remembered that the standards of comfort and cleanliness on passenger ships were lower then than they are now. Nevertheless great hardship resulted, and worse than mere hardship, disease.

The Apocalyptic Horsemen are accustomed to ride together. Early in the famine cholera appeared in Ireland, and conditions on ships overcrowded with undernourished passengers were probably ideal for its propagation. Those ships which sailed from uninfected ports were free from disease, while on board even the best ships coming from infected ports the disease was rife.[8]

The quarantine station in the St. Lawrence at Grosse Isle, a few miles below Quebec, was described by an observer a few years before: "The rocky isle in front, with its neat farm-houses at the eastern point, and its high bluff at the western extremity, crowned with the telegraph—the middle space occupied by tents and sheds for the cholera patients, and its wooded shores dotted over with motley groups—added greatly to the picturesque effect of the land scene." The rapid influx of immigrants in the spring of 1847 speedily caused the island to become overcrowded,[9] and those not obviously infected were sent on up the river in order to make room for more. Many subsequently contracted the disease or spread it along their path, and the quarantine station was merely the worst plague spot. Dr. Douglas, the medical officer at Grosse Isle, thus described the disease-stricken Irish immigrants arriving from Cork

8. The average mortality rates at sea and in quarantine, among migrants to Canada during the year 1847, in percentages, were:

Adults, 7.21
All migrants, including children, 8.84
Migrants from England, excluding Liverpool, less than 1.00
Migrants from Liverpool, 15.39
Migrants from Scotland, 3.12
Migrants from Ireland, 7.86
Migrants from Germany, 1.26

From the Annual Report of the Chief Emigration Agent in Canada. Enclosed with Elgin to Grey, No. 43, April 20, 1848. Dom. Arch. MS. Room. The average general mortality rate during the preceding five years had been slightly less than 0.6%.

9. Even in normal times this establishment had not escaped criticism. Lord Durham's Report refers to the "defects of the quarantine station at Grosse Isle."

and Liverpool: "I never saw people so indifferent to life; they would continue in the same berth with a dead person until the seamen or captain dragged out the corpse with boat-hooks. Good God! What evils will befall the cities wherever they alight."[10] Captain Boxer, an officious but trustworthy man, who visited Grosse Isle in the latter part of May, reported that the immigrants there were starving. In August the health authorities at Quebec expressed a fear that when winter came numbers of the sick Grosse Isle immigrants would be left on their hands.

In this fashion then, during that baleful year 1847, there poured into Canada the most polluted, as well as relatively the most swollen, stream of immigration in the history of that country. The chief emigration agent, A. C. Buchanan, reported that the "character of the Emigration to Canada in 1847, was exceedingly unfavourable. The large proportion of Irish which it comprehended, and the state of destitution in which the greater part of these people had embarked, presented features of inconceivable misery on their arrival in this country."[11] Another contemporary observer stated that "As a general rule, the English, Scotch, and north of Ireland men make much better and more independent colonists than emigrants from the south of Ireland."[12] The chief emigration agent for Upper Canada, A. B. Hawke, wrote in the autumn of 1847 that "more than three-fourths of the immigrants this year have been Irish, diseased in body, and belonging generally to the lowest class of unskilled labourers. Very few of them are fit for farm servants."[13] Gibbon Wakefield thought the Irish poor settlers, "who never colonize, but only emigrate miserably."[14] It may be noted that the Ger-

10. *Accounts and Papers, 1847–8,* XLVII.

11. Annual Report for 1847. Enclosed with Elgin to Grey, No. 43, April 20, 1848. (C.O. 42:550.)

12. Strickland, *Twenty-Seven Years in Canada West,* I, 138.

13. A. B. Hawke to the Civil Secretary, Sept. 20, 1847. *Accounts and Papers, 1847–8,* XLVII.

14. *Art of Colonization,* p. 456. Wakefield however was prejudiced. He refers to them elsewhere (p. 180) as "the careless, lazy, slovenly, dirty, whining, quarrelsome, Saxon-hating, Irish pauper emigrants."

man immigrants in 1847, very limited in number, were of the highest quality and free from disease. It would be interesting to know why the revolutions of 1848 did not visibly affect the emigration from Germany.

The colonists were not aware of the danger until it was close upon them. On May 7, 1847, Lord Elgin reported to the colonial secretary that "the prevalent feeling here is one of alarm lest it [immigration] sd be excessive this season: and lest disease should follow in its train."[15] The home government however, although after the fall of Peel in June, 1846, it did not suffer from what M. Maurois calls "la panique légumineuse," had nevertheless for a considerable time been well aware of the problem about to confront mother country and colonies alike. In December, 1846, the prime minister sent a warning to the lord lieutenant. "Those who are eager for emigration on a large scale," he wrote, "should recollect that the colonies cannot be prepared at once to receive large masses of helpless beings, and there is no use in sending them from starving at Skibbereen to starve at Montreal."[16] The governing authorities in England were very doctrinaire, and the effect of this was to paralyze action. The theories which bore on the case were *laissez faire* and the colonization gospel according to Gibbon Wakefield. The latter theory could not be put into practice in Canada, except in an exceedingly limited way; Lord Grey therefore adopted an attitude which was mainly though not completely negative. It was suggested that the famine sufferers might receive government assistance to emigrate. "The Government," said Grey, "cannot undertake to convey Emigrants to Canada because if it were to do so, if we were even to undertake to pay part of the cost, an enormous expense would be thrown upon the Treasury, and after all more harm than good would be done." He thought that it would

15. Elgin to Grey, May 7, 1847. Private Correspondence.

16. Lord John Russell to Lord Bessborough, Dec. 29, 1846. G. P. Gooch, *The Later Correspondence of Lord John Russell, 1840–1878,* I, 168.

undermine the morale of the assisted emigrants, and that "some 150,000 would have to be spent in doing that which if we do not interfere will be done for nothing."[17] He also urged the same policy on Elgin. Grey's attitude in this matter was that of his expert advisers, the colonial land and emigration commission, whose attitude is summed up in the following suggestion: "The best service which the Government can afford on this subject is probably that which it does now render, viz: to repress frauds on the poor Emigrants before they sail, to prevent abuses on the Ships by which they are conveyed, and in short to keep clear & sound the Channels in which Emigration flows, without undertaking itself to conduct the Stream."[18] Times have changed, and our more humane age has other ways of doing things. It is therefore very much easier to criticize than to appreciate Lord Grey's position. Gibbon Wakefield, who was a bitter and uncontrolled man and who hated Grey, spoke shortly afterwards of "the infinite superiority of systematic emigration to that 'spontaneous' scramble which Lord Grey now applauds, and which, often afflicting Canada with malignant fever, necessitates a lazaretto on the St. Lawrence."[19] This however was unfair and ungrateful, for, when it was written, a year after the event, Lord Grey had suffered much for Wakefield's sake.

In the colony men took a rather more pragmatic view of the situation. The provincial governments at this time, by contrast with those in London, were noticeably undoctrinaire. They were also less experienced in this particular matter, for the imperial government had but recently faced and was still facing a similar problem—but one more acute and on a far larger scale—in the case of Ireland itself. The colonial authorities undertook fairly extensive relief measures which were haphazard and not well

17. Extract of a letter from Lord Grey to Sir George Grey, Nov. 16, 1846. Grey Emigration Papers, 1823–50.

18. Copy of part of a memorandum by T. F. Elliott, the colonial land and emigration commissioner, of Jan. 23, 1847. Grey Emigration Papers, 1823–50.

19. *Art of Colonization,* p. 415.

thought out. Sickness and destitution offered two separate problems, and as always in such crises the measures required were partly of an immediate and partly of a more permanent nature.

Steps were taken in May to make use of military tents in order to provide shelter for the quarantined immigrants on Grosse Isle. A considerable number of so-called "Flanders" tents holding about twelve men apiece were erected on the island by the military authorities. In July further tents were asked for, which the military expressed their inability to provide. Friction always developed with comparative ease between the civil and military authorities in the colony. In the autumn, according to the ordnance authorities, the tents were so dirty "that the persons in the employment of the Department are unwilling to wash, or even touch them." The civil authorities promised to have the tents washed. In the spring of 1848 some of them were still in use.[20]

A not very important attempt was also made to bring chemistry to the rescue. A certain Colonel Calvert partially persuaded Lord Grey of the efficacy of a disinfecting fluid that he had, for dealing with the epidemic. He was sent to the colony and given a chance to show what he could do, with results which were unsatisfactory from the general point of view, and disastrous to himself.[21]

20. The details concerning these ordnance tents are in the Correspondence of the Civ. Sec., Nos. 4673, 4733, 4782, 4801, and 4950.

21. The "Decline and Fall" of Col. Calvert can best be told in quotation marks, from Grey's private letters to Elgin:—

July 19. "The reports of its efficacy in destroying infection are really wonderful."

Aug. 3. ". . . I . . . regret . . . that that pottering blockhead Col. Calvert contrived to lose his passage by the steamer with the disinfecting fluid."

Dec. 3. ". . . I am very sorry indeed to hear of more deaths by the emigrant fever, & that Col. Calvert is among those who have caught it. I hope poor man he may recover, tho' I begin to fear he is somewhat of a Charlatan. What is your opinion of the value of his fluid?"

Aug. 10, 1848. ". . . I think a gratuity of £100 . . . to . . . the widow of Colonel Calvert wd be very well bestowed."

Destitute immigrants crowded into the towns, and in some of the larger places conditions became very serious, and attempts were made to organize private relief. In May the citizens of Montreal, actuated no doubt by mixed motives of philanthropy and self-preservation, organized a committee to deal with the situation in that city. They expressed a fear that disease "soon will be amongst us to carry death into the bosoms of our families without precautionary measures are timely resorted to, to prevent the evil."[22] Their fears were justified. "A day scarcely passes," reported the *Pilot* a few weeks later, "without the intelligence reaching us of the death of some valuable and useful clergyman, some public-spirited and humane citizen, or some experienced and skillful captain of a vessel or steam boat." The unfortunate immigrants tended to remain in the larger cities and towns, and the problem was a difficult one. Work could not be provided for them there, yet many had not sufficient money to enable them to proceed further. They may have preferred the towns also, as the Irish migrant usually seems to do. It was not always easy for them to get work even in the countryside. Many of them were poor material for farm laborers, and the country people were afraid of them—"the doors of the farmhouses," wrote the governor-general, "are closed even against those who are reputed to be free from taint." A settler in the Peterborough district stated that "the typhus fever and dysentery have reached even this remote place. Wherever those wretched immigrants came they brought with them sickness and death. Some of the members of the board of health have already fallen under its malignant influence."[23] The emigration agent in Upper Canada was fairly optimistic in June: "We are getting on better—*much* better than I expected."[24] Later however his tone changed.

22. Montreal Immigrant Committee to the Governor-General, May 21, 1847. Correspondence of the Civ. Sec., No. 4670.

23. Eleanor Susanna Dunlop, *Our Forest Home* (Montreal, 1902), p. 218.

24. Hawke to the Civil Secretary, June 29, 1847. Correspondence of the Civ. Sec., No. 4722.

A problem similar to the one in Montreal, though less acute, arose in Toronto, where a citizens' immigration committee was also formed. The attempt to keep the immigrants moving out of the town as rapidly as possible seems to have been fairly successful, for by the middle of July, out of a total of sixteen or seventeen thousand migrants who had arrived in the town during the season, only two hundred and thirty-eight remained.[25] The local Board of Health reported the following year that during the season of 1847 up to February 1 of the following year, 38,560 immigrants had come into Toronto of which number 35,650 had been sent on. Of the remainder more than 1100 had died.[26] During the next two years cases of cholera were not uncommon in Toronto.

More systematic and uniform *ad hoc* arrangements for dealing with the crisis were made by the provincial government. There were no local rates to fall back upon, for ordinarily pauperism was practically unknown.[27] And so, early in June, arrangements were made for the setting up of a number of local boards of health. The corporation in each case was to appoint a board consisting of its own members. The board so constituted was authorized to draw up sanitary regulations, and to let contracts for bread and meat. A ration of three-quarters of a pound of bread and as much meat per adult, and of two-thirds of the amount for each child, might be issued to deserving immigrants during a period not to exceed six days in any one case. The corporation was to provide a hospital, and sheds for the healthy immigrants, and to appoint an attendant physician. The provincial government undertook to see that the bill was paid. Twenty-eight corporations were authorized to establish such boards.

Evidently the corporations and boards were given too

25. Report of an immigrant relief meeting, in the *Globe,* July 17, 1847.

26. Report of the Toronto Board of Health, Feb. 2, 1848, enclosed in Elgin to Grey, No. 16, Feb. 19, 1848 (C.O. 42: 549).

27. Lord Durham's Report refers to the absence of local authority in the North American colonies as a pronounced defect.

free a hand, and arrangements were not sufficiently uniform. The scheme was defective too, in that the boards were appointed by one authority in order to spend money derived from another. Buchanan recommended some surveillance over the boards and on the third of September Hawke set out on a tour of inspection. Before starting he asked for and received authority to abolish some of the boards of health, suggesting that half the existing number would be enough. A fortnight later he informed the civil secretary that he had taken steps to eliminate half of them. He had examined the accounts of a number of boards, and hinted that there had been extravagance and dishonesty. By the end of October most of them had been disbanded.[28]

The boards of health were far from superfluous, for there was obviously dire need of relief measures on an extensive scale. Nor had much time been given in which to consider the problem carefully. Yet, organized as they were the boards could hardly have been other than wasteful. The six-day limit on the supply of free food, on the other hand, seems to have been anything but recklessly extravagant. Hawke, however, like Lord Grey, feared lest the provision of free assistance might demoralize the recipients. In our age of lavish government relief of the aged, sick, and unemployed, what was then done in the province seems moderate enough; but to many contemporaries it did not seem so. Moreover, who even now can trace with precision a safe and certain middle road between *laissez faire* callousness and demoralizing generosity? Out of the whole story of the panic migration of 1847 the fact emerges clearly that public opinion, besides being far more afraid of paternalistic government action than it now is, was also less imaginative and sensitive in re-

28. These emergency boards of health are described in documents contained in the Correspondence of the Civ. Sec., Nos. 4770, 4804, and 4819, of which the following are the most important: Copy of Civ. Sec. to Hawke, Aug. 25, 1847, with enclosure; Copy of circular authorizing the establishment of boards of health; and Hawke to the Civ. Sec., Aug. 27, Sept. 20, and Oct. 16, 1847.

gard to human suffering. Public opinion in the colony was actuated to a much greater extent by fear than by compassion, in its attitude toward the unfortunate immigrants of 1847.

The expenses which resulted from the swollen immigration of that year were very large. In the province, the crisis being acute and close at hand, theories, if anyone had any, had gone by the board, and much money had been spent. The volume of private charity cannot be ascertained, but must have been extensive. As for the government, it spent money with a lavish hand, in the sure and certain hope that ultimately the burden might be placed upon other shoulders.[29]

The immigrant sheds included with the items of expense, were built for the purpose of affording temporary quarters to the new arrivals in the places where they most did congregate. The great aim of the service was to keep the immigrants moving as rapidly as possible away from the

29. Immigration expenses and receipts for the season of 1847, brought down to May 17, 1848 (from a statement signed by the deputy inspector-general. Correspondence of the Civ. Sec., No. 4985):

EXPENDITURES

| | £ | s. | d. |
|---|---|---|---|
| Sheds and fittings at Montreal, Quebec, and Grosse Isle | 27,644 | 9 | 0 |
| Transportation of immigrants inland, etc. | 46,443 | 13 | 7 |
| Boards of health | 67,965 | 6 | 9 |
| Quarantine | 15,465 | 17 | 6 |
| TOTAL | 157,519 | 6 | 10 |

RECEIPTS

| | £ | s. | d. |
|---|---|---|---|
| Immigration tax | 19,002 | 9 | 2 |
| From military chest, £30,000 stg., less £9500 stg. retained by commissary general for expenses defrayed by him, £20,500 stg. | | | |
| Amount placed by imperial government to credit of province in Bank of England on Dec. 31, 1847, £25,000 stg. Currency equivalent of £45,500 stg. | 55,358 | 6 | 8 |
| TOTAL | 74,360 | 15 | 10 |
| EXCESS OF EXPENDITURES OVER RECEIPTS | 83,158 | 11 | 0 |

towns and toward the farms. In normal years the expense of the immigration service had mainly been incurred in the process of forwarding from the ports to the interior those who were unable to pay their own way.

Under the existing law,[30] the colony levied a tax of five shillings a head on all immigrants. The imperial government was accustomed to make an annual contribution of between £1500 and £2500 sterling toward the immigration expenses of the colony. Ordinarily the revenue thus obtained was sufficient to defray the cost of the service. The unusual volume and character of the 1847 immigration, however, had thrown everything out of adjustment. The tax had sufficed to pay less than one-eighth of the expenses. It is an innate characteristic of bills to require payment, and the question very quickly arose of who was to do the paying.

Early in 1847 the British treasury authorized certain payments to be made from the commissariat chest. From the beginning however, the provincial government adopted the opinion that the whole extra expense occasioned by the immigration of that extraordinary year should be borne by the home government. Indeed, speaking in general, it may fairly be said that an abiding faith in the imperial treasury, and an instant readiness to plead for help from that source, were part of the provincial point of view. In this matter the Canadian government had the support of Lord Elgin, whose opinion invariably was that the spiritual bonds of empire were in no wise to be weighed in the balance against mere money. A memorandum of June 25, 1847, requested the governor-general to bring the subject of immigration expenses to the attention of the imperial government, and expressed a fear that "our Public revenues will have to be drawn upon to an extent that the Province cannot afford."[31] Three days later, Elgin informed Grey unofficially that "the Provincial Govt. are

30. 4 and 5 Vic., c. 13 (Prov.).

31. Two copies of this memorandum in Correspondence of the Civ. Sec., No. 4708.

doing all they can to mitigate their [the immigrants'] sufferings. Indeed, I think they are much more likely to exceed than to fall short in this matter, for all parties have a strong conviction that whatever they advance on this account will be reimbursed by the Imperial Treasury. In acknowledging the receipt of the memorandum from my Council which I have sent you officially I think it wd be well if you were to take occasion to impress upon me the necessity of caution and economy in administering relief." A petition to the throne, dated July 6, was sent by the legislative council of the province, asking that help be given by the imperial government.[32]

On August 13, Lord Elgin unburdened himself in a long letter to Lord Grey setting forth his views on the whole question.[33] He attacked what was at that time Grey's position, that only the minimum of governmental assistance should be given, and that such assistance as there was should be financed mainly or entirely by the province. Elgin thought that since a British colony, as such, was unable to exclude the immigrants, some compensation was due. He emphasized the unusual and desperate character of the situation, and felt that the ordinary theories and practices would not suffice. Since, moreover, the pauper immigrants could not be left to die in the streets, there had been no alternative to an expenditure of public funds. To the argument that since the province would in the long run benefit greatly from immigration, it ought to pay the cost of it, Elgin replied that the colonists would have shut out the "advantageous" immigration if they had been able to do so. He admitted that a system whereby the provincial government would spend the imperial government's money would be unsatisfactory, encouraging wastefulness. Characterizing as unfair the argument that emigration to the United States cost Great Britain nothing, he concluded: "It is a case in which on

32. *Accounts and Papers, 1847–8,* XLVII.
33. Elgin to Grey, Aug. 13, 1847. Private Correspondence.

every account I think the Imperial Government is bound to act liberally."

A further call for help was sent to the governor-general by his executive council.[34] It stated that "the Receiver General has no means of meeting further Warrants for the payment of the Immigration and Quarantine expenses, unless Your Excellency can afford relief by drawing on the Imperial Treasury." Upon one occasion too, at about this time, the inspector-general mentioned to Lord Elgin the possibility of having to call into play the imperial guarantee on the one-and-a-half million loan, the provincial funds being exhausted. By the end of September the province was more than thirty-five thousand in arrears on the immigration account, and it either could not or would not resort to additional taxation. The Bank of Montreal advanced the necessary amount, and the imperial government was asked for forty or fifty thousand pounds sterling wherewith to meet the deficit. Elgin reinforced this plea in a despatch of the ninth of October.[35] Grey replied that twenty thousand pounds sterling had been placed at the disposal of the colony, and that the balance, which amounted to about fifteen thousand, it was easily within the power of the province to pay. Elgin returned undaunted to the attack. "I do not see," he wrote, "how Great Britain can refuse to make good to the Province what she has expended in this [immigration] service during the current year. But for the future if Canada be permitted to enact such laws to guard herself against the evils of a pauper and diseased Immigration as she may see fit, I think the Mother Country may very properly decline to advance anything on this account."[36] Early in the following year, Lord Grey was able to announce that twenty-five thousand pounds sterling had been placed to

34. Memorandum of Aug. 20, 1847. Copy in Correspondence of the Civ. Sec., No. 4760.

35. Elgin to Grey, No. 90, Oct. 9, 1847. *Accounts and Papers, 1847–8*, XLVII.

36. Elgin to Grey, Dec. 24, 1847. Private Correspondence.

the credit of the province in the Bank of England, as an advance in aid of immigration expenses. Yet the colonial secretary still rejected the idea that the imperial government ought to assume responsibility for the whole of the Canadian immigration deficit, and suggested that Great Britain might pay a half. The imperial government's attitude was that the province should bear a part of the burden because the immigrants would ultimately be a valuable asset to it, and because the provincial authorities alone were in a position to prevent extravagance.

In the spring of 1848 however, the home government abandoned its position, and Elgin was so informed in a despatch of the fourteenth of April.[37] In this communication it was stated that in view of the exceptional character of the calamity, the government "are anxious that on this occasion the Province should not suffer pecuniary loss in consequence of the distress which reached it from this Kingdom. We are therefore prepared to recommend that Parliament should make provision for the expense which has been incurred so far as to relieve the Province entirely from any charge on account of the peculiar misfortunes of the year 1847." In future however, in order to avoid confusion and extravagance, and since a repetition of the crisis was scarcely to be feared, the province would have entire control of and responsibility for the immigration service. The customary annual grant by the imperial government would be continued. The despatch promised that with the consent of the Canadian government the imperial government would take the necessary steps to make the payment, and the consent of the provincial government was likely to be forthcoming. A considerable sum was paid to the province forthwith. In the middle of May the inspector-general proposed a payment of fifty thousand pounds sterling. Six weeks later Lord Grey acknowledged the receipt of the proposal, and stated that the amount asked for had been deposited to the credit of the province

37. Grey to Elgin, No. 197, April 14, 1848. Dom. Arch. MS. Room.

in the Bank of England.[38] Thus generously did the home government assume the whole weight of the financial burden.

Public opinion in the colony was, not without reason, stirred by the events of the year 1847. Lord Elgin reported that "an Immigrant with a shaven head is an object of terror in this neighbourhood." In June 1847, the provincial legislative assembly petitioned that conditions for immigration be improved, and that it be done at the expense of the imperial government.[39] A similar petition was addressed to the throne, bearing the signature of the mayor of Montreal. As so often in such cases, the blame was chiefly attributed to the government—in this instance the imperial government. Many wild and exaggerated statements were made. Louis Joseph Papineau hastened to enrich economic science by a generalization, the great merit of which lay in its extreme simplicity. He spoke thus of Ireland in the Bonsecours Market in Montreal: "Un quart de sa surface est inculte, parce qu'elle n'a jamais eu un gouvernement national."[40] Public opinion against immigration, when at its height in and soon after 1847, almost always failed to distinguish between undesirable, excessive immigration, and a normal and healthy influx of population like an infusion of fine new blood, which Canada, like all young colonies, needed so badly. It may very well be that the religion of the great majority of the immigrants strengthened the feeling against them in the English-speaking parts of the colony; but there seems to be no evidence that this was so.

The misfortunes of the year 1847 were not destined to be repeated. The chief emigration agent was able to make this statement at the close of the ensuing year: "The Emigration of 1848, so far as health and condition are concerned, bears a most favourable comparison with that of

38. Grey to Elgin, No. 241, June 30, 1848. Dom. Arch. MS. Room.
39. *Accounts and Papers, 1847–8,* XLVII.
40. *L'Avenir,* April 19, 1848.

1847."[41] This report gave the percentage of deaths on shipboard and in quarantine as 1.35: in the previous year the rate had been 8.84. A considerable proportion of all legislation, however, consists in closing the stable door. Both the home and provincial governments sought to take some precautionary measures for the future, lest by chance a second and similar calamity befall. In England an interesting report on the whole subject was made by the colonial land and emigration commissioners.[42] They were not sanguine on the subject of remedial legislation, and pointed out that British subjects could not be prevented from going from one part of Her Majesty's dominions to another. Their constructive suggestions were three in number—improved conditions on emigrant ships, a higher colonial emigration tax, and an increased tax in the case of ships held in quarantine. They recommended as a basic principle that it should be made the interest of shipowners to land migrants in a healthy condition. These ideas were elaborated by Lord Grey in a despatch of December 1, 1847. A provincial report also appeared, which drew the necessary distinction between acceptable and undesirable immigrants.[43] By an apparently undesigned coincidence the recommendations contained in the two reports were practically identical, and they were soon embodied in legislation.

The existing provincial law was repealed, and replaced by a new one.[44] This new law increased the tax on each immigrant from five shillings to ten, and the tax was to be collected on all immigrants, irrespective of age or country of origin. The rate was to be increased by two-and-sixpence per head, for each three days during which the ship concerned might be detained in quarantine. The maximum

41. Report enclosed with Elgin to Grey, No. 11, Jan. 17, 1849. (C.O. 42: 557.)

42. "Report of the Colonial Land and Emigration Commissioners," *Accounts and Papers, 1847–8,* XLVII.

43. Extract of a report by a committee of the Executive Council. Correspondence of the Civ. Sec., No. 4873.

44. 11 Vic., c. 1. (Prov.), Mar. 23, 1848.

tax on any one immigrant was not to exceed a pound. A penalty was provided for ships arriving after the tenth of September in any year. Arrangements were made to discourage the immigration of the physically and mentally unfit, and something was done to improve the environment of the passengers. This law was passed immediately after the immigration crisis, and the imperial government, and probably the business men of the province also, considered it to be too drastic. Some radicals on the other hand, thought that it was not drastic enough. The newspaper *L'Avenir*, uttered the following mournful prophecy: "L'émigration de morts et de mourans qui, l'année dernière, est venue porter la peste sur nos bords, va se renouveler cette année, car la loi n'offre aucune disposition pour arrêter ces flots de pestiférés."[45] The following year a more moderate law was substituted.[46] The tax remained at ten shillings; but this law established a kind of imperial preference in immigration, conforming to the wishes of the home government in this fairly important respect. Immigrants from the United Kingdom, coming with the sanction of the imperial government, would be admitted at two-and-sixpence less than the ordinary rate if adults, and at five shillings less, if children. Soldiers or pensioners and their families, coming out at the expense of the imperial government, would be admitted free. This legislation was soon afterwards altered in detail but not in principle.

In 1849 the quarantine law was also changed. In the same year too, a law was passed enabling the government to establish by proclamation local and central boards of health, and defining the nature, powers, and duties of such boards. This law would only come into operation in the event that the province were again threatened by "any formidable epidemic, endemic or contagious disease."

The immigration of the year 1847 subjected the colony to a very severe strain, and that too, at a time when its general economic condition was anything but satisfac-

45. *L'Avenir,* April 1, 1848. 46. 12 Vic., c. 6. (Prov.)

tory. The population of the province in that year was just over a million and a half. Of this number about half were English-speaking, and it was to the areas inhabited by these latter that the immigrants mainly went. So ninety thousand immigrants, among whom the proportion of destitute and diseased was extraordinarily high, landed almost without warning among a population of less than seventeen times their own number; and of these seventeen colonists per immigrant, nine bore the heavier part of the burden. It was, in proportion, approximately as if in the past year six hundred thousand immigrants, most of them poverty-stricken and many of them diseased, had landed in the Dominion. Not all the new arrivals stayed in the province; some of them passed on to the United States, but there were also some arrivals thence. There are no statistics to show the extent of the migration to and fro across the border; but there is reason to think that at this time the movements of population from Canada to the United States, and *vice versa*, came very close to balancing each other.[47] Qualitatively the United States got the best of the bargain in 1847, for they drew very heavily on the Germans, who were the cream of the immigrants of that year.

England has never had a more academically minded government than that of Lord John Russell from 1846 to 1852. It was composed to some extent of devotees—missionaries of the gospel of *laissez faire* which, being to them a panacea could be relied upon to cure the manifold social and economic ailments of a potatoless Ireland. Possibly the most doctrinaire man in the government was the colonial secretary. Yet if the influence of London was exerted against extensive relief measures in the colony, that influence was a brake on reckless and inconsistent action. The imperial government reflected the *Zeitgeist* much more accurately than did its colonial counterpart. Such mistakes as it made also were well-intentioned, and its princely generosity in finally paying the bill serves to

47. *Seventh Census of the United States,* pp. 120 and 132.

turn the edge of any criticism which might be made from the point of view of the province. For the colonist, nevertheless, the famine immigration was a sore trial, and he must be pardoned if, in the midst of the crisis, the highly theoretical advice of the home government appeared to him to be a trifle too detached. Indeed the case must have seemed to him to be very similar to that of Dr. Johnson's philosopher, who, when informed by a breathless neighbor that the latter's house was on fire, began to discourse calmly and with great erudition upon the nature and properties of flame. Had the province been an independent state it would have had an indisputable right to exclude any or all immigration. Yet it may be questioned whether in that case the right would have been exercised, since the United States, which was nobody's colony, did not exclude the famine immigration from its shores.

The migration of 1847 supplies a good historical instance of the tendency which the public has, to regard economic problems as though they were political ones. The Sovereign State could do nothing to prevent the potatoes from rotting; and political action could mitigate, but could not entirely relieve, the effects of the catastrophe. Famine relief on the necessary scale is an invention of our own century.

For those whose interest is mainly in things political, the whole episode is a fine illustration of the problems connected with the government of what is sometimes called the Second British Empire.

## IX

## MONTREAL IN 1849, AND THE ANNEXATION MOVEMENT

To render annexation by violence impossible, and by any other means as improbable as may be is, as I have often ventured to repeat, the polar star of my policy. LORD ELGIN.

THE foremost Canadian city of ninety years ago was Montreal. Born in misfortune, and baptized with the blood of martyrs, it had become preeminent by virtue of its favored position on the great river. It was a stone city that could boast of many fine buildings, among them the largest church on the continent. Contemporary accounts are agreed as to its beauty and impressiveness. An Englishman wrote: "In walking over the city, I could not but remark the beauty of some of the shops and the extent of the streets: Great St. James'-street would reflect credit on London, and the marble edifices of some of the banks were really most imposing."[1] According to another English visitor: "Many rows of good houses, of cut stone, are springing up in the suburbs, and there is a look of solidity about everything, pleasing to the English eye."[2] In the words of an American: "The sojourner for the first time at Montreal is struck with the beauty and strength of its wharves and quays, the substantial character of its buildings of thick stone walls, its magnificent churches, and no less with the beautiful smooth wooden pavements, than with the narrowness of the streets."[3] The latter were lighted by gas.

1. Lieut.-Col. Sleigh, *Pine Forests and Hacmatack Clearings* (London, 1853), p. 237.

2. G. Warburton, *Hochelaga* (London, 1846), I, 206.

3. Letter in the New York *Tribune,* Sept. 5, 1846.

Montreal, which had about fifty thousand inhabitants, was the capital of the province and no mean city.

Yet it was not a social unit, and from this came many troubles. Apart from its cosmopolitan character as a trade centre and seaport, Montreal was the home of two distinct cultural groups. The population was predominantly French and therefore Roman Catholic, while the commerce and wealth of the city were largely in the hands of an active, progressive, and in some ways dominant, English and Protestant minority. Two nationalities thus shared the city—the one strong in its numbers and ecclesiastical organization, yet a mere outpost of the army of *habitants* who lived in the valley around and below—the other possessing an effectiveness more than proportioned to its numbers, and conscious that it represented the dominant culture not only of the colony but of the continent. Here then were some of the most potent of the causes of strife among men—national, religious, and linguistic differences—and they generated heat due to proximity, and to hatred and fear. As a result the imposing little city was morally and spiritually disunited, and weaker than its buildings of solid stone.

Mass lawlessness and rioting were more common then than they are now; yet even for that time Montreal was a turbulent and troubled city. The French were law-abiding though sometimes provocative; but many of the English had a fascist confidence in direct action, and there were Irish in and near the city who were generally ready for trouble. The feuds of the Orange and Green had been transplanted to this newer soil and were flourishing there, and no adequate police force as yet existed.

Upon this rather abnormal city the economic depression of the late forties had fallen very heavily. Like most commercial communities its economic potentialities, whether for prosperity or misfortune, were great. Far more than any other place in the province, Montreal stood to gain or lose by the result of the St. Lawrence waterway experiment. Were it to succeed, she might well become as the point of trans-shipment, one of the great commercial centres of the world, and every advocate of the canals as well as every optimist had said something to raise her hopes. On the other hand, should the Erie Canal succeed under the new conditions in attracting not only the trade of the American northwest, but of Canada West also, it seemed certain that the results would be disastrous to Montreal; and in 1848 and 1849 as the completed canals waited for the ships that did not come, this was indeed the apparent prospect. In 1849 Lord Elgin wrote: "Property in most of the Canadian towns, and more especially in the Capital, has fallen 50 p.ct in value within the last three years. Three fourths of the commercial men are bankrupt."[4] These things were serious; they seemed more serious than they really were; and always there was close at hand a criterion of economic success. "How do these Americans thus become the usurpers of our trade?" asked the Montreal *Pilot*, and "how [can] land on one side of latitude 45 . . . remain unsaleable at a nominal price of 5s. to 10s. per acre, and right opposite on the other side of this mere imaginary line, within gunshot, be in quick demand at as many pounds per acre?" Canadians and others in fact were always asking this question.

Late in the month of April 1849, a political event took place which stirred this sorely tried community to its depths. In the previous year the Reform Party under the leadership of Baldwin and Lafontaine had carried the province by a large majority. Lord Elgin had in a general way foreseen the difficult situation which would arise, though the vision did not dismay him. He informed Grey that "the next Session of the Provincial Part is likely I think to be an interesting one and to throw considerable light on the prospects of British North America." A month later he added: "This Province is about to pass through an interesting crisis. I shall be required to accept as advisers persons who were denounced very lately by the

4. Elgin to Grey, April 23, 1849. Private Correspondence.

Secretary of State and the Govr Genl as impracticable and disloyal."[5] Indeed an interesting, important, and dangerous political situation was about to develop, the details of which have been very fully studied, and cannot be dealt with here.

The Rebellion Losses Bill was a piece of Reform legislation designed to provide compensation for persons in Lower Canada, other than former rebels, who had suffered property losses in 1837. A similar measure for Upper Canada had already been placed upon the statute book; but, though the bill now seems innocent enough, it was in fact heavily charged with explosives. As at some Hougoumont converging forces make of a single spot the symbol of success or failure; so over the Rebellion Losses Bill the whole issue between the deposed Tories and their Reform supplanters was raised and fought to a decision. The bill was passed by a Reform majority of 47 to 18, and on the afternoon of April 25, 1849, Lord Elgin drove to the legislature and gave the royal assent to it. This was colonial responsible government.

On the following day the leading Tory newspaper gave vent to its feelings:

"*The Rebel Bill Assented To—The First Blow Struck Against British Connexion—The Insult to the British Inhabitants of Canada, Perpetrated with the Assent of the British Government—Groans of the People.*"[6]

The bill was further referred to as "the infamous outrage, the damning insult to the loyal people of Canada, the Bill by which traitors, rebels, and murderers, are to be indemnified for supposed losses incurred by them in consequence of their crimes." Indeed the fury of the Montreal Tories knew no bounds, and found undelayed expression in what is perhaps the most lawless series of incidents in Canadian history. Like Paris of the revolutions, Montreal was a city where bold and purposeful mobs could be quickly collected. As Lord Elgin was leaving the

5. Elgin to Grey, Jan. 7, and Feb. 5, 1848. Private Correspondence.
6. *Courier,* April 26, 1849.

Parliament Buildings after sanctioning the Rebellion Losses Bill, there was a demonstration against him in the street and his carriage was pelted with eggs. In the evening a mass meeting of the British population was called together on the Champ de Mars, and hundreds if not thousands answered the call. Resolutions were passed, the crowd then adjourning to the Houses of Parliament, which were in session. There was "a loud shout, mingled with yellings," and a shower of stones began to strike the windows of the two Houses. Some of the mob then entered the assembly building, one of them seating himself in the speaker's chair, while others began to destroy the furniture and fittings of the buildings, and someone out-cromwelled Cromwell by running off with the mace. Then the buildings were set on fire by some person or persons whose identity remained a secret. So rapidly did the flames spread that many people were afterwards of the opinion that the incendiary act had been carefully prepared. Both the Houses, including their libraries and records, were destroyed. Further outrages were later committed, including attacks on the houses of Lafontaine and Hincks, and for some time afterwards the city was seriously disturbed. The newspaper *l'Avenir* complained that: "Il faut être continuellement armés, prêts à se défendre comme au temps mémorable des Iroquois."[7] Throughout this difficult time the French population was admirably law-abiding, in spite of great provocation.[8]

The wrath of the Montreal Tories was not quickly abated, and their press exhausted the language of vituperation. Indeed they were in a most unwholesome state of rage—oppressed by the multitude and violence of their hatreds. They hated their French fellow-citizens, and believed the government of the day to be in league with these for their oppression. They also hated all Reformers, the

7. *l'Avenir,* May 12, 1849.

8. Story of events in Montreal based on newspapers and personal accounts, and on the official material printed in *Accounts and Papers, 1849,* XXXV.

Rebellion Losses Bill, the new British commercial and colonial policy, the colonial secretary, and their sister cities, particularly Toronto. But most of all they hated Lord Elgin. In their view he was *ex officio* the guardian of their interests as the loyal party; yet he had gone over to the enemy in shameless surrender. He became the incarnation of all that they detested, and they poured upon him a torrent of scorn and invective. Like a College of Heralds they scrutinized his ancestry, and proclaimed that he was not a lineal descendant of the Bruce; but at most derived from a collateral branch. They implied that he came honestly by his defects, saying that the son of a man who was notorious as a "robber of the Greek temples," would himself be known as "the man who lost for England the noble Colony won by the blood of Wolfe." They swore, like Postumus to the Tarentines that "it will take not a little blood to wash this gown!" They threatened to reduce poor Elgin's salary "to as many dollars as he now gets pounds!" They alleged that at an auction sale fifteen-and-sixpence had been paid for a picture of Lord Metcalfe, while one of Elgin had only fetched sixpence. After an anti-French disturbance outside the principal hotel, the crowd, according to a Tory paper, gave "three tremendous cheers for the Queen, and as many dismal groans for Lord Elgin." One newspaper approached the lowest level of bad taste, by affirming that "Canada requires a man to govern it, who has other recommendations than poverty and a big uncle of his wife's." Mere prose proved inadequate, and lampoons like this were written and printed:

> And he sat, and he sat, by this and by that,
> Till he wore out six pair of trousers;—
> Endeavoring to trace who bagged the mace,
> And sacked the Parliament Houses.
>
> . . . . .
>
> But never a bit did anyone split
> On the kiddy what flashed the tinder.

Lord Elgin had been made an honorary member and patron of the St. Andrew's Society of Montreal. So strong did the feeling against him become that he was expelled from the society.

After the events of April 25, Lord Elgin retired to Monklands, and carefully refrained from any appearance in public which might savor of bravado, and tend to provoke excitement and violence. Public affairs were not his only anxiety at this time, as the following month Lady Elgin gave birth to a son. For thus remaining in seclusion he was subjected to fierce criticism, and his personal courage was questioned, even Lord Grey being apparently puzzled at first by his passiveness. In the midst of his troubles Elgin exclaimed in bitterness: "Montreal is rotten to the core and if all Canada be like it the sooner we have done with it the better."[9] For the rest, with great moral courage since he knew very well what was being said and was not a physical coward, he continued to follow the path which he had chosen. The lieutenant-governor of Nova Scotia prepared to send troops to Montreal; in the event however it was not found necessary to send them.[10]

Meanwhile the infuriated Tories, true to their recently acquired taste for establishing precedents, proceeded to set on foot an agitation as peculiar as anything in the history of Canada. The theory that colonies were certain to become independent sooner or later was widely held in England and elsewhere. In Canada however, independence was usually considered as involving something further, namely annexation to the United States. There were many reasons why this seemed to be an almost inevitable corollary to independence; while the political structure of the United States, since that country was organized for expansion, made the incorporation of new territory a very simple matter. There have always been in Canada, since it contained an English population, those who either desired or merely prophesied annexation, and their number,

9. Elgin to Grey, May 5, 1849. Private Correspondence.
10. Correspondence of the Civ. Sec., No. 5177.

never very great, seems to have varied inversely with the prosperity of the country.

It was to this exceedingly drastic proposal of annexation to the United States that the Montreal Tories now turned, as a way out of their troubles, and a whip wherewith to beat all their enemies. They who had so often and so proudly boasted of the superior quality of their loyalty, now forgot their former words, and began openly to advocate that which they had long been accustomed to attribute to their opponents as a secret and disgraceful wish. No *volte-face* could possibly have been more sudden or complete than this.

An annexation association was formed,[11] and the Tory press in Montreal began a serious and sustained annexation campaign. Appeals to reason alternated with violence of expression; but as time went on less heat was generated. Indeed the annexation movement, taken as a whole, was moderate and rational, as though the extreme character of the proposal afforded an outlet for emotions which had hitherto found expression in abusive language. The campaign was carried on throughout the summer, autumn, and winter of 1849, and into the following spring. The climax came with the publication early in October, of a manifesto addressed to the people of Canada,[12] examining the difficulties that beset them, discussing various proposed remedies, and pointing out the great advantages to be derived from annexation, as well as its inevitability. The concluding words were these: "If to your judgment and reason our object and aim be at this time deemed laudable and right, we ask an oblivion of past dissentions; and from all, without distinction of origin, party or creed, that earnest and cordial co-operation in such lawful, prudent, and judicious means as may best conduct us to our common destiny." Other manifestoes were issued from time to time.

11. Part of the records of the Montreal Annexation Association have been published in the *Canadian Historical Review,* V, 236–261.

12. See Appendix B.

The doctrine of "annexationism," to use what it is hoped may be a pardonable invention, was supported by various lines of reasoning in the manifesto, the annexationist press, and elsewhere. The argument in which the most confidence was placed, and which was more frequently used than any other, was an economic one. "Ceux qui désirent la prospérité du pays doivent désirer l'annexion, car il n'y a pas d'autre moyen de l'obtenir." The argument was that annexation to the most prosperous country in the world—a country which indeed seemed almost immune to economic disorders—would confer upon the province a like prosperity. It was indeed nothing else than the everlasting and familiar comparison with the United States; but the moral to be drawn was a new one. Again it was said that "English Free-Trade is a deathblow to the Colonial connexion." This argument was capable of development. "The truth is, that between the abandonment by England of her former system of protection to Colonial produce, and the refusal of the United States to trade with us on a footing of reciprocity, Canada, to use the old proverb, is between the devil and the deep sea, and we must own—it may be perhaps from our terrible blindness—that we can see no way to get out of the scrape, but by going to prosperity, since prosperity will not come to us." This argument sought to place on Great Britain the responsibility for whatever might happen. Nor, it was argued, would annexation involve the infliction of a wrong on Britain, since "without her consent we consider separation as neither practicable nor desirable." Nor would the necessary consent be withheld, for "we now know with certainty . . . that the people of Great Britain acknowledge the right of the inhabitants of this Province to choose for themselves and to establish the Government which they deem best adapted to secure prosperity and comfort for the greatest number." The political condition and institutions of the province were also alleged to be unsatisfactory, and notably inferior to those of the United States. "The simple and economical State

Government, in which direct responsibility to the people is a distinguishing feature, would be substituted for a system at once cumbrous and expensive." Indeed the annexationists, exaggerating the rôle of government, appear to have regarded the abounding prosperity of their southern neighbors as due, very largely at least, to their political constitution, and therefore as a further proof of the latter's excellence. Apart too from prosperity and convenience, it would be more honorable to be "*citoyens* Américains" than "*colons* Anglais," and we hear of the "enervating" influence of imperial rule.

Reference has frequently been made to the cultural similarity between Great Britain, Canada, and the United States. "We purpose on another day to ask you," said an annexationist newspaper, "what matter is it, whether you number yourself among the millions of Anglo-Saxons that obey our gentle Queen Victoria, or among those other millions who have delegated the supreme administration of their affairs for four years to plain old Zachary Taylor." The ethnological argument had two edges, either of which would cut. Undoubtedly one of the most compelling motives of the Montreal Tories in advocating annexation was that it would put an end for ever to what they called "French domination." It is probable that this idea was often in their minds, and that it found expression much more frequently in their speech than in what they wrote.

Two arguments based on the problem of international relations were sometimes used. One was the "entangling alliances" argument, so frequently heard at all times in the United States. Applied to the province it assumed the following form: "The Mother Country's foreign policy is avowedly that of non-interference in the affairs of Europe; but as it is difficult to shake off old habits and systems, she may yet think her honor and Eastern Empire require the sacrifice of her treasure and blood to sustain, or counteract, some one of the *émeutes*, or movements, of European Cabinets." More often it was represented that, supposing the province to be annexed, a war between

Great Britain and the United States "would not make the soil of Canada the sanguinary arena for their disputes, as under our existing relations must necessarily be the case." Annexation was represented, too, as a change which "we all believe to be inevitable," the argument being an expression of the "ripe fruit" theory of colonies, and sometimes uttered with Marxian finality. Moreover annexation if inevitable ought to be quickly carried out, since nothing could be worse than continued uncertainty. Appeals were also made to anti-slavery sentiment. Might not Canadian influence, exerted from within the American Union, be effectively used to free the slave or to mitigate his lot?

A very brief summary of the arguments of those who were opposed to annexationism, ought perhaps to be attempted. From the economic point of view the necessity of annexation was denied, on the ground that other remedies, such as reciprocity, would work equally well. The frequent statement that the cost of government in the States was less than it was in Canada was challenged, and it was argued that annexationism greatly exaggerated the seriousness of economic conditions. Facts were adduced to show that the province was, indeed, developing satisfactorily. The political arguments were that annexationism was a very serious and revolutionary idea which might end in bloodshed, that the military and naval protection afforded by Great Britain were entirely adequate, and the existing constitution of the province quite satisfactory.

A number of moral and sentimental considerations were also brought forward. Thus annexationism was said to be base ingratitude to the mother country, and its exponents were charged with unmitigated materialism, in that the claims of sentiment and of patriotism were entitled to consideration as well as those of profit and loss. It was argued too that an expanded United States might threaten the liberties of the world. Annexationists made use of the anti-slavery appeal; but it could be used far more effectively in the opposite direction. Thus annexation was opposed both on the ground that it would involve Canada in a degrading partnership with slavery, and also because an annexed Canada, having ceased to be a secure refuge for those escaped from bondage, would see in humiliation the enforcement of Fugitive Slave Laws throughout her territory.

Annexationism also suffered condemnation on the ground that it was not practical. The majority of Canadians, it was said, were opposed to annexation: nor would Great Britain give her consent, and it was a *sine qua non* of annexationism that this consent must first be obtained. Yet even if she did consent, it was very questionable whether acceptable terms of admission to the American Union could be arranged, and the annexationists were accused of conveniently ignoring a multitude of awkward details. They were also asked why steps should be taken to hasten annexation, assuming it to be inevitable as they claimed.

It was from members of the Tory Party that annexationism derived its chief support. There were many men in Montreal who as Tories, or as business men, or both, felt with apparent sincerity that in annexation lay their best, perhaps their only chance, to escape from an intolerable situation. Other elements in the community however supported the movement. There were a considerable number of Americans in the city, and in their case patriotism provided an additional and powerful motive for desiring annexation. The Irish element was sympathetic to annexationism, and even among the Orangemen the movement received considerable support. There were also a limited number of French annexationists. The movement never commanded anything approaching a majority; yet among the signatures to the manifesto, of which there were about a thousand, were many of the most important names in English Montreal.

Annexationism in Montreal had an excellent press, and this was one of its greatest assets, for the Montreal newspapers were well-known and widely-read, and possessed that extra measure of authority so often commanded by the press of a capital be it great or small. Four English newspapers, the *Courier*, the *Herald*, and for a time the *Gazette* and the *Witness*, and two French ones, *l'Avenir* and *le Moniteur* favored annexation. The *Pilot* and the *Transcript* took the opposite position. Early in the campaign a newspaper was projected expressly to advocate annexation,[13] and it was furnished with the admirable motto: "*Moderation in action and Force in argument.*"[14]

The French population as a whole held aloof from the movement, the Church authorities having unreservedly condemned it from the first. Indeed neither as Frenchmen nor as Roman Catholics had they anything in common with an agitation which if successful would have deprived them of their cherished safeguards, and delivered them over disarmed and bound to be de-nationalized at the hands of teeming Anglo-Saxon millions. For them the British connection had no sentimental appeal, yet as a minority group they recognized in it their greatest security. For this reason French Canada has always been ready to evince a kind of negative imperialism, and this came into play in 1849. Yet annexationism made some headway among the French in Montreal and Quebec, and in the latter place a short-lived French annexationist newspaper was started. Support too, and that of the most enthusiastic sort, was given to the movement by French radicalism of the *Rouge* school. These men were liberals of the nineteenth-century continental European type—prone to look at all things from a political angle, democratic, nationalist, and anti-clerical. They thrilled to the Revolutions of 1848, and saw in annexationism something similar. Like so many of the liberals of 1848 they had an almost religious veneration for the American system of government, "qui certainement est le plus parfait de l'univers."[15] Moreover, they considered Canada to be governed

13. See notice in the *Courier* of June 30, 1849.

14. For a detailed study of the Montreal press at this time, see C. D. Allin and G. M. Jones, *Annexation, Preferential Trade, and Reciprocity* (Toronto and London), chs. II and III.

15. *l'Avenir,* June 2, 1849.

tyrannically under an outworn and infamous form of government, and "que les institutions que l'Angleterre a imposées à ce pays [sont] un misérable replâtrage de son système aristocratique et constitutionnel."[16] It was pointed out that annexation would dissolve the union which was unpopular in Lower Canada. The economic argument they also used; but far less than the English did. A French annexationist, already quoted, had this to say about annexation as an antidote to priest-craft. "Enfin, Messieurs, si nous eussions été annexés aux Etats-Unis en 1815, vous ne verriez pas aujourd'hui le Clergé faire la propagande absolutiste; anathématiser le libéralisme; et lancer ses maigres ferrailleurs, désolantes médiocrités que les éclairs de génie ne tourmentent guère, sur ceux qui ont le malheur de trouver que les papes sont devenus un peu plus aristocrates que ne le comporte la formule 'serviteur des serviteurs de Dieu.' "[17] Yet, it must be repeated that these were not representative French Canadians, but an isolated group of political and religious heretics who were joined in a grotesque alliance to the right wing of the Tory Party.

Annexationism was not a phenomenon wholly confined to Montreal. It merely began and achieved its greatest successes there. The French population was largely immune to it; but the Townships and Upper Canada were inhabited by people very similar to the non-French of Montreal, and suffering like the latter, though not to the same extent, from economic depression. Great efforts were made to give publicity to annexationist ideas in those parts of the province, yet although for a time no man could foretell the result, annexationism proved to have no widespread or permanent appeal, though there were converts almost everywhere. The program proved distinctly less attractive to the country districts than to the towns, and outside of Montreal, though several newspapers

16. L. A. Dessaulles, *Six Lectures sur l'Annexation du Canada aux Etats-Unis* (Montreal, 1851), p. 196.
17. *Ibid.*, p. 22.

joined the campaign, they were not the most influential ones. Among them were the Kingston *Argus* and the Toronto *Mirror*, the latter an Irish Roman Catholic organ. The Toronto *Examiner*, without advocating annexation demanded a hearing for it. "However strongly," it said, "many may cleave to British Connexion as a matter of choice, all agree that the great interests of the country must be sustained even at the sacrifice of such a connexion."[18] Some editors were anxious not to commit themselves either way. A newspaper was started in Toronto for the express purpose of advocating independence, and it soon added annexation to its program; but it quickly joined the infinitely numerous company of newspapers that have ceased publication owing to lack of support. The great bulk of the press, including the most influential organs, opposed annexationism. The *Globe* was particularly uncompromising. "Every well informed person knows," it said, belittling annexationism, "that the true motives of the Tories who now cry for annexation, are to alarm Lord Elgin, and through him the Home Government, that they may have a change of Ministers, and the restoration of the Provincial patronage."[19] Many districts and organized groups publicly protested their loyalty to the Queen, and their dislike of annexationism.

In England the movement called forth the expression of a great variety of opinions; but considering the nature of the proposal it was received calmly enough, and opposition to it was less pronounced at first than later. Expressions of sympathy or indifference in England were quoted by the annexationists in support of their plan, and in the initial stages of the movement the colonial secretary made an unofficial confession to the effect that "looking at these indications of the state of feeling there [in Canada] & at the equally significant indications as to the feeling in the H. of Commons respecting the value of our Colonies I begin almost to despair of our long retaining those in N. America, while I am persuaded that to both

18. *Examiner,* Sept. 12, 1849.

19. *Globe,* April 14, 1849.

parties a hasty separation will be a very serious evil."[20] The Montreal correspondent of the *Times* made an early and accurate estimate of the situation, which he communicated to his newspaper. "I am of opinion," he wrote, "that those who wish to change the present Constitution at all are in a decided minority, even considering the British inhabitants alone. The Tories imagine that on the question of annexation they will be joined by the Upper Canada Liberals; in this I think they will find themselves mistaken, the Liberal Party being thoroughly satisfied with the acquisition of that for which they have been so long contending, viz. the administration of responsible government in all its integrity."[21] Commenting on the manifesto in an editorial that appeared several weeks later, the *Times*, while paying tribute to the earnestness and moderation of the document, said that the loss of a colony would not ruin England, that there would be no war over the issue, and wondered whether a confederation of the British North American colonies would not do as much as annexation to satisfy Canadian aspirations. The editorial added that the essential thing was whether or no the manifesto represented the general feeling of Canadians. "Meanwhile," it concluded, ". . . let us congratulate ourselves on the reflection that the document which we have quoted proves that the political training which England gives to her colonists is one which need neither make them ashamed of her, nor her of them; and that the future which awaits men thus trained can never be obscure nor dishonourable."[22] Later, when annexationism failed to develop any very wide support, the *Times* stuck to its own formula and opposed it. Other comments were more pessimistic, as for instance this, that "November has nearly passed without brightening the prospects of our Colonial empire in any corner of its wide horizon."[23] Some *laissez faire* organs merely thought that the "ripe fruit" theory

20. Grey to Elgin, July 20, 1849. Private Correspondence.
21. *Times*, Aug. 16, 1849. 22. *Ibid.*, Oct. 31, 1849.
23. *Tait's Edinburgh Magazine*, XVI, p. 753.

was being vindicated. Annexationism was also made the basis of charges against the Colonial Office. One constant critic of that department wrote: "The Colonial Office has been fairly beaten in Canada, and Canada is on the high road to independence."[24] Speaking generally, English opinion was opposed to annexation; but its expression was as restrained in tone as the manifesto itself.

Annexationism was not less important to the United States than to England, and the news from Canada aroused great interest there.[25] This was the period above all others when to the majority of Americans the almost indefinite expansion of their country was written in the stars. Nor is much imagination required in order to appreciate how the spirits of American patriots must have been stirred by the vision which was so often before their eyes of the most colossal nation ever seen on earth, stretching from Panama to the Arctic Sea.[26] Behind the vision too there lay a philosophy, for to those who believed in it, Manifest Destiny was an expression of the ethos. The tremendous expansive power of the United States would not be contained, since world progress demanded that the principles for which the Republic stood should triumph—light subduing darkness. "Thus, broad and marked, fall the portentous shadows of coming great events," wrote a New York newspaper, referring to the Canadian annexation movement. "The hour for a new conflict between the antagonistic principles of progress and conservatism steals on apace."[27] In the same strain is this: "It is arbitrary, unnatural, and contrary to the spirit of the age, that an Empire should thus be kept stretched beyond its legitimate territorial boundaries. That old system is exhausted and refuses to work longer."[28] The same newspaper remarked a trifle complacently: "The British Colo-

24. J. A. Roebuck, *The Colonies of England* (London, 1849), p. 220.

25. See Allin and Jones, *Annexation,* Ch. X.

26. Annexation would not of course have involved the Hudson Bay Territory.

27. New York *Herald,* April 4, 1849.

28. New York *Tribune,* Jan. 19, 1850.

nies are never-failing cares to keep the State-Physicians in practice."[29] The New York *Herald* saw in Canadian events a "significant resemblance to the movements and agitations which ushered in the era of 1776." Later, when nothing definite seemed to have happened, it began to suspect a difference. "But the men of seventy-six were not remarkably docile. . . . Does the same blood circulate in the veins of our Canadian heroes? We begin to doubt it."[30] American opinions of annexationism were however in many cases decisively influenced by the all-pervading slavery issue. Looked at through Southern eyes, Canada was simply a free-soil realm, which might weigh down the scales against slavery perhaps forever. It is true that Cuba entered into the discussion as a possible equivalent; but its acquisition was not certain, and so the irrepressible conflict prevented the project of Canadian annexation from receiving the unanimous welcome which might have been expected. Opinion in the United States therefore varied between the extremes of opposition and Dickensian "spread-eagleism." A fervent expression of the latter was given by some French-Canadians settled in the eastern states, who exhorted: ". . . ô canadiens, agrandissons la patrie aux proportions de l'hémisphère tout entier, . . . et nous verrons l'aigle américain dont les ailes trempent déjà dans les deux océans, embrasser le continent jusqu'au pôle, et emporter au plus haut des cieux la charte de l'Amérique du Nord émancipée!"[31]

At the beginning of the movement in Montreal, a Southern newspaper published a letter on annexation written by General Winfield Scott, the conqueror of Mexico, which naturally attracted considerable attention, being written by so eminent a man. It was republished in several Canadian newspapers.[32] The general prophesied widespread discontent in Canada, followed by independ-

29. *Ibid.,* Nov. 24, 1849.
30. New York *Herald,* April 28 and June 25, 1849.
31. Quoted in Allin and Jones, *Annexation,* p. 307.
32. E.g. *Examiner,* July 18, 1849.

ence, and probably by a desire for annexation. He pointed out how great would be the advantages to the United States of annexation, but emphasized the fact that his opinion was entirely unofficial and had often been expressed privately. He held that there must be no act of bad faith toward England, whose good-will was essential.

A Boston business man expressed in the following words an opinion probably but little colored by politics or "patriotics": "The Canadians, . . . seem to be rapidly approaching that point of discontent where they will not find any satisfaction, or relief from their disadvantages, real or imaginary, short of a revolution. It seems evident that the policy of England will be to yield gracefully to what must be, sooner or later, a matter of geographical and political necessity, and where nothing but harm could arise from resistance.—And further, supposing them independent, there can be but one opinion as to the desirableness to them, of their becoming a part of the United States."[33] In a letter written from New York, another of Messrs. Baring's correspondents said this of annexationism. "It would seem probable that if the present difficulties with the Mother Country cannot be adjusted—which really does not seem in a favorable way of settlement—by and bye, an amicable separation may occur, but whether, to become an independent Government, or a part of the United States, cannot now be told. Lord Ashburton told the writer in 1838, that England would interpose no obstacle, to a peaceable separation."[34] In 1849 the New York *Tribune* had an "Annexation Correspondent" in Montreal, who was of the opinion that annexation would be carried out, though not without some difficulty.[35]

Yet loudly though they clamored for annexation, the frayed nerves of the Montreal annexationists could not always brook expressions of American faith in the ultimate success of their project. On one occasion the strongly

33. Sam. G. Ward to Baring Bros., Aug. 28, 1849. Baring Papers—Official Correspondence.

34. James G. King and Sons to Baring Bros., Oct. 7, 1849. *Ibid.*

35. *Tribune,* Dec. 1, 1849.

annexationist *Courier* referred to such an expression as "a reckoning of chickens before they are hatched," and added: "If Canada is ever annexed to the United States, it will be by the action of Canada herself, with the consent of the Mother Country, freely given. If the Canadians do not choose Annexation, all the force which the United States could bring to bear, war being declared between her and England, could not make a forcible conquest."[36]

In the province the appearance of the manifesto, and its extensive signature in the capital, altered the status of the movement, and the authorities were then bound to take official notice of it. Robert Baldwin immediately nailed his colors to the mast by publishing a letter written by himself to Peter Perry, a supposed annexationist, in which he stated that "upon this question [severance of the connection] there remains in my opinion no room for compromise. It is one of altogether too vital a character for that. All should know therefore that I can look upon those only who are for the continuance of that connexion as political friends,—those who are against it as political opponents. The Mother Country has now for years been leaving to us powers of self-government more ample than ever we had asked—and it does appear a most impious return to select such a time for asking for a separation from her for ever." This unequivocal statement both gave a lead to the Reformers, and was a fore-shadowing of what their attitude would continue to be. Lord Elgin thought Baldwin to be "of more importance to the connexion than three regiments."[37] In regard to the manifesto Elgin's advice was that "the proper way to treat this document is to represent it to be, what in fact it is, an emanation from a knot of violent protectionists and disappointed party men."[38]

A considerable number of holders of official positions under the crown had admittedly signed the manifesto, and

36. *Courier,* July 28, 1849.
37. Elgin to Grey, Jan. 28, 1850. Private Correspondence.
38. Elgin to Grey, Oct. 14, 1849. Private Correspondence.

in all cases where it was legally possible to do so the government compelled these either to disavow annexationism or be removed from office, and the Colonial Office supported this action. In certain quarters these dismissals were criticized on the ground that men must be free to discuss anything, even the advantages of annexation; but it was not against mere discussion that the action complained of had been taken. The removal of the seat of government from Montreal to Toronto, which followed the events herein described, was no doubt influenced by the annexation campaign, though the scenes of violence that followed the enactment of the Rebellion Losses Bill, were the principal cause. The imprimatur of the imperial government was finally affixed to the policy of opposition to annexationism, when the prime minister in the course of a speech in the House of Commons said: "To that proposal, of course, the Crown could give nothing but a decided negative; and I trust, . . . it is not their intention to push their project of joining a neighbouring State to the ultimate result of endeavouring by force of arms to effect a separation from Great Britain; but that . . . they will acquiesce in the decision of the Crown."[39]

With the spring of 1850, a change began to come over the scene. In February an annexationist candidate contested a bye-election at Quebec, and was defeated by a decisive majority. Business conditions took a distinct turn for the better, reciprocity once more came up for official discussion in Washington, and annexationism began perceptibly to wane. In its final stages it was sometimes a simple independence movement, and split up at the last into numerous alternative projects, such as confederation, retrenchment, or reciprocity. In June we find that former bulwark of annexationism the *Courier*, urging that an attempt be made to increase the business of the St. Lawrence waterway, and incidentally of course of Montreal, by exempting from canal-tolls all produce intended for export from Montreal or Quebec. "The slug-

39. Feb. 8, 1850. *Hansard,* 3rd Ser., CVIII, 551.

gish nature of Lafontaine," said the *Courier* in this connection, "cannot appreciate the exigencies of commerce; yet accident invests him with the dominant voice in the Cabinet, and trade must travel the sinuosities which his heavy intellect imposes."[40] Two months later Elgin was able to state that "it is clear that annexation is dead for the moment." As the qualifying phrase implies however, the governor-general continued to regard annexationism as the greatest of his problems. Perhaps it is not too much to say that it was an obsession with Lord Elgin. A year later Montreal attempted the *amende honorable*, by officially inviting the governor-general to visit the former capital. He accepted and went, receiving and replying to a very courteous address from the city fathers. "All these follies" were thus "duly expiated in the most official and authoritative way possible."[41]

This curious episode in Canadian history, which offers many points of comparison with the better known Hartford Convention of 1814–15, was mainly due, it is evident, to racial and economic causes.

The legal position of annexationism appears to go through two separate stages. Keeping to the measured terms of the manifesto, we find certain subjects exhorting their fellow-subjects to assist in a peaceful agitation in order with the consent of their sovereign to sever their allegiance for the purpose of seeking incorporation with a foreign power. Whatever may be said of this as a practical program, it would seem to have been legal enough until such time as the official position of the crown had been ascertained. But after the decision of the crown had become known in Canada it seems probable that annexationism was seditious.

Certain factors undoubtedly made for the success of such a movement at that time. The economic situation was difficult, especially in Montreal, and many Canadians were sincerely convinced that the *laissez faire* policy of Britain was responsible for this, and all were seeking a remedy.

40. *Courier*, June 15, 1850. 41. *Examiner*, Oct. 1, 1851.

In very many ways Canada was less resistant to annexationist ideas then than she would be now. The agitators had moreover all the advantages usually enjoyed by the opponents of any existing arrangement. In other words a millennium might perhaps be defined as an imaginary picture of the future, beside whose rococo tints any actual state of affairs looks drab and faded. The story of the Canadian annexation movement of 1849 is an interesting instance of the limitations of the economic motive.

Yet in a movement which does not succeed we may expect to find weaknesses. "Outside of Montreal and Quebec, and the border districts in the eastern and western extremes of the province, the movement had not obtained a firm hold upon any considerable portion of the population. The number of signatures to the various manifestos did not amount to 5,000, an insignificant fraction of the total population."[42] An attempt to assign some reasons for the failure of the movement does not imply a belief that human motives can be fully enumerated, weighed on the scales, and labelled with precision and finality. The annexationists started with a moral handicap, being led by the men who had put themselves in the wrong in the matter of the Rebellion Losses Bill. Moreover the passage of that very measure, with all that it implied, had left the Reform Party, decidedly the strongest party in the province, well satisfied, and the Reformers had thus become for the time being conservatives. Responsible government, too, like democracy of which it was merely a particular form, tended to render revolutionary minority agitations of that sort innocuous, for to some extent it undermined the logic of a resort to violence. The whole influence of powerful organizations like the Roman Catholic and Anglican churches, was wielded against a project which for very different reasons they were bound to oppose. The movement had this fatal weakness, also, that excepting in the case of the *Rouges*, the arguments used on behalf of annexation were almost entirely mate-

42. Allin and Jones, *Annexation,* p. 327.

rialistic ones. It is of course true that idealism, divorced from supposed self-interest, cannot hope for general acceptance; but it is also true that a propaganda appealing to self-interest alone, lacks driving power. The English-speaking annexationists offered their audience no thrills, but only statistics and an uninspiring doctrine of alleged necessity. Unlike their *Rouge* allies what they preached was not a crusade but a foraging-party. In modern societies there is no force stronger than that of nationalism,[43] the power of which over the hearts and actions of men it is difficult to exaggerate. It was with this tremendous sentiment, which thrives on misfortune and is impervious to reason, that the annexationists had ventured to match their inadequate strength. Nor were the economic troubles of the colony either as widespread or as likely to persist as the annexationists supposed, and the event showed that they had been crying ruin where there was no ruin. The movement had derived its vitality to a great extent from economic distress, and did not long survive the return of prosperity.

43. Nationalism in the province is described elsewhere in this work as having been weak. The word, as applied to the province, may comprise either local or imperial sentiment. It is of course used here in the latter sense.

# X

## CONCLUSION

And the waters returned from off the earth continually: and after the end of the hundred and fifty days the waters were abated.
GENESIS, viii, 3.

BETWEEN the years 1783 and 1926, the constitutional status of the colonies of settlement in the British Empire was wholly changed by a gradual evolution toward a far less logical but more workable organization. This political transformation was accompanied, and was to some extent caused, by economic changes of a far-reaching character. The most important phase of the whole evolution occurred after 1846. Here the political development led to responsible government, and thence to dominion status. During the same period the economic pathway led almost immediately to commercial independence, and thence toward industrial self-sufficiency. Yet the most important step of all those which were taken along this economic pathway was the abolition of the old commercial system in the interest of free trade, because everything else resulted from this change as though of necessity. Any adequate attempt to study a particular colony during that decisive period from 1846 to 1851 must treat its subject not only as a separate phenomenon, but also and chiefly as a colony, an integral part of a larger political and economic unit. During that period moreover, the practice and even the principles of colonial administration underwent important modifications, partly because the general economic crisis and the new commercial policy were prolific of new problems, and partly because the colonial policy of the imperial government was very liberal. The character of colonial administration at this time is therefore unusually interesting.

In the history of Canada during that brief period of transition, an effective comparison can be made between the older colonial administrative system, and that of dominion autonomy which was to take its place: such a comparison revealing in the earlier arrangement a number of serious defects from which the later one is almost wholly free. In dealing with colonial questions under the old system, it was impossible to draw a satisfactory line, or indeed to draw a line at all, between those matters which affected the interests of Britain or the empire at large, and those which only concerned a particular colony. As a result the colonial office often felt itself obliged to take sides over an issue which the colonials considered to be entirely or mainly a local one, and thus to become the ally of one or other of the political parties in the colony—usually of that party which was the more conservative in its attitude toward the issue concerned. Consequently flag-waving became a normal feature of colonial politics, every reform movement was certain to be branded as treason, and almost every important domestic question involved a discussion of the connection with Great Britain.

At its best autocracy has great advantages—it is steady and effective; but it lacks the safety-valves possessed by the fully representative form of government. Men are proverbially prone to blame "the government" for all their tribulations, and it is one of the greatest merits of the representative system that it provides a harmless outlet at the polls for such feelings, and indeed utilizes them in the interests of the state. An unpopular government may thus be belabored to the heart's desire of the electorate without any strain whatever being imposed on the constitution of government itself. Under the old imperial system the Colonial Office received a very large share of the blame when anything went wrong in a colony, and its authority was not representative. This was an important matter in democratic colonial communities whose social order predisposed them to accept without reserve the basic political principles of the French Revolution. A chronic strain on the imperial tie resulted. Nor was the authority of the Colonial Office by any means autocratic enough to be decisively and efficiently exercised in colonial affairs. It therefore labored under the disadvantages both of the autocratic and of the representative systems, without possessing the advantages of either. In these circumstances every little hill of difficulty became a mountain, and a colonial governor was, as Wakefield said, among the least enviable of mankind. In Canada the arrangement was being continually subjected to unfavorable comparison with the political constitution of the United States, so much admired of contemporary liberals.

The parasitic attitude of the colonists has also been noticed. They took too mercenary a view of the connection, and Lord Grey once referred to "that disposition wh. is so universal in all the Colonies to throw upon the B^sh^. Treasury any charges they possibly can."[1] As a consequence, the imperial government was continually being put in the invidious position of having to refuse favors. Decentralization and an increased degree of autonomy worked a great improvement in this respect, though many years later Goldwin Smith found the Canadians too client-minded to suit him, and so did John Bright. The colonial point of view was also very sectional and introversive, which tended to produce opportunism in action. The imperial government, on the other hand, had to administer a host of colonies as well as maintain reasonably harmonious relations with the rest of the world, and there were two important consequences of this complex responsibility. The first was the difficulty, overemphasized by Charles Buller, of understanding the conditions and problems of communities so numerous and so diverse in character. The second consequence was that the imperial authorities nearly always acted in accordance with some principle or theory, a thing which the provincial government almost never did, though it often quoted principles in support of its policy. This difference in the methods of

1. Grey to Elgin, Nov. 18, 1847. Private Correspondence.

action, which no doubt is the reason why despatches from the Colonial Office often seem so pedantic, and why the provincial government was such a frequent advocate and practitioner of the convenient expedient, was probably due also to the existence of distinct types of political leader in Great Britain and in Canada. The Stanleys, Greys, and Russells were land-owning aristocrats, and their knowledge of economic matters was mainly theoretical. Their Canadian counterparts, Hincks, Merritt, and MacNab, for instance, were practical business men. Incidentally, it is worth noting that Grey, the doctrinaire, and Hincks, the realist, were alike accurate in prophesying, like the good free traders which they were, that all would come right in the end.

The faults of the system were inherent in it, and did not result from the way in which it was worked, for there was plenty of good-will on both sides. That of the old country is sufficiently shown in connection with the guaranteed loan, the passing of the Canada Corn Act, and the assumption of the expenses which grew out of the famine migration. The failure of the annexation movement on the other hand, bears witness to the popularity of the connection in the colony, for, although independence had little enough to offer, annexation to the United States must have seemed economically and perhaps politically advantageous to an entirely unprejudiced observer between 1845 and 1851.

Yet, though the transition from the old to the new was no doubt inevitable, and even though it was on the whole desirable also, the old system carried with it certain advantages. The present commonwealth system, if system it may be called, presents many stark problems, not only to the political scientist, but to the statesman charged with the working of it. Decisions on matters of general imperial policy can now be reached only after much delay. Occasionally unanimous agreement cannot be arrived at. Nor is it possible to foresee the result over a long period of time of the pursuit of policies in which all the partners do not concur, or of different policies, or of policies which may in practice conflict with each other.

It is certain that under the old system the colonies derived a valuable advantage from the restraining influence of London on ill-advised or hasty action on the part of local governments and legislatures. This often wise and almost always conservative influence, for example, probably saved the Canadians from duplicating the costly monetary blunders and the morally indefensible Indian policy of their American neighbors. The authority of the Colonial Office was exercised by men of strict integrity and impartiality, and both these invaluable virtues were alike protected and enhanced by thousands of miles of salt sea water. Sometimes too this authority was exercised by men of very outstanding ability like Gladstone or Sir James Stephen.

For the forming of intelligent judgments all the necessary information was at the disposal of the officials at the Colonial Office, excepting only, whatever it may be worth, that intimate knowledge of local conditions which prolonged residence in the community concerned alone can give. These officials had access at all times to copies of colonial statutes, sessional papers, and official gazettes; to the governor's despatches and the enclosures which they contained; to statistical material, and to some of the more important colonial newspapers. The Record Office, for example, possesses the most complete file in existence of the earlier issues of the Toronto *Globe*. It is interesting to notice in this particular connection, the importance attributed by Lord Grey to colonial newspapers as a source of information. In a circular despatch of Feb. 9, 1847, he said to the colonial governors: "I find that for many years there have been regularly transmitted to this Office, from the several British Colonies, Copies of the principal Newspapers published in each. I am happy to find this practice existing, and I attach much importance to its regular observance. . . . There are many small circumstances connected with the feelings of those under your

Government, and with the general leaning of public opinion with which daily habit has rendered you so familiar, that they pass unobserved before your eyes. Yet, to a person at a distance from the scene, such circumstances may be full of significance, and may merit deliberate attention in the decision on the policy to be followed by Her Majesty's Government.

"Upon these grounds I have made arrangements for ensuring a more regular examination than has hitherto been attempted, of the Newspapers which reach this Office from the several Colonies."

During the period just mentioned the old economic policy was abandoned, and its successor introduced. The latter decentralized the constitutional authority to regulate commerce, a step which no doubt was inevitable. The practical result was that there developed within the empire two distinct types of commercial policy, each following a different path. It is probable that this too could not have been avoided; but avoidable or not it has raised important problems, for in the field of commercial policy widely varying interests have developed within the empire. Yet it is certain that Lord Elgin's prophecy has been fulfilled, and that the new policy has obviated more difficulties than it has created.

Under the old imperial economic system the greater part of the external trade of Canada had been with the old country by way of the St. Lawrence. Not very successful attempts had been made to build up a trade between the British North American colonies and the West Indies, similar to that which had flourished for so long between those islands and New England. It had been supposed that the Canada Corn Act of 1843, together with the complementary provincial legislation of the preceding year, would stimulate the trade of the St. Lawrence, not only in Canadian breadstuffs, but also in flour ground in the province from American wheat. On the strength of this anticipation, an uncertain but probably small amount of investments was made in mills and warehouses along the

St. Lawrence River. The subsequent repeal of the Corn Law, which took effect in 1847, removed all preference from colonial breadstuffs, and deprived the province of whatever benefits may have been conferred upon it by the Canada Corn Act. The death-sentence of the colonial preference was immediately followed by a severe depression in the province, which lasted until 1850. The consequence was that the change in commercial policy was regarded by a majority in the colony, particularly in Montreal, as the principal or even the sole cause of the hard times which followed. This is not surprising since *post hoc ergo propter hoc* is a very seductive form of reasoning, nor had the arguments necessary to disprove the theorem as yet revealed themselves. As a result a very serious view of the situation was taken by many, for, if the depressed state of trade were due to the new commercial policy, prosperity might not return until the old system should have been re-established—a most unlikely event. The prospect therefore seemed black enough, and only an unquestioning faith in the beneficence of Providence or of free trade was proof against the general gloom in those parts of the province where this view prevailed. So plausible was the *post hoc* view moreover, that it has never disappeared, and the catch-words of that time have very often been presented as its history.

While it may be admitted that the change in commercial policy was important, it was far from being the sole or even the main cause of the economic troubles of the province. In the first place the Canada Corn Act, during the very short time that it operated, does not seem to have tempted increased quantities of American breadstuffs to seek an outlet by way of the St. Lawrence. Indeed it has been shown that in the long run it might have had precisely the opposite effect. The repeal of the Corn Law therefore did not deprive Canada of great and certain advantages which that colony had possessed while the Canada Corn Act was in force. Nor did the adoption by Great Britain of the policy of free trade in raw materials leave the province in the serious position of having a permanent unmarketable surplus of wheat and timber, and no means wherewith to pay for its imports. When all is said and done the province was raising good competitive wheat, for producing which it possessed great advantages, since in the requisites of soil, climate, and rainfall, Upper Canada was well favored, and the western portion of it might have invited comparison with any part of the continent. In the timber trade, as it has been shown, market conditions generally speaking were exceptionally good, and the depression of that trade after 1845 was both a by-product of past success and a prelude to an era of further prosperity.

Yet the advent of the new commercial policy was not without its effects on the province. The first and most immediately serious of these was the resulting atmosphere of uncertainty and gloom. Business conditions are exceedingly sensitive to fear, which may cause the consumer to spend less, the merchant to curtail his orders, and the producer to diminish his output or have an unsold surplus on his hands. The metabolism of the body economic is thus retarded, and prices fall. The psychological effects of the new policy were serious, and many instances of this have been given. After the year 1845 the economic future of the province was full of unknowns which seemed to many to be adverse certainties, and these for a time exercised a "bearish" influence on almost every phase of economic life. A second result of the change in policy was that trade became dislocated during the period of readjustment—an unavoidable result of any such change, and in this case of no great consequence. These two effects were temporary only; there were however two others which have hitherto proved to be permanent, and which are more important. One was that under the new conditions the St. Lawrence was never able to regain its monopoly of the Canadian trade with Britain. The other was that after the change in policy the external trade of Canada became much more widely diffused than it had been before.

The protection afforded to the St. Lawrence route by the old preferential system had enabled that waterway to monopolize the trade of the province, and until the year 1845 the competitive effectiveness of the unimproved waterway had never been put to the test and was therefore unknown. The American Drawback Law of 1845 entered the Erie Canal as an avowed contender for the trade of Canada West. The magnificent new St. Lawrence canals however were finished by 1848, and Canadians were hopeful that the superiority of these canals, more especially if the Navigation Laws could be repealed, would turn the scales in their favor, and not only restore to the St. Lawrence the monopoly of the provincial trade, but also attract to it the much larger commerce of the American lake region. Yet neither of these hopes were fulfilled, for the lower ocean freight rates obtaining at New York more than compensated for the superiority of the Canadian canals, and this situation was not altered by the repeal of the Navigation Laws which went into effect at the beginning of 1850. Even in 1851 the contest between the two routes was not regarded as finally settled; but confidence in the eventual success of the St. Lawrence had abated considerably by that time. It so happened that the improved provincial waterway had been put to the test shortly after the inauguration of the new commercial policy, to which its failure was widely attributed. In considering the effect of the new policy on the waterway, it should be remembered that that project had aimed at two distinct objectives. The waterway was expected to handle the whole of the provincial trade. It was intended also to provide an outlet and an entrance for a considerable part of the trade of the American Northwest.

Under the old colonial system, until 1845, the St. Lawrence had monopolized the overseas trade of the province, because provincial exports going down the St. Lawrence or the Rideau obtained the colonial preference and avoided paying the American import duty. This monopoly however began to break down in 1845 with the enactment of the American Drawback Laws, and the change in imperial policy seems only to have accentuated the tendency already existing, a tendency which the new provincial canals were not sufficient to overcome. Probably the principal effect of free trade upon the waterway came from the encouragement offered to increased trade between the province and the United States. It should be noted too that the shipping at the ports of Montreal and Quebec suffered much less than might be supposed after the middle of the century. The timber trade continued to support Quebec, while the railways came to the rescue of Montreal. The secondary aim of the canal-builders on the St. Lawrence was visionary. It was extremely unlikely that the Canadian route could have obtained any large part of the western trade, even had the old system remained in force, unless American breadstuffs might have been admitted free into Canada, and thence into Britain at the preferential colonial rate—a manifest impossibility.

Yet the failure of the Canadian waterway did surprisingly little harm to the colony. It inflicted no serious injury upon the English-speaking farmers, while the *habitants* did not need the waterway owing to the fact that they were practically independent of staple and imports. As compared with most of the competing wheat lands of the American West, Upper Canada was advantageously situated with respect to distance from the overseas market, as well as from that of the eastern states, from which however it was separated by a tariff barrier in favor of its rivals. After the passage of the American Drawback Laws the farmer and the merchant of Canada West had the choice between two export and import routes, and they could, like their competitors, use whichever might be the cheaper at any given time. Indeed the opening of the Erie to their trade did more good than harm to the people of Upper Canada,[2] and had they been unable to use that route after 1846 the results might have been very serious

2. The advantage which the Erie Canal was capable of conferring upon Upper Canada was pointed out in Durham's Report, II, 187–188.

for them. An increasing benefit also was derived from the fact that the two routes were competing for a very lucrative trade, the result being a gradual reduction of tolls. This was advantageous to the grain-growers of Canada West as against distant competitors in the British market who depended on entirely different channels of transportation. As consumers, too, the Upper Canadians profited from being able to import by the cheaper route, though a part of what they would otherwise have saved went by way of import duties to pay the interest on the debt incurred for the construction of the provincial canals. These great advantages Upper Canada derived from her commanding position at the place where the two waterways diverged. When in addition her favorable soil and climate are considered, it is evident that that part of the province possessed assets which, while very far from constituting a natural monopoly, were sufficient to guarantee to her inhabitants in normal times, a high level of prosperity. Before the year 1845 the old colonial system and the American tariff had made the province dependent on her river to an extent that was artificial. The American Drawback Laws and the new imperial commercial policy had laid bare the competitive inferiority of the St. Lawrence; but had also revealed the natural advantages of Upper Canada.

The Canadian canals, which were government-owned, had cost a lot of money, and it had been hoped that they might prove to be a profitable investment; but this hope was not fulfilled, for the income was in proportion to the traffic. In consequence the province had to bear the weight of what was, for a young colony, a heavy burden of debt. Yet the financial problem though temporarily embarrassing was not at any time radically serious, for the colony continued to pay its way. Its almost complete fiscal dependence on revenue from customs, together with lack of credit, in a period of business depression, account for its financial difficulties, which disappeared after 1849 more as a result of improved business conditions generally than of any action of the government. The burden of largely unremunerative debt incurred on behalf of the waterway remained. Apart from the hope that the provincial treasury might benefit by a revenue derived from tolls, the debt had been incurred for the supposed benefit of the English-speaking people of the province; yet the French had no serious cause for complaint on that score, since the money for payments on interest and sinking fund was derived chiefly from import duties, and, because the English-speaking inhabitants consumed most of the imports, the duties were largely paid by them. They had wanted to establish communication with the sea as cheaply as possible. If the St. Lawrence had obtained the western trade their waterway would have cost them nothing, returning a profit; while if it had retained a larger share of the total trade it would have cost them less than it did. In the event, be it St. Lawrence or Erie, they had their waterway; but the expense had exceeded expectations. With the return of prosperity however the debt proved not to be a grievous burden, and its weight to be negligible in the long run, as the colony grew in size and wealth.

It is no wonder therefore that many of the commercial men in Upper Canada regarded the success of the Erie–New York route with perfect composure, and it was advantageous to them to have the option of dealing through business firms other than those of Montreal. Yet the mercantile class of the colony as a whole, which was very largely English-speaking, was not uniformly affected by the failure of the waterway scheme. Montreal and the Eastern Townships for a time suffered severely from this cause, and, had it not been for the advent of the railways, Montreal would have been injured even more than it was. There were also a number of business men who lost money in investments made on the strength of their belief in the ultimate success of the waterway and of the Canada Corn Act. For merchants in general the whole period was an uncertain one, the year 1847 especially being difficult and dangerous for those engaged in the grain trade. Where the merchants suffered the town population did also. The course taken by the annexation movement throws a good deal of light on this whole question, though it would be a serious mistake to suppose that all who did not become annexationists were prosperous and contented.

In short, the province as a whole suffered much less from the failure of its waterway than the loud complaints of the pessimists would indicate. Lower Canada did not need the waterway, and Canada West was able to make profitable use of the American route to the sea. Though the farmers suffered but little from the failure of the waterway, many of the commercial men were not so fortunate. A large but by no means crushing public debt remained to remind the colony of its carefully planned but unsuccessful undertaking. The ambitious aim of securing the western trade for the St. Lawrence was impracticable; yet this could scarcely have been foreseen. The Erie Canal conferred an almost magic prosperity on parts of New York State—a prosperity which would no doubt have fallen to the lot of the province had the St. Lawrence route justified the hopes of its advocates.

During the years from 1846 to 1850, and therefore synchronizing with the change in commercial policy and the resulting adjustments, and with the early years of the waterway experiment, there was a worldwide depression in trade, accompanied as usual by scarcity of money and low prices. It came at the end of a long and gradual decline in prices, and was itself a period of acute distress in very many parts of the world, when demand was low and the constant tendency of prices to fall discouraged business enterprise, and diminished the flowing currents of commodities and capital by means of which prosperity is fed. The Province of Canada was not immune to so epidemic a complaint: in fact the characteristic structure of its economic life, since it was not industrialized and was therefore unusually dependent on its exports and imports, made it especially sensitive to conditions in the world at large. Indeed, so closely did the economic state of the province conform throughout to the course of trade elsewhere, that there can be no possibility of accidental coincidence. The internal trade of the province also was profoundly affected by the prevailing conditions. The general depression bore heavily upon the farmers, although they were neither desperately nor permanently injured by the events of these years, and the high wheat prices which prevailed in the year 1847 must have been helpful to the grain-growing portion of the colony. The *habitants* suffered less severely than did the English-speaking farmers of Upper Canada and the Townships, on account of their economic aloofness. Cheap exports were in a measure balanced by cheap imports, yet low prices are always feared by producers, and agriculture, partly because it is an unorganized industry, is seldom able to adjust production to demand on a sufficiently wide basis. The commercial class of the colony was affected as the farmers were by general trade conditions—probably more so indeed. Their numbers were small, yet in the province they formed the bulk of that middle class which in a complete social democracy of the British colonial type is always extremely powerful, and better able to make its wants known than any other economic group.

The province therefore from 1846 to 1850, was suffering from an ordinary cyclic depression. This was the basic cause, and the principal one, of the distempers of those troubled years. The change in imperial policy and the difficulties accompanying the readjustment of trade which resulted, the failure of the waterway, and the famine migration of 1847—these things merely aggravated a malady which existed independently of them, and which would have occurred had they been absent. The apparently very serious economic disturbance which resulted was the chief though not the only cause of the political tension which accompanied it.

By the latter part of 1849 the worst of the depression was over, and in the following year the tide of prosperity was once more rising. In the autumn of the former year, a

Montreal newspaper was able to report that "Il s'est fait beaucoup plus d'affaires dans la cité de Montréal durant l'automne que les années précédentes. Les marchandises se sont vendues à des bons prix et en grandes quantités."[3] The government very naturally made the most of this change for the better, and indeed it was beginning to have sore need of any strength which returning prosperity might be able to lend to it, and the speech from the throne in the spring of 1850 struck a moderate note of optimism. In 1851 Hincks began a speech in the assembly by congratulating the committee of supply on "the great prosperity which prevails throughout the country." The Census Report of 1852 makes the following statement: "It is believed that a very general feeling prevails, not only in the Mother Country, but even in Canada, that her growth and prospcrity arc not commcnsurate with that of the United States, and without any intention to deny or conceal the rapid progress of our neighbours, it may be well, by a few facts, compiled from Statistical Returns, to prove how erroneous such an impression is,—the growth of Upper Canada, taking it from the year 1800, having been nearly *thrice* that of the United States."[4] An equally confident foreign opinion was expressed in 1850 by I. D. Andrews: "No permanent injury . . .," says his report, "can result to the colonies from the change in the commercial policy of Great Britain . . ., their trade will gradually conform to the change, and it will compel them to greater self-reliance, and to seek new channels for their commerce."[5] In the province where there were practically no industries, and where revenue duties were levied on imported manufactured goods, the customs revenues are probably the most accurate index of the general level of prosperity. Another good indication is afforded by the statistics of the sales of crown lands. In a more mature agricultural country where all available land was in private hands, land values would be a reasonably dependable

3. *La Minerve,* Oct. 18, 1849.
4. *Census Report of 1851–2,* I, p. x.
5. *First Report,* p. 13.

guide; but the provincial government was offering land at a fixed price, which fact tended to stabilize the value of all agricultural land. The amounts of land sold by the government year by year however, are an approximate measure of agricultural prosperity, public confidence, and available capital. The table given below affords impressive evidence of rapidly increasing material well-being after the year 1849.[6]

It is quite evident that with the year 1850 prosperity returned to the colony. Thus the doctrinaire free traders like Gladstone and Grey had proved to be entirely correct in their main contention that in the end all would be well. It is a nice instance of the use of economics as an applied science. Nevertheless the prophecies of the pessimists, when they said that the provincial waterway would not succeed under a régime of free trade, were fulfilled also. Agriculture however, and the timber trade recovered an ample measure of prosperity, so that exports as well as imports began to show a steady and generous increase. Even Montreal, after its failure to establish itself as the entrepôt of the western trade, or to monopolize that of its Canadian hinterland, or even to retain its rank as the provincial capital, recovered a reasonable degree of prosperity, and began to set its heart upon more moderate successes, which proved to be much easier of attainment.

It is natural that economic depressions should, and they always do, call forth a plethora of suggested remedies, and Canada of the late eighteen-forties was no exception to

6.

| *Year* | *Customs Revenues* | | | *Crown Land Sales* |
|---|---|---|---|---|
| | £ | *s.* | *d.* | (*Acres*) |
| 1847 | 381,063 | 11 | 10 | 62,881 |
| 1848 | 304,358 | 7 | 4 | 34,838 |
| 1849 | 412,626 | 18 | 5 | 25,444 |
| 1850 | 583,530 | 10 | 3 | 164,307 |
| 1851 | 703,700 | 14 | 0 | 197,855 |
| 1852 | 705,517 | 15 | 10 | 68,210 |
| 1853 | 986,597 | 16 | 10 | 256,059 |

Figures from annual financial statements of the province, and from *Accounts and Papers, 1854–55,* XXXVI.

the rule. Repeal of the Navigation Laws, annexation, and reciprocity had their advocates, and among many other suggestions were retrenchment in public expenditure, political independence, a confederation of the British North American colonies or free trade between them, a return to the old commercial policy, tariff autonomy, and the construction of railways. Of all these the last mentioned only, which was mainly a matter for private enterprise, and which was not taken up extensively before 1850, was appreciably effective as a measure of relief. The whole story suggests the limited power of political action to affect economic life, since not only did the discarding of the old commercial policy fail to have any permanently bad effect, but legislative attempts to cure the temporary ailment miscarried. Yet this generalization ought not to be pushed too far, since the economic life of the province was too simple and too fundamentally sound to require the intervention of the state to adjust and to stimulate, or to benefit very much from such intervention. The essential requirements were a market for the staples together with adequate transportation facilities; and given these two things and some outside capital now and then, all was likely to be well. *Laissez faire* therefore justified itself; but had the circumstances been less inherently favorable to its operation the inference might be more difficult to draw.

Many causes combined to bring prosperity back to the province after 1849. The first of these was the very sudden and sustained improvement everywhere in prices and trade at that time, and this was the most important cause of all, since general depression had been the main reason for the economic troubles of the province in the first place. The recovery was greatly facilitated too by the fundamentally sound material condition of the colony. The productive facilities of the province were adequate and it was very favorably situated with respect to trade routes, the result being that it produced good staples at a marketable price. Its wealth was widely distributed, its population was rapidly increasing—a fact which alone goes some way toward accounting for prosperity in a colony—and it was practically immune to the more serious distempers of industrialized societies.

After 1845 a gradual readjustment was taking place to a new trade equilibrium which was to prove to be in some ways superior to the old one. The external trade of the province, no longer surrounded by the barrier of the old commercial system, began to seek diversified outlets, without however breaking its long-established and desirable connection with the market of Great Britain. Before the year 1847 it had been almost entirely an intra-imperial trade, the amount of smuggling over the American border being certainly insufficient to modify this statement seriously. The great bulk of the trade both in exports and imports had been with Great Britain itself; that part carried on with the United States having been small, and having increased much less rapidly than had the trade with Great Britain. After 1846 the provincial trade with Great Britain diminished; but with the return of prosperity it began once more to increase. Under the new commercial system, however, the United States obtained a much larger share of the provincial trade than ever before. Under the new conditions too, the total trade with the United States increased more rapidly than did that with Britain. Indeed it was during these years that Canada began to develop those intimate economic relations with the United States, which have been continued ever since to the extent that tariff policies have permitted—economic relations which free traders find so natural, but which to many imperialists seem so pernicious, and which are open to attack, if at all, on political grounds alone. The provincial imports from Great Britain in the period immediately after 1849 increased faster than the exports to that country, and at least as fast as did the imports from the United States. This is of course to be expected, in view of the superiority in manufacturing then enjoyed by Great Britain. There was a rapid growth in the trade with other colonies, much of which was carried on by way of the United States, and also in the trade with foreign countries other than the United States, though in this case the total remained small. The entire external trade of the province after 1848 showed a steady increase. This whole readjustment of trade connections, although made necessary and easy by imperial and provincial legislation, should nevertheless be regarded as the work rather of the merchant in his office than of the draftsman of laws in a government department.

In the years immediately following 1849, the value of imports into the province greatly exceeded that of its exports. Colonies have a tendency to present such trade returns, and at this particular time improved conditions increased the tendency in Canada to a marked degree. The colony had no invisible exports, and the excess of its imports was paid for by money or credit imported in various ways. There was an increase in the amount of public securities held outside the province during these years. The expenditure by the imperial government to maintain the military forces in the province amounted to a considerable sum each year, as did also the money brought into the province by immigrants. In a period of expanding trade, the credit facilities accorded to individuals and firms in the province, by those with whom they did business in Great Britain and the United States, must have been greatly extended. Probably the most important of all was the capital, chiefly from Britain, invested during these years in private business undertakings in the province, notably railways. Indeed railway investments were a considerable factor in the general improvement which was noticeable after 1849.

At the same time there was a marked change for the better in the general monetary situation. Money became plentiful, enabling the provincial government as well as private enterprises to borrow much more easily than before the capital which they needed, and making possible the extensive railway investments to which reference has just been made. This was accompanied by a rapid and sustained rise in prices, and an increase of production and trade. It was in fact simply one phase of that general recovery[7] which was mainly responsible for the revived prosperity of the colony. Economic depressions, like many of the diseases which affect the body, establish the conditions which are necessary to their own cure. One of their characteristics, in other words, is that they come to an end. This particular depression however seems to have terminated precisely when it did because of the discoveries of gold, and especially of those mines in California which began in 1849 to pour an abundant stream into the world's reservoir of precious metal.

In September 1849, the *Examiner* reported that: "The harvest just gathered is far more abundant than any with which Canada has been blessed in any previous year."

Along with the returning prosperity of which it was both a cause and an effect, went a very noticeable improvement in morale. An exuberant optimism is more natural to a young country with great resources and few serious problems, than the querulous despondency which had been so noticeable in Canada during the difficult years that had gone before. It has been pointed out that the annexation controversy necessitated a careful investigation, whereby the more cheerful aspects of the picture were discovered and emphasized, and the latent tendency to optimism asserted itself once more in those parts of the colony where there had been such great discouragement. Moreover the dawn of the day of railways was already in the sky. In the new technique of rail and steam the Canadians thought that they saw the solution for many of their problems, and in the enthusiasm for railways the former despondency was quite forgotten. The dream of El Dorado, too, has often proved to be demoralizing but has never yet been productive of dismay, and away to the westward on the shores of the Pacific Ocean that dream had come true. In

7. The Baring Letter Book for 1850 offers reiterated evidence of the swiftness and striking character of the change which was taking place.

1849 a resident in Canada West wrote: "There is a great *fever* about California now raging in this neighbourhood. Several young men have made up parties to go there."

The provincial government was not strengthened by the return of good times—on the contrary it grew weaker and had lost its hold on the country by 1851, finding as others have done that the French Canadians can have nothing in common with real liberalism. Yet returning prosperity was like oil on the troubled political waters. Early in 1850 Sir Allan MacNab the arch-Tory called on Lord Elgin for the first time since the signing of the Rebellion Losses Bill, and was received in friendship and peace. The political events of the preceding years began to be regarded as closed incidents, and the warfare between parties was now being waged with a moderation and even a listlessness to which the province was not accustomed. "Very many years have passed away," said the *Globe* in the autumn of 1850, "since the Province of Canada enjoyed the same public tranquillity it does at this moment. The harvest has been abundant and prices are remunerative; trade has been very good, and mercantile accounts promptly met; the summer has been an unusually healthy one, the public exchequer is filled to repletion, money is plentiful in commercial circles, and on every side are springing up fresh evidences of successful enterprize and increased social comfort among the masses. Is it wonderful that the din of political strife should be unheard in the midst of such general prosperity? . . . We are glad that so many grounds of strife are removed; but as believers in party government we wish the lines separating parties were more clearly drawn on great questions of public policy."[8] This was indeed a far cry from the days of the Rebellion Losses Bill eighteen months before.

The year 1850 marks the end not only of a political era but of an economic one also. In the following decade the scene has been changed, and the problems and issues are for the most part new ones. The railway comes to tie

8. *Globe,* Oct. 8, 1850.

farm and market more closely together, to supplement the waterway as well as to modify its functions, and eventually to open up the Canadian prairies and so create a new hinterland vastly larger and more productive than the earlier one, and to make possible that confederation of the provinces which has helped to solve so many of their earlier problems both political and economic.

The wheel of life as it rolls forward turns around also, and the familiar things of an earlier time become the innovations or the fresh experiences of today. Essentially the same, though changed in detail since an altered environment perforce changes them a little, they reappear like familiar actors in a new scene. These latter years have known the dismay of a great economic crisis, and have heard the voices raised to protest, or to advocate this or that means of salvation. The same years have seen revived in Great Britain a belief in the virtues of the old commercial system, and a partial re-establishment of that system. They have seen Canadian governments negotiating in Washington for a reciprocity treaty, and the signing of such a treaty. Also they have heard from many mouths both in Canada and in the United States, weighty arguments favoring the use of the Great Lakes and the St. Lawrence on a continental scale. So powerful moreover has been the support accorded to this scheme, that the next few years seem very likely to witness an improvement of the St. Lawrence waterway such as would enable ocean-going ships to carry cargoes all the way from Chicago or Fort William to the sea.

# APPENDIX A

## ADDRESS OF THE PROVINCIAL LEGISLATIVE COUNCIL AND ASSEMBLY ASKING FOR REPEAL OF THE NAVIGATION LAWS. JAN. 29–30, 1849.

Printed in *Accounts and Papers, 1849,* XIV. Also in the *Assembly Journal, 1849,* pp. 44–45. (C.O. 45:235.)

"To the Queen's Most Excellent Majesty.
Most Gracious Sovereign,

We, Your Majesty's most dutiful and loyal subjects, the Legislative Council and Commons of Canada, in Provincial Parliament assembled, humbly approach Your Majesty for the purpose of assuring Your Majesty of the devoted loyalty of the people of this province, and of their sincere attachment to Your Majesty's Person and Government, and we beg to represent to Your Majesty that we feel it to be a duty incumbent upon us to take the earliest opportunity to assure Your Majesty that the sentiments of the people of this province on the subject of the repeal of the British Navigation Laws, which were expressed to Your Majesty in a joint Address from the two Houses of the Provincial Parliament in the month of July, One thousand eight hundred and forty-seven, remain unchanged; that delay in removing the present restrictions on the employment of foreign shipping, would, in our opinion, be highly injurious to the carrying trade of the St. Lawrence; that, in order to secure this trade, the province, relying on the continuance of the protection which was then enjoyed by colonial products in the markets of Great Britain, incurred a large debt for the construction of a line of ship canals, by means of which the cost of inland transport has been very materially reduced; that owing to the difficulties attending the navigation of the St. Lawrence, the greater length of the voyage, and the higher rates of insurance, freights are likely at all times to range higher at Quebec than at New York, but the practical effect of the Navigation Laws is not only to prevent the possibility of a fair competition between the two routes, but actually to give direct encouragement to American shipping, not only through the canals of the state of New York, but at the sea-ports of the United States; that at the sea-ports of the United States, shipping can generally be procured to carry any quantity of produce that may be offered without a material increase of freight, but that even in case of scarcity, as the navigation is open throughout the year, foreign shipping can readily be procured in Europe at fair remunerative rates of freight, and without serious inconvenience or loss of time; that at Quebec, on the other hand, the exporter is compelled to rely on the regular traders to the port, so that when an unusual accumulation of produce takes place, vessels cannot be procured, and freights immediately rise to most exorbitant rates; that no means exist of engaging British shipping to meet the sudden demands which the nature of the trade causes, as such shipping is seldom to be met with at American ports, unless under specific orders, or the engagements of a charter; that the early closing of the navigation of the St. Lawrence renders it difficult, if not impossible, to obtain shipping from England to supply the sudden demands which, from the nature of the trade, are constantly arising, and which could readily be supplied at the American sea-ports, whence vessels would at any time come round to the St. Lawrence if assured of remunerative freights; that the uncertainty which at all times prevails as to the route by which the products of the West will be transported to the sea-board, must operate to prevent British vessels coming to the St. Lawrence in sufficient numbers to ensure moderate freights during the shipping season, while the scarcity of shipping, and the immediate rise of freights to England whenever a large supply of products is sent by the St. Lawrence, has the effect of diverting those products through the Erie canal to New York.

We beg further to represent to Your Majesty, that the Navigation Laws have likewise had a most injurious influence on the import trade of the province; that it has not unfrequently happened that Canadian importers of sugars, being unable to procure British vessels on any terms at Havana and other foreign ports, have been compelled to import their cargoes in American bottoms to New York, and thence through the American canals to Canada, when, but for the restrictions imposed by the Navigation Laws, they would have imported them by the St. Lawrence in foreign bottoms, which could have been readily procured.

We have observed with much satisfaction that a Bill was introduced into the House of Commons during the last Session of the Imperial Parliament for the repeal of the Navigation Laws; and, being of opinion that the provisions of that Bill are calculated to remove those restrictions from which the trade of this province is now suffering, we most humbly pray that Your Majesty will be graciously pleased to recommend the subject of the repeal of the Navigation Laws to the favourable consideration of the Imperial Parliament.

And we would further humbly pray, that Your Majesty will be graciously pleased to authorize the Governor of this province to permit foreign vessels to navigate the St. Lawrence above Quebec, under such restrictions as his Excellency may, in his wisdom, see fit to impose."

# APPENDIX B

## THE ANNEXATION MANIFESTO

Printed in *Accounts and Papers, 1850,* VII.

"To the People of Canada,

The number and magnitude of the evils that afflict our country, and the universal and increasing depression of its material interests, call upon all persons animated by a sincere desire for its welfare to combine for the purpose of inquiry and preparation, with a view to the adoption of such remedies as a mature and dispassionate investigation may suggest.

Belonging to all parties, origins, and creeds, but yet agreed upon the advantage of co-operation for the performance of a common duty to ourselves and our country, growing out of a common necessity, we have consented, in view of a brighter and happier future, to merge in oblivion all past differences, of whatever character, or attributable to whatever source. In appealing to our fellow colonists to unite with us in this our most needful duty, we solemnly conjure them, as they desire a successful issue and the welfare of their country, to enter upon the task, at this momentous crisis, in the same fraternal spirit.

The reversal of the ancient policy of Great Britain, whereby she withdrew from the colonies their wonted protection in her markets, has produced the most disastrous effects upon Canada. In surveying the actual condition of the country, what but ruin or rapid decay meets the eye! Our provincial Government and civic corporations embarrassed; our banking and other securities greatly depreciated; our mercantile and agricultural interests alike unprosperous; real estate scarcely saleable upon any terms; our unrivalled rivers, lakes, and canals, almost unused; whilst commerce abandons our shores; the circulating capital, amassed under a more favourable system, is dissipated, with none from any quarter to replace it! Thus, without available capital, unable to effect a loan with foreign states or with the mother country, although offering security greatly superior to that which readily obtains money both from the United States and Great Britain, when other than colonists are the applicants. Crippled, therefore, and checked in the full career of private and public enterprise, this possession of the British Crown—our country—stands before the world in humiliating contrast with its immediate neighbours, exhibiting every symptom of a nation fast sinking to decay.

With superabundant water power, and cheap labour, especially in Lower Canada, we have yet no domestic manufactures; nor can the most sanguine, unless under altered circumstances, anticipate the home growth, or advent from foreign parts, of either capital or enterprise, to embark in this great source of national wealth. Our institutions, unhappily, have not that impress of permanence which can alone impart security and inspire confidence; and the Canadian market is too limited to tempt the foreign capitalist.

Whilst the adjoining States are covered with a net-work of thriving railways, Canada possesses but three lines, which, together, scarcely exceed 50 miles in length, and the stock in two of which is held at a depreciation of from 50 to 80 per cent.—a fatal symptom of the torpor overspreading the land.

Our present form of provincial Government is cumbrous, and so expensive as to be ill suited to the circumstances of the country; and the necessary reference it demands to a distant Government, imperfectly acquainted with Canadian affairs, and somewhat indifferent to our interests, is anomalous and irksome. Yet, in the event of a rupture between two of the most powerful nations of the world, Canada would become the battle-field and the sufferer, however little her interests might be involved in the cause of quarrel or the issue of the contest.

The bitter animosities of political parties and factions in Canada, often leading to violence, and, upon one occasion, to civil war, seem not to have abated with time; nor is there, at the present moment, any prospect of diminution or accommodation. The aspect of parties becomes daily more threatening towards each other, and, under our existing institutions and relations, little hope is discernible of a peaceful and prosperous administration of our affairs, but difficulties will, to all appearance, accumulate until government becomes impracticable. In this view of our position, any course that may promise to efface existing party distinctions and place entirely new issues before the people, must be fraught with undeniable advantages.

Among the statesmen of the mother country—among the sagacious observers of the neighbouring republic—in Canada—and in all British North America—amongst all classes, there is a strong pervading conviction that a political revolution in this country is at hand. Such forebodings cannot readily be dispelled, and they have, moreover, a tendency to realize the events to which they point. In the meanwhile, serious injury results to Canada from the effect of this anticipation upon the more desirable class of settlers, who naturally prefer a country under fixed and permanent forms of government to one in a state of transition.

Having thus adverted to some of the causes of our present evils, we would consider how far the remedies ordinarily proposed possess sound and rational inducements to justify their adoption:—

1. 'The revival of protection in the markets of the United Kingdom.'

This, if attainable in a sufficient degree, and guaranteed for a long period of years, would ameliorate the condition of many of our chief interests; but the policy of the empire forbids the anticipation. Besides, it would be but a partial remedy. The millions of the mother country demand cheap food; and a second change from protection to free trade would complete that ruin which the first has done much to achieve.

2. 'The protection of home manufactures.'

Although this might encourage the growth of a manufacturing interest in Canada, yet, without access to the United States market, there would not be a sufficient expansion of that interest, from the want of consumers, to work any result that could be admitted as a 'remedy' for the numerous evils of which we complain.

3. 'A Federal Union of the British American Provinces.'

The advantages claimed for that arrangement are free trade between the different provinces, and a diminished governmental expenditure. The attainment of the latter object would be problematical, and the benefits anticipated from the former might be secured by legislation under our existing system. The markets of the sister provinces would not benefit our trade in timber, for they have a surplus of that article in their own forests; and their demand for agricultural products would be too limited to absorb our means of supply. Nor could Canada expect any encouragement to her manufacturing industry from those quarters. A Federal Union, therefore, would be no remedy.

4. 'The independence of the British North American colonies as a Federal Republic.'

The consolidation of its new institutions from elements hitherto so discordant—the formation of treaties with foreign powers—the acquirement of a name and character among the nations—would, we fear, prove an over-match for the strength of the new republic. And, having regard to the powerful confederacy of States conterminous with itself, the needful military defences would be too costly to render independence a boon, whilst it would not, any more than a Federal Union, remove those obstacles which retard our material prosperity.

5. 'Reciprocal free trade with the United States, as respects the products of the farm, the forest, and the mine.'

If obtained, this would yield but an instalment of the many advantages which might be otherwise secured. The free interchange of such products would not introduce manufactures to our country. It would not give us the North American continent for our market. It would neither so amend our institutions as to confer stability nor ensure confidence in their permanence; nor would it allay the violence of parties, or, in the slightest degree, remedy many of our prominent evils.

6. Of all the remedies that have been suggested for the acknowledged and insufferable ills with which our country is afflicted, there remains but one to be considered. It propounds a sweeping and important change in our political and social condition, involving considerations which demand our most serious examination. This remedy consists in a 'Friendly and peaceful separation from British connexion, and a union upon equitable terms with the great North American confederacy of sovereign States.'

We would premise, that towards Great Britain we entertain none other than sentiments of kindness and respect. Without her consent we consider separation as neither practicable nor desirable. But the colonial policy of the parent state, the avowals of her leading statesmen, the public sentiments of the empire, present unmistakeable and significant indications of the appreciation of colonial connexion. That it is the resolve of England to invest us with the attributes, and compel us to assume the burdens of independence, is no longer problematical. The threatened withdrawal of her troops from other colonies—the continuance of her military protection to ourselves only on the condition that we shall defray the attendant expenditure, betoken intentions towards our country, against which it is weakness in us not to provide. An overruling conviction, then, of its necessity, and a high sense of the duty we owe to our country, a duty we can neither disregard nor postpone, impel us to the idea of separation; and whatever negotiations may eventuate with Great Britain, a grateful liberality on the part of Canada should mark every proceeding.

The proposed Union would render Canada a field for American capital, into which it would enter as freely for the prosecution of public works and private enterprise as into any of the present States. It would equalize the value of real estate upon both sides of the boundary, thereby probably doubling at once the entire present value of property in Canada, whilst, by giving stability to our institutions and introducing prosperity, it would raise our public, corporate, and private credit. It would increase our commerce both with the United States and foreign countries, and would not necessarily diminish to any great extent our intercourse with Great Britain, into which our products would for the most part enter on the same terms as at present. It would render our rivers and canals the highway for the immigration to, and exports from, the West, to the incalculable benefit of our country. It would also introduce manufactures into Canada as rapidly as they have been introduced into the Northern States; and to Lower Canada especially, where water privileges and labour are abundant and cheap, it would attract manufacturing capital, enhancing the value of property and agricultural produce, and giving remunerative employment to what is at present a comparatively non-producing population. Nor would the United States merely furnish the capital for our manufactures. They would also supply for them the most extensive market in the world, without the intervention of a Custom-House officer. Railways would forthwith be constructed by American capital as feeders for all the great lines now approaching our frontiers; and railway enterprise in general would doubtless be as active and prosperous among us as among our neighbours. The value of our agricultural produce would be raised at once to a par with that of the United States, while agricultural implements and many of the necessaries of life, such as tea, coffee, and sugar, would be greatly reduced in price.

The value of our timber would also be greatly enhanced by free access to the American market, where it bears a high price, but is subject to an onerous duty. At the same time there is every reason to believe that our shipbuilders, as well at Quebec as on the Great Lakes, would find an unlimited market in all the ports of the American continent. It cannot be doubted that the shipping trade of the United States must greatly increase. It is equally manifest that, with them, the principal material in the construction of ships is rapidly diminishing, while we possess vast territories, covered with timber of excellent quality, which would be equally available as it is now, since under the free trade system our vessels would sell as well in England after annexation as before.

The simple and economical State Government, in which direct responsibility to the people is a distinguishing feature, would be substituted for a system at once cumbrous and expensive.

In place of war and the alarms of war with a neighbour, there would be peace and amity between this country and the United States. Disagreement between the United States and her chief, if not only, rival among nations would not make the soil of Canada the sanguinary arena for their disputes, as under our existing relations must necessarily be the case. That such is the unenviable condition of our state of dependence upon Great Britain is known to the whole world, and how far it may conduce to keep prudent capitalists from making investments in the country, or wealthy settlers from selecting a fore-doomed battle-field for the home of themselves and their children, it needs no reasoning on our part to elucidate.

But other advantages than those having a bearing on our material interests may be foretold. It would change the ground of political contest between races and parties, allay and obliterate those irritations and conflicts of rancour and recrimination which have hitherto disfigured our social fabric. Already in anticipation has its harmonious influence been felt—the harbinger may it be hoped of a lasting oblivion of dissentions among all classes, creeds, and parties in the country. Changing a subordinate for an independent condition, we would take our station among the nations of the earth. We have now no voice in the affairs of the Empire, nor do we share in its honours or emoluments. England is our parent state, with whom we have no equality, but towards whom we stand in the simple relation of obedience. But as citizens of the United States the public service of the nation would be open to us—a field for high and honourable distinction on which we and our posterity might enter on terms of perfect equality.

Nor would the amicable separation of Canada from Great Britain be fraught with advantages to us alone. The relief to the Parent State from the large expenditure now incurred in the military occupation of the country—the removal of the many causes of collision with the United States, which result from the contiguity of mutual territories so extensive, the benefit of the larger market which the increasing prosperity of Canada would create, are considerations which, in the minds of many of her ablest statesmen, render our incorporation with the United States a desirable consummation.

To the United States also the annexation of Canada presents many important inducements. The withdrawal from the borders of so powerful a nation, by whom in time of war the immense and growing commerce of the lakes would be jeopardized,—the ability to dispense with the costly but ineffectual revenue establishment over a frontier of many hundred miles,—the large accession to their income from our Customs,—the unrestricted use of the St. Lawrence, the natural highway from the Western States to the ocean,—are objects for the attainment of which the most substantial equivalents would undoubtedly be conceded.

FELLOW COLONISTS:

We have thus laid before you our views and convictions on a momentous question, involving a change which, though contemplated by many of us with varied feelings and emotions, we all believe to be inevitable,—one which it is our duty to provide for and lawfully to promote.

We address you without prejudice or partiality,—in the spirit of sincerity and truth,—in the interest of our common country,—and our single aim is its safety and welfare. If to your judgment and reason our object and aim be at this time deemed laudable and right, we ask an oblivion of past dissentions; and from all, without distinction of origin, party or creed, that earnest and cordial co-operation in such lawful, prudent, and judicious means as may best conduct us to our common destiny."

# APPENDIX C

## POPULATION OF THE PROVINCE OF CANADA IN ALTERNATE YEARS, 1842–52 INCLUSIVE

The figures, some of which are estimates only, are taken from The Blue Books of Statistics of the colony, (C.O. 47).

| YEAR | LOWER CANADA | UPPER CANADA | TOTAL |
|---|---|---|---|
| 1842 | 693,000 | 486,055 | 1,179,055 |
| 1844 | 691,193 | 545,438 | 1,236,631 |
| 1846 | 761,602 | 628,214 | 1,389,816 |
| 1848 | 770,000 | 723,292 | 1,493,292 |
| 1850 | 840,000 | 791,000 | 1,631,000 |
| 1852 | 890,261 | 952,004 | 1,842,265 |

# APPENDIX D

## COMPARATIVE STATEMENT OF TONNAGE AND TOLLS ON THE ERIE, WELLAND AND ST. LAWRENCE CANALS, 1850–56 INCLUSIVE

From a Table in *Sessional Papers, 1863,* No. 3 (C.O. 45: 351).

| YEARS | ERIE CANAL | | ST. LAWRENCE ROUTE | | | | *Total Tolls by St. Lawrence Route* |
|---|---|---|---|---|---|---|---|
| | | | WELLAND CANAL | | ST. LAWRENCE CANALS | | |
| | *Tons* | *Tolls* $ | *Tons* | *Tolls* $ | *Tons* | *Tolls* $ | $ |
| 1850 | 3,076,617 | 3,273,899 | 399,600 | 151,704 | 288,103 | 81,872 | 233,576 |
| 1851 | 3,582,733 | 3,329,727 | 691,628 | 201,841 | 450,401 | 91,252 | 293,093 |
| 1852 | 3,863,441 | 3,118,244 | 743,060 | 233,094 | 492,575 | 88,077 | 321,171 |
| 1853 | 4,247,852 | 3,204,718 | 905,516 | 269,916 | 561,601 | 102,411 | 372,327 |
| 1854 | 4,165,862 | 2,773,566 | 767,210 | 208,304 | 639,000 | 110,110 | 318,414 |
| 1855 | 4,022,617 | 2,805,077 | 849,333 | 223,747 | 541,254 | 74,493 | 298,240 |
| 1856 | 4,116,082 | 2,748,203 | 976,556 | 272,050 | 634,536 | 85,535 | 357,585 |

# BIBLIOGRAPHICAL NOTE

## *SOURCE MATERIAL*

### OFFICIAL

THE COLONY: The Correspondence of the Civil Secretary is the file of the official correspondence of the governor-general's secretary, other than with the Colonial Office. It consists of letters, memoranda, and other papers. Almost all matters of public business came before the governor-general, usually through his immediate assistant the civil secretary, consequently this material is authoritative and covers a wide range of subjects. The papers are arranged chronologically in numbered bundles, and are in the MS. Room of the Dominion Archives.

The *Sessional Papers* of the province are listed in the Public Record Office as C.O. 45. The first two or more volumes in each year are the Council and Assembly *Journals*. The official papers laid before the legislative assembly of the colony and ordered to be printed, are attached as appendixes to the assembly journal of their year, usually in separate volumes. The best approach to these documents is through Alfred Todd's *General Index to the Journals of the Legislative Assembly of Canada.* One volume (1855) covers the period from 1841 to 1851; a second (1867) the period 1852–1866. A third (1848) indexes the journals of the Upper Canada assembly, 1825–1840. Certain of these papers, or categories of papers, have been particularly useful for this study. Among them are the Annual Reports on the Public Accounts of Canada, and the Annual Reports of the Board of Works or Commissioners of Public Works. Many, if not all, of the manuscript originals of these latter are in the Dominion Archives. Especially full of information are C.O. 45:237, App. B.B. (1849); and C.O. 45:247, App. T. (1851). Official correspondence relating to the Canada Corn Act, is printed in C.O. 45:215, App. O (1843); that dealing with the Navigation Laws, with enclosures, in C.O. 45:236, App. C. (1849). Some official correspondence relating to migration, with enclosures, is contained in C.O. 45:237, App. E.E.E. (1849). Very useful papers of the same date, also, are the Appendix to the Report from the Board of Registration and Statistics, C.O. 45:236, App. B., and the

Second Report of the Committee on the Lumber Trade, C.O. 45: 238, App. P.P.P.P. Worth mentioning, too, are the Reports of the Committee on Public Income and Expenditure, C.O. 45:243, App. B.B. (1850); and the Report of the Committee on Trade, C.O. 45:284, App. D.D.D.D. (1854–55).

For reports of council and assembly debates, contemporary newspapers must be relied on for the most part. The *Globe* paid special attention to the debates, and reported them more fully than any other newspaper. Its reports, however, are neither complete nor entirely unbiased. A negative defect is due to the fact that the parliamentary correspondent understood no French; but recourse may be had to the French press. The *Globe* file in the Record Office begins in 1847, and for the period is the most complete that exists. The debates during part of the year 1846 are contained in the *Mirror of Parliament of the Province of Canada* (Montreal, 1846). The intention was to print the debates in and after 1846 in a continuous series of volumes; but only one appeared at that time. It covers the second session of the second parliament, i.e. from March 20 to June 9, 1846. A small *Mirror of Parliament* volume had been published in 1841, and another appeared in 1860.

The *Acts of the Provincial Legislature* are printed; but the Record Office file (C.O. 44), for the period is in manuscript, as the custom of making transcripts for the Colonial Office was adhered to after the colony had begun to print its statutes.

The Blue Books of Statistics, C.O. 47, one volume a year, give an annual statistical account of the colony, under some twenty or twenty-five headings. They are not entirely dependable, and in general the official statistics of the province in this period require careful handling. Figures may be gathered from many sources, and most conveniently of all from the *Sessional Papers*. The statistics of shipping contained in *Tables of the Trade and Navigation of the Province of Canada* are helpful, particularly those covering the period 1850 to 1855, C.O. 47: 195–199. This series was published annually from 1850 to 1858. The *Census of the Canadas, 1851–2*, 2 vols. (Quebec, 1853, 1855) is an obvious source of information.

Certain military records in the Dominion Archives are indispensable to a study of the early history of the provincial canals. Series C., 38–62, in manuscript, consists mainly of official correspondence carried on by officers of the Royal Engineers in the colony, and tells the story of the Ottawa and Rideau canals. It also contains some information about the origins of the St. Lawrence canals. Selections are printed in the *Report on Canadian Archives,* 1890. Some documents contained in the Archives report for 1897, note C, also deserve to be mentioned. Lieutenant-Colonel George Phillpotts' Reports on the Inland Navigation of the Canadas, 1839 and 1840, C.O. 42:498, also in the Dominion Archives, are a mine of information. Useful source material is accessible in H. A. Innis and A. R. M. Lower, *Select documents in Canadian Economic History, 1783–1885* (Toronto, 1933).

The provincial official documents of the year 1849 were slightly affected by the burning of the Parliament Buildings and the hasty removal of the seat of government from Montreal to Toronto.

Great Britain: An obviously important source of information is the official correspondence between the colonial secretary and the governor-general C.O. 42 (also in the MS. Room of the Dominion Archives). These despatches, with their enclosures, supply continuous and authoritative information on a wide range of subjects concerning the colony. Some are printed in *Accounts and Papers* and in the provincial *Sessional Papers.*

Among the Parliamentary Papers classed as *Accounts and Papers,* vol. XXVII, 1846, contains official correspondence in regard to the forthcoming repeal of the Corn Laws. A number of memorials and addresses concerning the Navigation Laws, from Canada and other colonies, are printed in vol. XXXVII, 1847; official correspondence on the same subject is printed in vol. LIX, 1847–48, and vol. LI, 1849. Vol. XLVII, 1847–48, contains documents relating to the famine migration. Material on the annexation movement and related events is to be found in vols. XXXIV and XXXV, 1849, and vol. XXXVIII, 1850. Several of the *Reports from Committees* require special mention. Vol. V, 1831–32, contains the Report from the Committee on Canal Communications in Canada. Lord Durham's famous Report on the Affairs of British North America is printed in vol. XVII, 1839; for the sake of convenience, however, references are to Sir C. P. Lucas edition, 3 vols. (Oxford, 1912). Very useful are the Reports from the Committee of the House of Lords on the Navigation Laws, in vol. X, 1847 (vol. XX, pt. I, 1847–48 is almost identical with the above), and vol. XX, pt. II, 1847–48, Apps. K. and FF., contains official correspondence with Canada. The Appendix to the Final Report of the Decimal Coinage Commissioners, in *Reports from Commissioners,* 1860, XXX, throws light on the question of the use of money in the colony.

Imperial statutes, and *Hansard's Parliamentary Debates,* have been used extensively in the present work. Less important are the Entry Books of Correspondence, C.O. 43:107–112, containing correspondence of the Colonial Office with the Board of Trade, Treasury, and Foreign Office, and the Treasury Out Letters—Colonial Affairs, 1849–50, T. 7:1.

THE UNITED STATES: American documents of various sorts are an important ingredient in the mixture, though less so than those originating in the province or in Great Britain. The *Congressional Documents* form the most useful single category. Important among these documents are a Report on Trade with the British Colonies, *House Reports,* No. 650, 27th Cong., 2nd Sess., vol. III (1842); also Report concerning the River St. Lawrence, *House Reports,* No. 295, 31st Cong., 1st Sess., vol. II (1850). Official correspondence on the subject of reciprocity is printed with the Presidential Message on Reciprocity with Canada, in *House Ex. Docs.,* No. 64, 31st Cong., 1st Sess., vol. VIII (1850). The Report on the Trade of the British American Colonies, *Senate Ex. Docs.,* No. 23, 31st Cong., 2nd Sess., vol. IV, and Report on the Trade of the British North American Colonies, *Senate Ex. Docs.,* No. 112, 32nd Cong., 1st Sess., vol. XI (also *House Ex. Docs.,* No. 136, 32nd Cong., 1st Sess., vol. XV), are Israel D. Andrews' two reports. The author was a very intelligent U.S. consul in Canada and other B.N.A. colonies whose reports present a detailed and well-informed economic analysis of the colony. Andrews was strongly in favor of free trade. Among American statutes the most important are the Drawback Laws of 1845 and 1846, 28th Cong., 2nd Sess., LXX; 29th Cong., 1st Sess., CII; and the tariff law of 1846, 29th Cong., 1st Sess., LXXIV. Other relevant sources are *The Seventh Census of the United States,* 1850 (Washington, 1853), and William M. Malloy, *Treaties, Conventions, International Acts, Protocols and Agreements between the United States of America and Other Powers,* 2 vols. (Washington, 1910).

## CONTEMPORARY MAPS

Among the documents in this class, three, all of which are in the Dominion Archives, have been particularly useful. T. C.

Keefer, chief engineer of the Board of Works, made a map, dated 1855 (*Dom. Arch. Map Catalogue,* No. 3859), to be shown at the Paris Exhibition. It was designed to show the communications of the Province, and is the map referred to on p. 57. The second map (Correspondence of the Civ. Sec., No. 3870) is dated 1844. It shows the Rideau, Ottawa, and St. Lawrence canals, finished and otherwise. Lieutenant Colonel Holloway, R.E., and Captain Boxer, R.N., the harbor master at Quebec, conducted a survey of the canals, and this map was handed in with their report. The course of the Welland Canal and its feeder, is shown on a fairly large scale map dated 1837 (*Dom. Arch. Map Cat.,* No. 2886), endorsed by Captain Bonnycastle, R.E. The map following the index is partly based on the Keefer and Holloway maps.

## UNOFFICIAL

Letters and Papers: The most important group of materials in this class is the Grey Papers. These unpublished manuscripts were a part of the third Earl Grey's private papers, and were given by the fourth Earl to the late Dr. A. G. Doughty, the Dominion Archivist, to be unofficially published. They are bound in twelve volumes, and may be divided into seven categories: (1) Five volumes of private letters from Lord Elgin to Lord Grey, 1847–52 inclusive. These are originals. Extracts are printed in Theodore Walrond, *Letters and Journals of James, Eighth Earl of Elgin* (London, 1872). (2) Two volumes of private letters from Lord Grey to Lord Elgin, 1846–52 inclusive, most of them being transcripts made by Lady Grey. Lord Grey was the second Lady Elgin's uncle, and this correspondence is a fairly intimate one. It is almost entirely concerned with public affairs, for both men took their official duties very seriously. The letters are therefore complementary to the official despatches, whose subject matter they discuss in a wholly untrammelled way. In 1849 this correspondence was objected to in parliament as being contrary to the public interest. (3) One volume of miscellaneous papers—clippings, memoranda, notes, pamphlets, etc. (4) One volume of Navigation Laws papers, chiefly manuscripts, and pertinent to the colonies, especially Canada, and to the movement for repeal. (5) One volume of papers relating to emigration. They cover the period from 1823 to 1850; but are mainly concerned with the latter part of it. (6) The manuscript of Grey's *The Colonial Policy of Lord John Russell's Administration,* bound in one volume.

(7) A small volume containing a long letter written by Lord Elgin, criticizing and appraising the above.

The firm of Baring Brothers, in addition to being the leading London financial house, were the principal financial agents of the province in London. Everyone familiar with the Canadian field knows that a large section of the voluminous Baring records was obtained for the Dominion Archives a few years ago by the late Dr. Adam Shortt. These Baring Papers, as might be supposed, throw much light on the course of world trade and on the provincial finances in the period. The American correspondents of the Barings make interesting reports on public opinion in the United States. The Papers consist of In-Letters to the firm from its agents all over the world, Letter Books, and Miscellaneous Correspondence. The last-named series, together with the Letter Books, contains the correspondence between the firm and the provincial inspectors-general. The Merritt, Askin, Baldwin, and Lafontaine Papers are also relevant. The Merritt Papers in the Dominion Archives, and the Provincial Archives in Toronto, are the private records of William Hamilton Merritt. His varied and essentially economic interests, are of course reflected here. In the period Merritt's two great enthusiasms were the waterways and reciprocity. Askin was a business man, living in Upper Canada, and the Askin Papers in the Dominion Archives are helpful to an understanding of the conditions of life in the province at that time. The papers of Lafontaine and Baldwin in the Dominion Archives and the Toronto Public Library respectively, are too exclusively political to be of great importance for the present work. George Peabody Gooch, *The Later Correspondence of Lord John Russell, 1840–1878,* 2 vols. (London, 1925), comes into direct contact with the present subject at several points.

Personal Accounts: There is a large supply of contemporary literature of this type, and it has been used fairly extensively in the present work. It consists, almost entirely, of accounts written by old-country people who either were living in the colony or had visited it. These, because they were comparative strangers and were writing chiefly for an old-country audience, took note of circumstances which the native regarded as commonplaces not calling for pen and ink. It is to this fact, more than anything else, that the special value of these accounts is due. Their authors were for the most part very appreciative of the colony—

slow to chide and swift to bless. Only those accounts which have been particularly useful are included here.

Sir Richard Bonnycastle was a senior engineer officer who knew his Canada well. He wrote three books of two volumes each—*The Canadas in 1841* (London, 1841–42), *Canada and the Canadians, in 1846* (London, 1846), and *Canada, as it was, is, and may be* (London, 1852). Bonnycastle has much to say about the canals, and his descriptions of places that he had seen are extraordinarily good. The third of these works, published posthumously, is less relevant and helpful than the other two. The members of the Strickland family were valiant writers of memoirs. The literary work of Susannah Moodie (*née* Strickland), is well-known in Canada. Mrs. Moodie wrote two personal accounts of which the first, *Roughing it in the Bush,* 2 vols. (London and New York, 1852), is the better and the better known. The author was a highly cultured English gentlewoman. The Moodies settled in Canada for financial reasons and the book is well-named. It is critical, without being unreasonable, is full of interesting information, and has been republished three times. Susannah Moodie also wrote *Life in the Clearing versus the Bush* (London, 1853). Her brother, Samuel Strickland, wrote *Twenty-Seven Years in Canada West,* 2 vols. (London, 1853). He came to Canada at the age of twenty, and, unlike his more gifted sister, he adapted himself very quickly to the settler's way of life. Catherine Parr Traill, the author of *The Female Emigrant's Guide* (Toronto, 1854), was a sister of Strickland and Mrs. Moodie. G. W. Warr, *Canada as It is* (London, 1847), contains much interesting information about the details of life in the colony. Warr was an Anglican clergyman in Oakville, Canada West, and he lived in the colony from 1843 to 1846. Sir Francis Hincks, *Reminiscences of his Public Life* (Montreal, 1884), is not the work of a *genre* painter; but it is important because of the leading part played by the author in the public life of the colony in the period. Not quite contemporary, but valuable because written from an unusual point of view, is William Thomson, *A Tradesman's Travels, in the United States and Canada* (Edinburgh, 1842). The author, an extremely intelligent Scottish textile-worker, spent several weeks in the southern part of Upper Canada in the autumn of 1841. James Johnston, *Notes on North America, Agricultural, Economical, and Social,* 2 vols. (Edinburgh and London, 1851), is the record of a tour made about 1848–49 by a scientist. James B. Brown, *Views of Canada and the Colonists* (Edinburgh and

London, 1851), is an enlarged and improved edition of an anonymous work published in 1844. Extracts from the correspondence of Frances Stewart, who lived in the Peterborough district of Upper Canada, are contained in E. S. Dunlop, *Our Forest Home* (Montreal, 1902). Several other accounts may be mentioned without comment: James Beavan, D.D., *Recreations of a Long Vacation* (London and Toronto, 1846); Lieutenant Colonel Sleigh, *Pine Forests and Hacmatack Clearings* (London, 1853); James Taylor, *Narrative of a Voyage to, and Travels in Upper Canada* (Hull, 1846); Hugh Seymour Tremenheere, *Notes on Public Subjects, made during a Tour in the United States and in Canada* (London, 1852); George Warburton, *Hochelaga; or England in the New World,* edited by Eliot Warburton (London, 1846). French visitors to the North American continent seldom went to Canada. Xavier Marmier in *Lettres sur l'Amérique,* 2 vols. (Paris, 1851), devotes several chapters to Lower Canada in vol. I of his work. So does J. J. Ampère in vol. I of his *Promenade en Amérique,* 2 vols. (Paris, 1855). Both these writers were academicians. Ampère is not strictly within the period.

NEWSPAPERS: Contemporary newspapers are, needless to say, a requisite, if limited, type of source material for a study of this kind. The chapter on the annexation movement is particularly dependent upon them. For that movement did not at any time go beyond the stage of propaganda, and a study of it is therefore, to a considerable extent, a study of opinion. Of those newspapers used, the more important are given in alphabetical order. *L'Avenir* (Montreal) was Papineau's newspaper. It favored free trade, was republican and anti-clerical, and was inspired with the ideals of the revolutions of 1848. The *Canadian Economist* (Montreal) was founded in 1846 in order to preach free trade. *Le Canadien* (Quebec), was the best newspaper published in that city. The *Courier* (Buffalo), possesses considerable interest because the western end of the Erie Canal entered Lake Erie at Buffalo. The *Morning Courier,* later the *Courier* (Montreal), was Tory and influential, and is very important for a study of the annexation movement. The *Examiner* (Toronto), was an able radical newspaper, much given to discussing economic matters. The *Globe* (Toronto), George Brown's great newspaper, was independent, and strongly liberal and Protestant. Established in 1844, it quickly became the best English newspaper in the province. The *Herald* (New York), had James Gordon Bennett for its editor at this time. *La Minerve* (Montreal), moderate, and worthy of its title, was the best of the French journals. The *Pilot* (Montreal), was owned by Francis Hincks. The *Times* (London), threaded its way through the uncertainties of the annexation movement more sure-footedly than did any other newspaper. The *Tribune* (New York), was edited by Horace Greeley. It was protectionist, pacific, and overflowing with moral purpose. The *Witness* (Montreal) supported free trade.

### CONTEMPORARY WORKS

Practically all the material referred to in this section is, for present purposes and to some extent, source material.

BOOKS: In the field of colonial policy, two essential works are, Earl Grey, *The Colonial Policy of Lord John Russell's Administration,* 2 vols. (London, 1853), and Edward Gibbon Wakefield, *View of the Art of Colonization* (London, 1849). Wakefield's ideas were not always sound; but he knew the colonies. Moreover the ideas which he had been advocating, and which are expressed in his *Art of Colonization,* had exerted great influence, and Lord Grey's book describes a colonial policy which was, in part, an attempt to put into practice some of Wakefield's theories. John Arthur Roebuck, *The Colonies of England* (London, 1849), and Judge Haliburton, *Rule and Misrule of the English in America* (New York, 1851), the latter published anonymously, are critical treatments of the same topic. William H. Smith, *Canada: Past, Present and Future,* 2 vols. (Toronto, 1851), is an elaboration of *Smith's Canadian Gazetteer* (Toronto, 1846 and 1849). It is full of interesting and, in the main, accurate details, especially those of a local character; but it deals only with Upper Canada. A general economic picture of the colony is presented by an eminent Canadian in J. C. Taché, *Esquisse sur le Canada considéré sous le Point de vue Economiste* (Paris, 1855). It is very optimistic in tone, for the depression was past, and the book was intended to advertise the province at the time of the Paris Exhibition. A well-known social and economic survey of Great Britain, and to some extent of the colonies, at the middle of the century, is the third edition of G. R. Porter, *The Progress of the Nation* (London, 1851). Two very profitable studies of the Navigation Laws in general, are by "A Barrister" [Sir Stafford Northcote], *A Short Review of the History of the Navigation*

*Laws of England* (London, 1849), and by John Lewis Ricardo, *The Anatomy of the Navigation Laws* (London, 1847). Ricardo was a member of the commons committee on the Navigation Laws, and a convinced free trader. A rich source of information about conditions in Ireland during the famine, is *Transactions of the Central Relief Committee of the Society of Friends during the Famine in Ireland, in 1846 and 1847* (Dublin and London, 1852). L. A. Dessaulles, *Six Lectures sur l'Annexation du Canada aux Etats-Unis* (Montreal, 1851), presents the *Rouge* point of view. These papers were read before the Institut Canadien. Prophets of the far-off event were the authors of three books: F. A. Wilson and Alfred B. Richards, *Britain Redeemed and Canada Preserved* (London, 1850); Allan Macdonnell, *A Railroad from Lake Superior to the Pacific* (Toronto, 1851); and Millington Henry Synge, *Great Britain One Empire* (London, 1852). They advocated, among other things, the construction of a railway which should run, on British soil, right out to the Pacific.

PAMPHLETS: Relevant contemporary material in this category is abundant; but its quality, generally speaking, does not match its quantity, and only a few pamphlets will be mentioned. Several general pictures are presented. J. Sheridan Hogan, *Canada* (Montreal, 1855), won the first prize for an essay on the colony, offered by the Paris Exhibition committee of Canada. A. M. Morris, *Canada and her Resources* (Montreal and London, 1855), won the committee's second prize. The Hon. A. T. Galt, *Canada: 1849 to 1859* (London, 1860), is an interesting retrospect. The author holds that the depression of 1846–50 was wholly due to the repeal of the Corn Laws. Two pamphlets by J. Houston Browne, *The Navigation Laws: their History and Operation* (London, 1847), and *The Navigation Laws, a National Question* (London, 1848), strongly oppose the repeal of those laws. The second one is a criticism of Ricardo's *Anatomy*. Authoritative and very good is T. C. Keefer, *The Canals of Canada: their Prospects and Influence* (Toronto and Montreal, 1850). William Cayley, *Finances and Trade of Canada at the Beginning of the Year 1855* (London, 1855), by the financial expert of the Tory Party, is useful for a study of provincial finance. Statements of the provincial revenue, expenditure, and debt, during the period from 1842 to 1854 inclusive, are given in tables compiled from the annual financial reports of the province, which are printed in the *Sessional Papers*. The Hon. Francis Hincks,

*Canada: its Financial Position and Resources* (London, 1849), was published by Hincks in order to improve the credit of the province, during his visit to London in 1849. Six other pamphlets may be mentioned without comment: James Buchanan, *Letter on Free Trade and Navigation of the St. Lawrence* (Toronto, 1846); "A Projector" [Merritt?], *A Concise View of the Inland Navigation of the Canadian Provinces* (St. Catharines, 1832); William Hamilton Merritt, *Brief Review of the Origin, Progress, Present State, and Future Prospects of the Welland Canal* (St. Catharines, 1852); Hon. Adam Ferrie, *Letter to the Rt. Hon. Earl Grey . . . embracing a Statement of Facts in Relation to Emigration to Canada during the summer of 1847* (Montreal, 1847); Rt. Rev. G. J. Mountain, *Thoughts on "Annexation," in connection with the Duty and the Interest of Members of the Church of England* (Quebec, 1849); Millington Henry Synge, *Canada in 1848* (London, n.d.).

## *SECONDARY MATERIAL*

Books: The amount of more or less pertinent secondary material is very great, because the subject dealt with impinges upon so many fields. No attempt will be made to do more than give a severely pruned selection of essential books. Among biographies, J. L. Morison, *The Eighth Earl of Elgin* (London, 1928), comes first. Two volumes in the "Makers of Canada" series are especially useful: Sir John George Bourinot, *Lord Elgin* (London and Toronto, 1905); and Stephen Leacock, *Baldwin, Lafontaine, Hincks* (London and Toronto, 1907). J. P. Merritt, *Biography of the Hon. W. H. Merritt, M.P.* (St. Catharines, 1875), is not a good book; but it helps. A great deal of exceedingly interesting information is to be found in Edwin C. Guillet, *Early Life in Upper Canada* (Toronto, 1933). Much technical information regarding the St. Lawrence River was obtained from a *Statement and Engineering Report by the Hydro-Electric Power Commission of Ontario* (Toronto, 1925). Of late years there has been a spate of articles and books dealing with the St. Lawrence waterway; but looking to the future rather than to the past. A. Barton Hepburn, *Artificial Waterways and Commercial Development* (New York, 1909), contains a good account of the early days of the Erie Canal. Robert Chalmers, *A History of Currency in the British Colonies* (London, n.d.), is the standard work. Bernard Holland, *The Fall of Protection 1840–1850* (London, 1913), ought perhaps to be mentioned. An excellent background for the famine migration is supplied by William Forbes Adams, *Ireland and Irish Emigration to the New World from 1815 to the Famine* (New Haven, 1932), also by George O'Brien, *The Economic History of Ireland from the Union to the Famine* (London, 1921). Cephas D. Allin and George M. Jones, *Annexation, Preferential Trade and Reciprocity* (Toronto, and London, n.d.), contains the fullest account of the annexation movement. The very difficult work of writing a general economic history of Canada has been done by L. C. A. Knowles, in *The Economic Development of the Overseas Empire,* II (London, 1930), and by Mary Quayle Innis, in *An Economic History of Canada* (Toronto, 1935), of which the latter is to be preferred.

ARTICLES: As already stated, the material in this category is voluminous. Only a few essential articles are cited here. On the subject of the waterways see W. A. Mackintosh, "Economic Factors in Canadian History," *Canadian Historical Review,* IV, 12–25; T. C. Keefer, "The Canals of Canada," *Proceedings and Transactions* of the Royal Society of Canada (1893), Sec. III, 25–50; George W. Brown, "The St. Lawrence Waterway in the Nineteenth Century," *Queen's Quarterly,* XXXV, 628–642. Questions arising from the Navigation Laws, and similar restrictions, are dealt with in J. H. Clapham, "The Last Years of the Navigation Acts," *English Historical Review,* XXV, 480–501, and 687–707, and in George W. Brown, "The Opening of the St. Lawrence to American Shipping," *Canadian Historical Review,* VII, 4–12. For some effects of Corn Law repeal, see D. L. Burn, "Canada and the Repeal of the Corn Laws," *Cambridge Historical Journal,* II, 252–272. A good short account of Hincks as a financier is to be found in R. S. Longley, "Francis Hincks and Canadian Public Finance," *Report* of the Canadian Historical Association (1934), pp. 30–39. There are a number of articles on the currency of the colony in the *Journal* of the Canadian Bankers' Association. On the famine migration, see Frances Morehouse, "The Irish Migration of the Forties," *American Historical Review,* XXXIII, 579–592, and by the same author, "Canadian Migration in the Forties," *Canadian Historical Review,* IX, 309–329. The activities of Israel D. Andrews in connection with the movement for reciprocity are critically examined in William D. Overman, "I. D. Andrews and Reciprocity in 1854," *Canadian Historical Review,* XV, 248–263. A view of the annexation movement from within is afforded by documents published in Arthur G. Penny, "The Annexation Movement, 1849–50," *Canadian Historical Review,* V, 236–261.

# INDEX

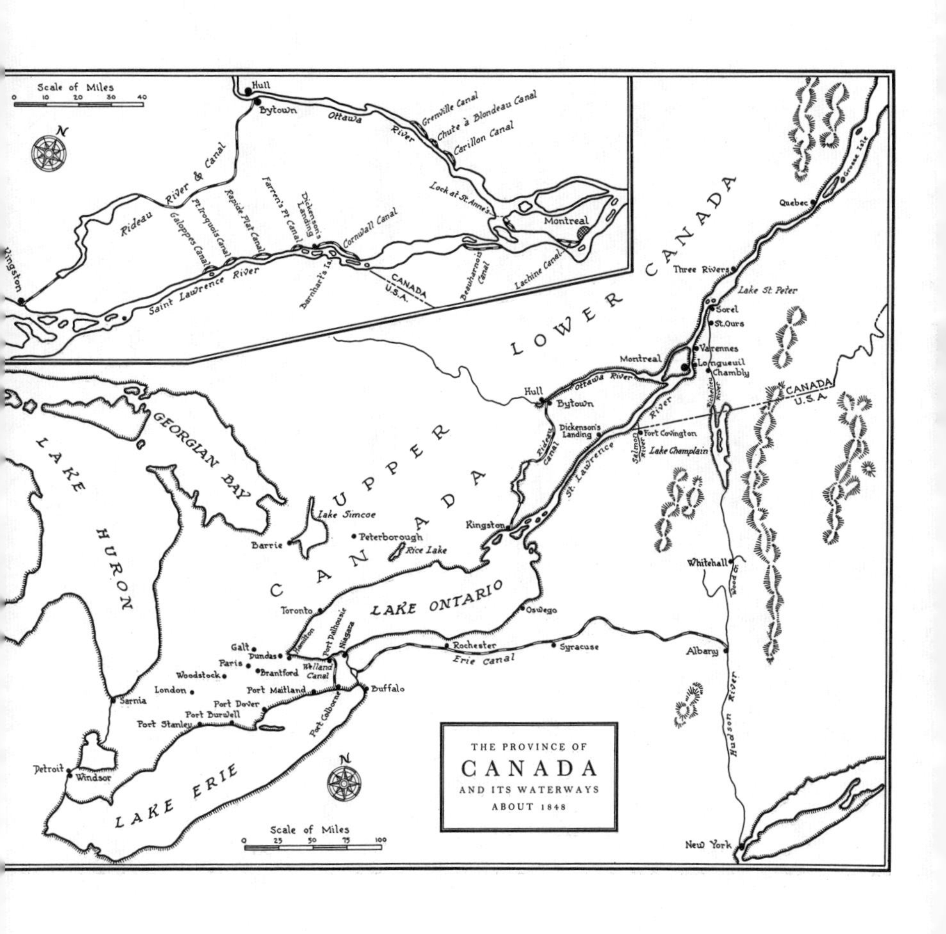

THE PROVINCE OF
CANADA
AND ITS WATERWAYS
ABOUT 1848
Scale of Miles
Hull
Bytown
Ottawa River
Grenville Canal
Chute à Blondeau Canal
Carillon Canal
Lock at St. Anne's
Montreal
Rideau River & Canal
Galoppes Canal
Pt. Iroquois Canal
Rapide Plat Canal
Farren's Pt Canal
Dickenson's Landing
Cornwall Canal
Barnhart's Is.
Beauharnois Canal
Lachine Canal
CANADA
U.S.A.
Saint Lawrence River
Kingston
LOWER CANADA
UPPER CANADA
Quebec
Grosse Isle
Three Rivers
Lake St. Peter
Sorel
St. Ours
Varennes
Longueuil
Chambly
Richelieu River
Ottawa River
Rideau Canal
St. Lawrence River
Salmon River
Fort Covington
Lake Champlain
Whitehall
Wood Cr.
Albany
Hudson River
New York
GEORGIAN BAY
LAKE HURON
Lake Simcoe
Barrie
Peterborough
Rice Lake
Toronto
LAKE ONTARIO
Oswego
Hamilton
Port Dalhousie
Niagara
Welland Canal
Rochester
Syracuse
Erie Canal
Galt
Dundas
Paris
Brantford
Woodstock
London
Port Maitland
Buffalo
Sarnia
Port Dover
Port Burwell
Port Stanley
Port Colborne
Detroit
Windsor
LAKE ERIE